DATE DUE

JY 3 1 '08			

DEMCO 38-296

ELECTRONIC TECHNOLOGY, CORPORATE STRATEGY, AND WORLD TRANSFORMATION

K

ELECTRONIC TECHNOLOGY, CORPORATE STRATEGY, AND WORLD TRANSFORMATION

Maurice Estabrooks

QUORUM BOOKS
Westport, Connecticut • London

Library of Congress Cataloging-in-Publication Data

Estabrooks, Maurice.
    Electronic technology, corporate strategy, and world
transformation / Maurice Estabrooks.
        p.   cm.
    Includes bibliographical references (p.   ) and index.
    ISBN 0–89930–969–0 (alk. paper)
    1. Information technology—Economic aspects.   2. Information
technology—Management.   3. Computer networks.   4. Information
networks.   5. Business enterprises—Communication systems.
6. Strategic planning.   I. Title.
HC79.I55E85   1995
658.4'038—dc20   94–39336

British Library Cataloguing in Publication Data is available.

Library of Congress Catalog Card Number: 94–39336
ISBN: 0–89930–969–0

First published in 1995

Quorum Books, 88 Post Road West, Westport, CT 06881
An imprint of Greenwood Publishing Group, Inc.

Printed in the United States of America

The paper used in this book complies with the
Permanent Paper Standard issued by the National
Information Standards Organization (Z39.48–1984).

10 9 8 7 6 5 4 3 2

In memory of Lottie Muriel Estabrooks

Contents

Preface

The subject of electronic superhighways has been the focus of intense media attention in recent years because of the dramatic impacts these are expected to have on people, businesses, and the structure and organization of economic society. The truth is that electronic technology, electronic communications, and electronic networks have played a profound role in the development of an advanced industrial society especially in the postwar period. In fact, they transformed it into an information and communications society. This book provides a sociotechnical and economic history of this transformation with specific emphasis on the microchip and computer and telecommunications revolutions as viewed from the Schumpeterian process of "creative destruction." That is, it focuses on those dynamic mechanisms and behavioral elements of capitalist systems that result in the creation of new production processes, new products and services, new markets and new organizational forms and how it destroys others. It advances the premise that these are not "ordinary" technologies in any sense of the word. To appreciate their true significance, these technologies must be seen as generic and fundamental to the way businesses, the economy, and our society are structured and organized, and the way they operate.

Microelectronics and computer and telecommunications technologies are truly transformative in the sense that they are capable of being applied universally to all manner and variety of business and economic and social activity.

They are contributing in this way to a transformation of the basic technological underpinnings of economic society, and, through these, they are initiating a profound transformation of the socioeconomic and institutional foundations of the society.

The principal thesis is that corporations and individuals all over the world, acting as designers and developers and as users of hardware, software, and systems are pushing the entire envelope of technologies—which encompasses everything from microchips, computers and optical fiber, satellite and wireless communications systems to software, workgroup, and multimedia technologies and robotics—along an evolutionary course and making them converge and coalesce into a single "intelligent technology." This technology is differentiated from those of the past by its powerful, automatic, information-processing, communications and artificial "intelligence" capabilities. It is these multifunctional attributes which give these technologies, in combination, their universal application to every kind of business activity and throughout society.

Viewed from a Schumpeterian perspective, all manufacturers and suppliers of software and service and business users are engaged in a process of creative destruction on a grand scale to engineer, integrate, and synthesize all of the these technologies into a new kind of infrastructure that has the capabilities to mediate, either directly or indirectly, all business and economic activity. They are creating a radically new "intelligent," knowledge-based infrastructure to mediate the design, development, and production of all products, equipment, and machinery, the trading and exchange of all goods and services, as well as the all-important information-processing, communications, and decision-making activities that are so integral to the way organizations, economic systems, and society operate and are structured.

Corporations are using intelligent technology to re-engineer and transform the nature of work and management and the structure and operation of business organizations. They are contributing to a great convergence of industrial activities worldwide and the fusion of economic systems and world civilization into a cohesive and interactive whole. In the process, they are initiating a profound decentralization of decision-making and economic power throughout the world and the globalization of everything.

ACKNOWLEDGMENTS

I would like to thank Dr. Harry Trebing, Professor Emeritus (economics) at Michigan State University for his invaluable assistance in bringing this book to publication. I would also like to acknowledge the contribution to Max Melynk, a senior engineer with many years of experience and expertise in telecommunications engineering, management, and economic matters, who edited the entire manuscript and provided helpful comments and suggestions to improve it. I would like to thank as well the many dozens of personal friends, business acquaintances and university professors who spent many hours of their valuable time discussing the subject matter on numerous occasions over the past eight years or more. Finally, I would like to thank the staff of Strategy & Intelligence for their assistance in preparing the manuscript for publication.

ELECTRONIC TECHNOLOGY, CORPORATE STRATEGY, AND WORLD TRANSFORMATION

Chapter I

Technology, Corporate Strategy, Public Policy, and the Transformation of the World

Wherever we look in the world today, we see the unmistakable signs of social, economic, and political upheaval and, indeed, revolution. In the time span of just three years, for example, between 1989 and 1992, a dozen or more events occurred that fundamentally altered the balance of military, economic, and political power in the world. Some have even argued that they changed the course of world history and world civilization. The most notable of these events were the demise of communism, the fall of the Berlin Wall, the breakup of the Soviet Union, and the end of the cold war. The world is also witnessing the rise of more democratic, market-oriented regimes throughout Eastern Europe, Africa, South America, and Southeast Asia. Even China has become caught up in this maelstrom because it too can no longer insulate itself from the forces of global change. South Africa freed Nelson Mandela and began dismantling apartheid during this period and has now achieved majority rule. And the Israeli government and the Palestine Liberation Organization signed an historic peace accord in 1993 ending over four decades of conflict that threatened to engulf the world. Spectacular upheavals such as these are transforming the old political order everywhere and hold for the first time in this century the possibility of creating a new world economic and democratic political order.

Western nations are also in the throes of an economic and political revolution of their own making—a revolution that has been brought about by the same forces of liberal democracy and capitalism that made them so great. It is these two forces in combination that are propelling a profound technological transformation of the economy and the creation of a global, knowledge-based services economy. The implications of globalization should not be underestimated. For it means more than growing social, economic, and political interdependence among the nations of the world. In some cases like Europe, it means economic integration to the point where national economies are becoming one. One of its most significant implications is a dramatic decline in the economic, political, and even cultural power and sovereignty of nation states—everywhere. The globalization of economic activity is so significant that it calls into question the concept of the nation-state, the role of government, and the industrial model that has served Western nations for over two hundred years.

A growing body of social scientists and, indeed, even business leaders and politicians argue that the concept of industrial society and all that it stood for throughout this century and before is already obsolete. They argue that industrial society has been transformed over the course of the last quarter century or more by innovations in technology, work, management, and organization. We are told that we now live in a new postindustrial age in which information and knowledge, rather than land, labor, and capital, are the pre-eminent factors of production. This debate is not an academic one. For it has extremely important, practical implications for the way we live and make a living and the way we organize and govern ourselves as a society. One of the consequences is that many of the concepts of industrial management and organization developed throughout this century must be radically revised or discarded altogether.

Certainly no one can disagree that we now live in a new technoeconomic and knowledge-based economy. The evidence is everywhere about us, and it is indeed compelling. It is exhibited by the rise of the new biological sciences of genetic engineering and gene therapy and the new materials and information and communications sciences that are moving into the mainstream of economic life. By far the most distinguishing feature of the new economy is the ubiquitous presence of microchips and computers and the millions of devices, equipment, machines, and household products that contain them. Microcomputers also constitute the brains of telephone switches and banking, securities and commodity trading systems, as well as the optical fiber and satellite and radio communications networks which tie all of them together. Offices are literally being transformed into a distributed network of multimedia computers and communicating machines that allow people from all over the world to work together and communicate, cooperate, and interact with one another. State-of-the-art factories are dominated by intelligent, programmable robots, flexible manufacturing systems, and automated guided vehicles.

Another characteristic of the new economic age is the scarcity of factory workers. Many of them have already been replaced by robots and various intelligent machines and networks, but this process of substituting machines for workers has not yet completely run its course. Blue-collar as well as a growing number of white-collar workers, managers, and executives dread what they see as the inevitable destruction of jobs that will be brought about as the computerization of society speeds to its ultimate end.

The new economy, above all, is characterized by the ultra-rapid pace of technological and economic and social change and the obsolescence of everything. Entire bodies of knowledge have become or are becoming outdated and obsolete in shorter and shorter periods of time. Many of the technologies, machines, and ideas and even some of the institutions that have served us so well for the greater part of this century are either outmoded or obsolete altogether. And the skills of vast numbers of office and factory workers and many middle managers are being completely written off. The great industrial corporations of the world are themselves engaged in a process of self-destruction, only they call it by such names as restructuring and business process re-engineering. They are downsizing and shedding millions of workers, managers, and executives at rates that are unprecedented in recent history. And all indications point to the fact that there is more to come.

But not everything has become obsolete. Certain cornerstones of our way life and certain institutions have come to play a far more dominant role in our lives and in our society. Take markets, for example. Markets still exist, and they still carry out their important information, communications, and trading, exchange, and resource allocation functions. They still serve to coordinate economic activity, and money is still the great medium of exchange it has always been. But that is about where the similarities with the past end because money and markets play much more important roles in our society, and they exert much greater influence over the lives of everyone than ever before. The markets of today are also global in scope and their players come from all parts of the world. They are also extremely competitive and efficient by the standards of the past, and, to an increasing degree, they are electronic in nature. Money and information and information-processing, communications, and trading and exchange activities must be electronic to operate at the extremely high speeds and high volumes to make global commerce feasible and efficient. And it has been developments in technology, in information-processing and communications technologies, in particular, that have made many of these innovations in the operation and organization of global markets possible and make them so efficient.

Information and communications technologies have allowed us to create an instant world that recognizes no limits to geography, time, or information-processing, communications or decision-making capacities, or economic or political boundaries for that matter. And it is they more than any other single factor that are facilitating the integration of world commerce, exposing national markets, industries, and companies to competition and introducing great instabilities in international financial markets. It was the automation of the world's securities and options trading systems and their linking together by telecommunications networks that triggered the great stock market crash of 1987 when the leading stock exchanges of the world experienced their biggest plunge in history. The signals reverberated back and forth across the Atlantic and Pacific oceans between the stock exchanges in New York, London, and Tokyo, over the global computer-communications networks. These global electronic securities, commodities, currency, and futures trading systems and the global telecommunications networks which have made them possible have become much more sophisticated and powerful since then. Some would argue that it is they that are really in control. Estimates are that over one trillion dollars in foreign currencies were trading hands in these electronic markets in 1993 by traders, speculators, and institutional investors located all over the world. The speed and volumes of these flows already threatens the financial stability of the world economy and they are continuing to grow.

It was the work of speculators, in particular, operating in these international currency markets that sabotaged efforts by members of the European Community to create a single currency market in 1992 and 1993. Using complex program trading software written by some of the brightest mathematicians, physicists, and engineers they could find, they were able to pounce on the British pound, the Italian lira, and the French franc in succession, driving them down below the price floors established in European central banking system. Central banks lost billions trying to support their currencies while the speculators made their get-away with billions in profits. The lesson these global trading systems have taught us and continue to teach us day by day is that traders, speculators and institutions have much more power than most governments especially when they work together. They can defeat the intentions of almost any government, when there is money to be made, and when they act together. The second conclusion is that these global, information, communications, and financial, and trading and exchange infrastructures have become the means through which economic power and control over the world are wielded and where much of the world's wealth is channeled and invested. They have given rise to huge pools of "stateless" money and "stateless" securities, and they have facilitated the creation of "nomadic" or "stateless" corporations. And it is they, as much as any other factor, that have eroded much of the economic power of governments and nation states.

These observations highlight several critical points. Innovations taking place in the development and application of electronic technology are in effect contributing to the creation of a global electronic infrastructure. This infrastructure comprises hundreds of millions of microchips, computers, storage devices and displays, telephone switches and optical fibers, satellites, and microwave and radio communications transmission systems which interconnect manufacturers, suppliers, distributors, retailers, banks, stock exchanges, and offices and homes everywhere. To an increasing degree, all are being integrated in a variety of ways so they can operate as a single interdependent global entity. This evolving electronic information-processing and communications infrastructure already represents the new medium for global communications, and, increasingly, it is evolving as the basic medium for the global sharing of information and knowledge, for trading and exchanging the goods and services of the world, and for investing the world's wealth.

This electronic infrastructure also represents the new medium for the evolution of a new form of capitalism—a capitalism that is not confined by geography or land masses or to nation states—a capitalism that is electronic, optical, and photonic, and, therefore, instant and global as well. The new economic order could, indeed, be called "telecapitalism," "computer-capitalism," or "electronic-capitalism." And, it is affecting literally everything.

The structure and operation of business enterprises and even the nature, meaning, and concept of organization itself are also being fundamentally altered by innovations in work and management, and many of these are being made possible by the application of information and communications technologies. The new infrastructures that companies are creating are also instant and electronic and have incredible information processing and communications capacities. And they are expanding by orders of magnitude the capabilities of organizations to efficiently produce, store and access, process, and communicate information, knowledge, and intellectual products, and engage in almost any kind of activity.

Corporations are using the technology, for example, to create and communicate complex engineering and architectural designs and publish materials and interact, share information, make decisions, coordinate their activities with one another, and trade and transact business throughout the global marketplace. Through cooperative and collaborative computing and workgroup technologies, hundreds of scientists, engineering designers and developers, and marketing specialists in separate locations around the world can work simultaneously on the same document, design, or problem and pool the expertise and ideas of everyone. This way they can take advantage of incredible synergics and realize productivity enhancements that were previously impossible. They can also operate three consecutive shifts in the three principle economic time zones of the world in any twenty-four-hour period. All work and work-related activities are, in fact, becoming mediated by computers and telecommunications networks in ways such as these.

Information and communications technology allows corporations to create new kinds of information-intensive, and knowledge-intensive learning organizations. They can design and engineer their information-processing and communications infrastructures to delegate decision making down and out into the organization to worker-managed teams located around the country and around the world in ways that enable them to achieve optimum strategic competitive advantage. The new corporate information infrastructure holds the potential to empower workers and people everywhere. They are also breaking down the barriers that separated work activities within and between companies and fusing them into a new interactive supraorganizational model. What is evolving is a new form of postindustrial "telecorporation" that has a minimum of hierarchy and a maximum of horizontal, intracompany and intercompany flows of information, communications, coordination, and decision-making activities. These are loosely structured, amorphous organizations which are continually changing and evolving in response to changes and demands placed on them by customers, markets, suppliers, competitors, and government policies.

The computerization of corporate organizations and the marketplace is also eliminating the boundaries between industrial activities and causing previously separate industries and sectors of the economy to converge and compete with one another. This so-called "convergence" phenomenon is synonymous with the collapse of the technological, geographical, legal and regulatory boundaries that separated industries in the industrial age, and it is forcing a great restructuring and transformation on the entire economy. In the seventies, the focus of convergence was on the merger of computers, telecommunications, and office and factory systems. It precipitated the deregulation of the telecommunications industry and culminated in the American Telephone & Telegraph Company breakup. In the eighties, the banking and financial services sector became the focus of convergence as banks, brokerage houses, insurance companies, big retailers, and information service suppliers began using the technology to demolish the boundaries that separated their industries. Here again the institutional repercussions and impacts of convergence have been phenomenal. The result has been the obsolescence of most of the legal and regulatory boundaries that separated these industries in the United States, the United Kingdom, Canada, and elsewhere.

The convergence of computers; telecommunications, consumer electronics; cable television; and information, publishing, broadcasting, and entertainment industries was the most newsworthy event of 1993. For it initiated a no-holds-barred struggle among giant telephone, cable television, publishing, motion picture, and entertainment companies operating competitively and cooperatively through mergers and acquisitions and joint ventures and strategic alliances to gain as much control as possible over these evolving electronic markets and electronic and photonic distribution systems into homes and throughout national and global economies.

The leaders in these industries are attempting to use technology to create a variety of national and global conglomerates with strengths in as many of these industries as possible. They include giants like Time Warner Incorporated, Tele-Communications Incorporated, and News Corporation of Australia that control huge cable television, broadcasting, entertainment, and publishing portfolios; telephone and telecommunications companies like AT&T, Bell Atlantic, and BellSouth; and world-scale manufacturers like General Motors/Hughes Electronics, General Electric and IBM; as well as software companies like Microsoft Corporation, Apple Computer, and Novell; and banks, retailers, and many others. These players are gambling hundreds of billions of dollars in an all-out effort to create and control the electronic superhighways that will deliver everything imaginable into the homes of every nation in the next decade and beyond. These are but a few examples of how companies are using computers, telecommunications, and their capital and knowledge resources to compete and create and take advantage of the opportunities in the new economy. The effect of the actions of all of them together will be to further restructure and transform economic activity in yet another dimension.

THE VIRTUAL ECONOMY

The development and application of microchips and computer and telecommunications technologies is contributing to the creation of a strange and abstract new world. Indeed, the new language and the new concepts that are being used to describe this new world have been borrowed from the computer industry. We are told that the new frontiers of work, organization, and of economic activity are in a "cyberspace," a "hyperspace," or "virtual space," as it has been called, that exists in the space inside computers, microchips, and telecommunications networks, and that many of us already work in this space, which is not confined or constrained by the usual physical and economic realities of the industrial age. Scientists and engineers are actively building sophisticated models of real and imaginary designs, concepts, products, and systems in this virtual space and simulating them in a completely artificial or virtual environment. And they have complete control over everything that takes place in this imaginary virtual world. This new and emerging domain of "virtual reality" is one of the most important consequences of the microchip and computer revolutions. It is rapidly evolving as the focal point of the new factory, the new office, and the new workshop of the world.

Virtual laboratories already exist that operate within the confines of the most advanced computer networks of the world, and they do not recognize national boundaries, or time zones, or any spatial or temporal barriers of any kind. And growing numbers of scientists, engineers, artists, and program producers are operating in this virtual workplace, sharing ideas, communicating and cooperating with one another, and creating incredibly complex designs and program content and new knowledge with tremendous speeds and efficiencies and with a minimum expenditure of energy and materials. Leading-edge companies in the United States, Japan, and Europe are investing huge sums to develop applications of virtual reality technology in business, entertainment, and education and training. Scientists, engineers, architects, artists, educators, software developers, program producers, and many other knowledge workers all over the world are involved in this effort to create "virtual worlds" that exist in pure software inside "silicon" chips in computers, computer networks, and the private and public information infrastructures that are being created. The ultimate product of their efforts will be the creation of a "virtual economy."

Advancing technology is indeed already giving rise to a new form of organization which has been called the "virtual corporation." It is an organization that has no formal structure in the usual sense. It is highly networked and flexible and interactive. It exists as a network within and a part of a variety of other networks, including the biggest one of all, that is, the network that constitutes the global marketplace and the global economy.

All of this serves to point out that the innovations taking place in the application of the microchip and computer and telecommunications technologies, aided and facilitated by innovations in work and organization, have already transformed much of the world in which we live and work, into something new and strange and different from anything most of us have ever conceived of in the past—something that is closer to science fiction than physical reality in terms of its structure organization and operation. And this demonstrates, once again, the need to recognize and understand the scientific, economic, and organizational principles and laws that now underpin the new kinds of work and production processes, as well as the structure and behavior of the new organizations and economic systems that are evolving.

Increasingly, we are living in a virtual economic system that recognizes no physical, geographical, temporal or organizational boundaries. And there may no longer be any limits to the kinds of wealth that we can create in the future by exploiting the new economic opportunities that are being opened up by the application of these technologies. The fundamental economic laws of the evolving virtual economy recognize that the basic factors of production are no longer land, labor, and capital or even energy and matter at a more fundamental level. Ultimately, the only real factors of production and the only real limits to economic growth and prosperity are knowledge, creativity, imagination, and intelligence. And the technologies embodied in the microchip and the computer and telecommunications networks could provide the means to harness these factors of production for the good of mankind.

KNOWLEDGE AND SCIENCE AND TECHNOLOGY AS AGENTS OF SOCIAL CHANGE, ECONOMIC GROWTH, AND CREATIVE DESTRUCTION

This line of argument brings us back once again to the subject of knowledge, the prime mover and principal agent of social and economic change in Western societies, and its discovery and application. Knowledge has always been the quintessential factor of production and of social and economic change and development but seldom has its influence on society been quite so pervasive as it is today. Knowledge is special because it knows no bounds and literally no action or economic activity can be accomplished without it. Knowledge has application to literally everything. Knowledge is omniscient. And our society invests enormous sums in its creation, recording, communication, and management and application, by maintaining enormous libraries in which to store it, as well as spending vast sums on education and training and scientific research and development. The application of this knowledge plays fundamental roles in work and management and in the creation and operation of organizations, institutions, markets, cultures, and society as a whole because human beings are intelligent, learning creatures, creators, appliers, and communicators of knowledge. Everything we do, including all of the social, economic, and political organizations and institutions we create, is the result of the knowledge we create or learn or acquire through experience, education, experimentation, and discovery. And this is why it is, indeed, true that we live in a knowledge society.

No wonder everything is changing so rapidly. All of the changes taking place at the present time are the result of the collective revolutions in wisdom and knowledge over the ages and their application to all things. And the more we invest in knowledge, the greater is its impact on society in terms of the speed, scope, and pervasiveness of change. The result is ever-growing mountains of knowledge and the knowledge-intensive activity that are becoming obsolete over shorter and shorter periods of time.

Here again the information-processing and communications infrastructures that are being created within organizations and throughout society are playing a critical role in the creation and management of a knowledge-based society. The computer in all of its myriad manifestations along with all of its various software tools and telecommunications networks and all of the programmed content that they contain and are capable of mediating are amplifying our abilities to create, communicate, and apply all of these growing volumes of knowledge. Consequently, these technologies too are the great facilitators and the great instigators of change, and all of them are playing a most critical role in the creation of a knowledge-based society.

All of this goes to point out that knowledge, in all of its various manifestations, including its embodiment in technologies and social and economic infrastructures, as well as economic production processes and organizations and institutions, are all-important because they are sources of wealth, power and control in economic society. This search for and application of knowledge, including its manifestation as technologies and organization, for example, and through the pursuit of invention and discovery and, therefore, change itself, are integral to the very social, economic, and political fabric of Western societies. They are programmed into our constitutions and our systems of learning and legislation and our laws, regulations, and political systems, and they represent the basic elements of democratic, capitalist institutions. Democracy and capitalism in point of fact together constitute a unique kind of social and economic organization that never is, and perhaps never will be, in a state of equilibrium.

When examined over a sufficiently long period of a time, of a century or more, and often over shorter periods of time, of a decade or less as is the case today, it is clear that our society is in a constant state of disequilibrium, of continuous change, growth, and evolution. Controlled chaos or managed chaos, or, "creative destruction," as Joseph Schumpeter[1] described it, is the best way of describing the combined effects of capitalism and democracy on society. And it is to an understanding of these dynamics and the interplay between technology, capitalism and society to which the remainder of this chapter is devoted.

FROM AN INDUSTRIAL TO AN INTELLIGENT ECONOMY

The reality is that rapid technological and economic change and creative destruction have always been essential to economic growth and development as well as the competitive advantage of corporations and of nations but never perhaps more than they are today. Over the centuries, Western societies have been transformed by literally hundreds and thousands of distinct technological and organizational and economic innovations and discoveries in a process that has been relatively continuous at times, discontinuous at other times, and relatively static over long periods at other times. Certain kinds of knowledge, certain ideas, and certain technologies have had such unique and omnipotent attributes that their impacts on the economy and on society are so great that the adjective "transformative" is the only word to adequately describe them. Intelligent technology is one of these transformative technologies.

By intelligent technology, I mean the technology that is the foundation of "thinking machines." These are machines that have the capability to collect, process, store, retrieve, and communicate information on their own, automatically, with tremendous speed, efficiency, and accuracy, and to act on this information in a "rational," and "purposeful," manner, without human intervention. This action and this control is achieved indirectly, that is, through stored program control.

Intelligent technology is a much more advanced and sophisticated control technology than any previous technology. The industrial and information societies of the past depended on manual, mechanical, and analogue technologies to facilitate economic production processes as well as those of creating, processing, and communicating information and knowledge and making decisions. Their technological underpinnings were based on passive, physical, analogue technologies (such as cogs, belts, levers, gears, wheels, hammers, and pistons, for example) which had relatively limited application. The industrial economy also depended on physical motion and enormous amounts of energy and materials to operate.

By contrast, the intelligent technologies and intelligent machines of today are "active," digital, programmable entities and are capable of capturing, producing processing, and communicating information in all of its many forms, so they have universal application to all human socioeconomic activity. And, to an increasing degree, they are solid-state devices. That is to say, they operate by simulating the real world through the control and manipulation of electrons and photons. They operate "inside" materials rather than "outside," in the electronic and optical or photonic domain,[2] so they use a minimum of energy and physical resources and this has phenomenal importance to the economy and society in the future.

The newest unique factor of production and many of the new commodities of the evolving postindustrial economy are characterized by their nonmaterial and, therefore, invisible software existence. This is due to the existence of a fundamental "dematerialization" and "intellectualization" force that seems to underpin all economic activity, and it is propelling the current technological and economic revolution. This force is synonymous, first of all, with the creation of machines in the form of computers with increasingly powerful intelligence capabilities and, second, with their miniaturization in the form of ever-smaller microchip devices and their incorporation into all machinery and equipment. This same force is resulting in the substitution of physical production processes by information, communications, and human intellectual processes and, finally, the substitution of physical products by invisible, nonmaterial, and nonphysical, software-based intellectual products. The result is the replacement of bulky electromechanical machines by miniature, solid-state intelligent machines and the rise of an intellectual or software economy. It is this intelligent technology and its capability to mediate all socioeconomic intelligence activities that give the evolving postindustrial economy its unique character and differentiate it from both the industrial and information economies of the past.

All of those factors and characteristics that make the emerging postindustrial society unique are thus derived from its technological underpinnings, its basic machinery and socioeconomic infrastructures, and its communications media which exhibit ever-more powerful and sophisticated degrees of this automatic, programmed intelligence. To one degree or another, these machines and infrastructures exhibit a growing spectrum of intelligent functionality ranging from relatively simple information processing and communications capabilities (i.e., involving logical and text manipulation, for example) to the more sophisticated capabilities of seeing, speaking, and recognizing spoken commands, shapes and images, and, ultimately, of thinking, perhaps in a manner that may some day put it on a par with the human brain. The basic commodities of the new economic system and the new postindustrial society are implemented in, and represented by, software, and these together with its intelligent hardware machines and infrastructures represent its new form of capital and wealth.

By facilitating and mediating its information and communications activities, its banking and financial services, its production, distribution, and trading and exchange activities, intelligent technology constitutes the foundation of the evolving "twenty-first century" corporation and the "twenty-first century" economy. To the extent that its underlying technological underpinnings exhibit this same degree of artificial machine intelligence, it is more proper to call this an "intelligent economy" or an "intelligent society."

To understand how this transformation of society occurs, we need a model or paradigm that links all of these corporate, technological, and organizational entities with one another and with the social, economic, and institutional dimensions of society, including the market system, the economy, and society itself. And it is the development of this model to which I shall now turn beginning with the link between technology and the economy.

TRANSFORMING THE TECHNOLOGICAL AND
ECONOMIC UNDERPINNINGS

Of all the factors influencing economic growth and development and the structure and organization of economic society, none has more profound impacts than science, technology, and knowledge and institutions devoted to their discovery, application, and diffusion throughout society. In their book *How the West Grew Rich,* Nathan Rosenberg and L. E. Birdzell wrote "Western economic innovation owes much to the interaction between economic and scientific spheres. Underlying the geometric growth in output of Western economies has been a geometric growth in scientific knowledge, linked to a variety of institutions that transmute the growth in scientific knowledge into growth in material welfare. This growth of scientific knowledge has shaped, nurtured, and fuelled Western economic growth. It offers a key to understanding the growth process."[3]

Within this context, however, it is the corporation as an institution that is the principal agent of change as much as any other factor.[4] It is the corporation, after all, which brings all of the factors of production together to supply the needs of society. The corporation is forced by competitive pressures to use knowledge, technology, information, people, and organizations to achieve strategic competitive advantage of one kind or another. It can do so by employing or embodying technology in its essential design, development, or production processes; in its distribution, marketing, or sales systems; or in its communications, coordination, and decision-making processes, which are essential for them to operate. Or it can use technology in all of these ways in combination. If it is successful, then every other corporation is forced to adopt these same innovations or suffer an inevitable fate. And the economy advances to another stage of development and evolution through this step-by-step process.

But how can these strategies and these technologies be made to transform the world? Just how do corporations use technology to accomplish this incredible feat? And what is so special about intelligent technology that it can be used to transform the world in such profound ways?

Figure 1.1 illustrates the principle that the transformation of business and economic society is being driven by the strategies of leading corporate enterprises in the context of the market economy as well as institutions and the policies of governments and that it is science, technology, and knowledge and their discovery and application that are playing key roles in propelling economic society forward into ever-increasing degrees of technological and organizational complexity and sophistication.

All of the essential elements to the explanation have been described above. One is that the microchip and computer and telecommunications technologies are truly flexible, intelligent, programmable technologies. That is, they exhibit a wide variety of intelligent functionalities that have, shall we say, "universal," practical applications to all social, economic, and organizational activities. These

Figure 1.1
A Paradigm for the Transformation of Economic Society

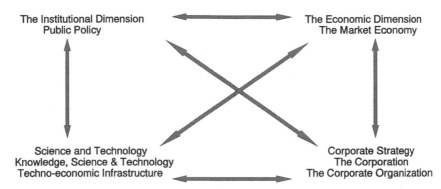

features enable corporations to design and apply these technologies to change the nature of the goods and services they produce and the ways they produce and distribute them to serve their customers. To take truly effective advantage of the opportunities offered by this technology, corporations are forced to change the nature of work, management, and their organizational structures to better compete, that is, to re-engineer and reinvent themselves. Ultimately, they transform the basic information-processing, communications, production, distribution, and trading and exchange systems and infrastructures of society. Intelligent technology in combination with corporate strategies and public policies ultimately affect the way society is operated and organized from both an economic, institutional, and political perspective.[5] Technology even has an effect on our demands for natural resources so it affects our natural environment in profound ways.

For all of the many component parts and players in economic society, including all of its individuals and organizations and all of the activities they engage in, and all of its industries and sectors, and its socioeconomic infrastructures, and the natural environment itself are linked together in a great matrix of interdependencies to form a single integrated system or organism. That is to say, all are part of an enormous anthropological, cybernetic feedback and control system. It is knowledge, intellectual technologies, and information and communications technologies, in particular, as well as organization and institutions that permeate and bind all of these together into one cohesive entity so that changes in any one can induce changes in one or more or all of the others in a chain reaction.[6] These factors and forces interact in such a way as to influence the structure, operation, and organization of the economic society as illustrated in Figure 1.1.

All of these entities can be seen to be organized in a hierarchy consisting of at least four components as illustrated in Figure 1.2. The first, the sociopolitical system, serves a vital control, coordination, communications, decision-making,

Figure 1.2
The Hierarchial Organization of Economic Society

The Sociopolitical System
$\updownarrow$
The Economic System
$\updownarrow$
The Technology Platform
$\updownarrow$
The Natural Resource Platform

and intelligence purpose. By specifying the rights and freedoms of individuals, private organizations, and governments, the political system gives legitimacy to all of their activities as well as the organization and operation of society. The second level in this hierarchy consists of the economic systems of production and distribution and trading and exchange which serve to provide for the material and nonmaterial welfare of society. At the bottom of this hierarchy are two foundation elements which I have called the technology and the natural resource platforms. Intelligent technology is the product of the interaction among all four elements. On the other hand, it is through its impacts on each and all of these elements that intelligent technology is able to transform society.

The technology platform embodies the practical application of knowledge and state-of-the-art science and technology developed by society to all manner of things to serve useful, practical, productive objectives and pursuits. This platform constitutes the foundation of the basic infrastructures of economic society, including its production and distribution systems, its trading and exchange systems and its information and communications systems. The technology platform is of fundamental importance because it serves to transform primary natural resources into finished products, including food, clothing, and machinery and equipment. It also serves as the means for mediating its information and communications activities. To one degree or another, the technology platform determines the scope of possibilities for structuring and organizing economic society, for creating wealth, and for raising its standard of living.

The technological changes described in previous sections can now be seen in this context. The technology platform is clearly undergoing a transformation from one dominated by electromechanical machinery, paper, and transportation infrastructures to one increasingly dominated by the computer, the microchip and telecommunications networks, software, artificial intelligence, and intellectual commodities. A distinct trend is also taking place towards the use of electronic and optical or photonic and optoelectronic technologies and machinery and equipment and infrastructures based on them. Complementing this change is an equally significant change in the material and biological underpinnings of society. The new material sciences, for example, are making it possible to create "artificial," "smart" materials that have "supernatural" properties. Smart materials can absorb, convert, store, and conduct energy much more efficiently and even learn and react to their environment. And biotechnology and genetic engineering are giving mankind the power to intervene in the natural biological processes by which living organisms are engineered. This makes it possible to create "artificial" living organisms through the manipulation and programming of the genetic code.

The technology platform dictates what is economically feasible and efficient to produce in the context of society's needs. It thus determines the demands on the stock of its natural resources. Fundamental changes in the technology platform, therefore, initiate changes in the demands for natural resources which, in turn, can have dramatic effects on the natural environment. The ensemble of natural resources on which economic society depends at any one time constitutes what I have called its natural resource platform. It consists of all of the primary resources and raw materials, including ores, wood, water, and energy, and plants and animals, including grains, fruits and vegetables, and other foodstuffs, as well as fish, game, and other animals. The technology platform of the economic system of production has evolved over the centuries from that of the preindustrial agricultural age, based on the use of animals, including the ox and the horse, and wind and water power, along with human muscle, for example, to that of the industrial age, based on mechanical and electromechanical technology and the intensive use of energy and materials. This technology platform ultimately became the basis of the factory system, which came to constitute the most visible and most dominating and influential institution of the industrial age. And it is this technological platform that is now undergoing dramatic changes today to one that is energy- materials- and manual-labor conserving and this in turn is creating an economic system that is intellectual labor-enhancing and intellectual capital-intensive.

TRANSFORMING THE STRUCTURE, ORGANIZATION, AND OPERATION OF ECONOMIC SOCIETY

This transformation of the technological underpinnings of industrial society, in turn, is precipitating a transformation in the structure, organization, and operation of the economic system itself. It is contributing to the creation of new industries, the destruction of old industries, and the transformation of most of those that remain in one way or another. And it is propelling economic activity into the invisible electronic, cybernetic domain of things where all activity can take place independently of geography and space and time and even material and energy constraints. The electronic superhighways that are evolving today thus represent a powerful force for coordinating, rationalizing, and restructuring economic activity on a global scale.

Corporate enterprises throughout the world are using technology and organization to create and take advantage of new business opportunities by penetrating new geographical and product and service markets in every sector of the economy. Manufacturers, banks, brokerage and investment houses, and retailers are using the technology to create electronic, information, and communications linkages with their suppliers and their customers. In these and other ways, intelligent technology represents a powerful integrating force that is fusing formerly separate, competing, and noncompeting enterprises, industries, and sectors of the economy. And it is erasing the distinctions and the boundaries between companies and industries and sectors of the economy.

Technology is also changing the factors that determine the efficient size and scale of operation of corporate enterprises and the nature and number of activities in which they can efficiently engage. By affecting the size of companies and the nature of the activities they engage in, it influences the relative efficiency of both markets and corporate organizations in mediating economic activity. In some cases, the effect is to complement, extend, and enhance the efficiency of the market as the great mediator and allocator of economic resources. In other cases, however, its effect is to enhance the efficiency and superiority of the corporation over those of the market, thereby subordinating competitive market forces and the market itself to the control of private enterprises.

The consequence is that competition is increasing and predominating in some sectors while, in others, corporations are internalizing more and more transactions and in some cases what used to be entire markets. In the latter case, it is resulting in much greater industrial concentration.

Ultimately, all of these technological, organizational, and economic operating forces in combination create the conditions whereby the legal, regulatory, and institutional structures that are designed to administer and control industrial activity at the level of the national economy become incompatible with the underlying economic and technological realities at the level of the corporation, the industrial sector, and the marketplace. Through their effects on the production, distribution, and information-processing and communications systems of individual enterprises, they are precipitating a process of industrial rationalization and restructuring of all economic activity on both a national and a global scale.

The rise of the computer-mediated economy in which all design, production, and distribution systems are based on information-processing and communications systems can also be linked to the relative decline of the traditional manufacturing base, that is to the phenomenon of "deindustrialization" that many nations have been experiencing in recent years. A related phenomenon is the "hollowing out" of the modern manufacturing corporation, which is synonymous with the transformation from hardware to software, the "outsourcing" of many manufacturing activities to newly industrializing countries, and the rise of a new international division of labor.

THE GLOBAL ECONOMIC AND POLITICAL DIMENSION

The economic dynamics described above are having some of their most dramatic impacts at the political level. The rise of global optical and electronic infrastructures that efficiently and inexpensively mediate the flows of information, knowledge, and educational and entertainment content of all kinds throughout the world are contributing to the creation of near-perfect national and global markets. They are making it possible for individuals to invest their money and wealth, through pension funds and mutual funds, for example, in world markets where the return is greatest. The size of these global pools of capital has exploded in recent years to the point that they are knocking down the doors of entry into almost every developing country. Mutual funds, according to *The Wall Street Journal*, have even taken over the financing role of big banks and quasi-governmental institutions such as the International Monetary Fund and the World Bank. Through their impacts on the global flows of information, knowledge, money, and wealth, these information and communications infrastructures are redistributing economic and political power and wealth throughout the world. They are distributing it away from governments and nation states to global markets, global corporations, and global investors and speculators. At the same time, new international institutions like the World Trade Organization are being created to oversee the implementation of the new trading regime established under the General Agreement on Tariffs and Trade signed in December 1993. War is also becoming obsolete. In some respects, the technological and economic revolutions constitute one of the most powerful democratizing forces the world has ever seen.

I will go so far as to argue that these same technological and economic dynamics have played a profound direct as well as indirect role in the demise of communism. It is widely recognized that the transborder flows of Western radio, television, video, and print media played an important role in the fall of communism, the consequences of which continue to reverberate around the world. Greed and corruption had also permeated the very core of political power in the Soviet Union. Much of the decay has also been linked to its excessively centralized and authoritarian economic and political system. The institutions for generating and harnessing technological and organizational innovation and change in the Soviet Union as well were incapable of keeping pace with those of the West at a time when the pace of change had accelerated to the point that many nations in the West were, themselves, having trouble keeping up. The production and distribution systems of the Soviet Union continued to be based on those of the industrial age of the past and, hence, were utterly obsolete. Its state-owned enterprises and its institutions had failed to make the transition to the new technological and intellectual standards based on microelectronics, computers, software, and telecommunications. The system, in effect, collapsed under its own weight. It collapsed because it was obsolete.

But capitalism itself is changing and adapting to the times and circumstances. In addition to an American capitalism, a European capitalism, and a Japanese capitalism, we already have the makings of an Eastern European capitalism, a South American capitalism, an Asian capitalism, and possibly even an African capitalism. Each has its own distinctive features. Western capitalism is changing as well. Employee ownership schemes are on the rise in many capitalist countries including the United States, and the wealth of the citizens of Western countries in the form of pension and mutual funds, for example, is transforming developing nations and indeed the world. Technology and capitalism are proving to have the potential to empower knowledge workers everywhere. Peter Drucker has referred to the new order as "information capitalism." I referred to it above as "electronic capitalism" and in a previous publication as "programmed capitalism." Some economists have even gone so far as to conclude that the "perennial gales of creative destruction" that are powering the current revolutions are also poised to transform capitalism, ironically, into a kind of people's capitalism, not entirely unlike that which Karl Marx foresaw over a century ago. If so, nations everywhere and capitalism itself are truly poised on the threshold of a new era.

NOTES

1. Joseph A. Schumpeter, *Capitalism, Socialism and Democracy* (London: Allen and Unwin, 1943).

2. George Gilder has called this domain the "microcosm." See George Gilder, *Microcosm: The Quantum Revolution in Economics and Technology* (New York: Simon and Schuster, 1989).

3. Nathan Rosenberg and L. E. Birdzell, Jr., *How the West Grew Rich: The Economic Transformation of the Industrial World* (New York: Basic Books, 1986), p. 333. Robert Solow, who won the Nobel Prize in economics in 1979, provided statistical evidence in the fifties that technological change contributed more to economic growth than the savings rate or capital investment.

4. For a treatise on the relationship between corporate strategy and industrial market structure, I highly recommend Alfred Chandler, *The Invisible Hand* (Cambridge: Harvard University Press, 1977) and *Strategy and Structure* (Cambridge: Harvard University Press, 1990).

5. For an economic analysis of the relationship between information technology and the economy, see *New Technologies in the Nineties: A Socio-Economic Strategy* (Paris: Organization for Economic Cooperation and Development, 1988) and *Technology and the Economy: The Key Relationships* (Paris: Organization for Economic Cooperation and Development, 1992).

6. James Beniger has demonstrated that economic revolutions can be linked to developments in information process, communications, and control technologies. Refer to James R. Beniger, *The Control Revolution: Technological and Economic Origins of the Information Society* (Cambridge: Harvard University Press, 1986).

Chapter 2

The Role of Electronic Technology in the Creation of the Advanced Industrial Society

Some of the greatest organizational and socioeconomic revolutions in history occurred as a result of innovations in communications technology and media. The invention of the printing press, for example, in the mid-fifteenth century by the German typographer Johann Gutenberg initiated the knowledge revolutions in science and technology, commerce, engineering, law, and politics. Indirectly, the print medium gave rise to the market economy based on paper and contributed to the industrial revolution. The development of electricity in the nineteenth century initiated a series of other revolutions which transformed industrial society in profound ways. It led to a broad range of electrical and electromechanical inventions, including the light bulb, the dynamo, the electric motor and hundreds of electric machines based on it, as well as the telegraph, the telephone, radio, and television. These diffused throughout the economy, influencing the nature and location of production, the structure and operation of business organizations, including offices and factories and the marketplace itself.[1] Ultimately, they came to constitute the technological underpinnings of the hydroelectric and communications and transportation infrastructures we know today. These, in turn, influenced the evolution of the mass production, mass consumption, and mass communications society of the twentieth century.

TELEGRAPHY AND THE FIRST ELECTRONIC COMMUNICATIONS REVOLUTION

The invention of the telegraph initiated the first truly electronic communications revolution and gave rise to the age of instant global electronic communications. Although the British team of William Fothergill Cooke and Sir Charles Wheatstone built and tested a telegraph in 1837, the credit for inventing a practical one and commercializing it goes to the American Samuel Morse, a painter, and his partner, Alfred Vail, an engineer. With Vail's assistance, Morse developed a crude prototype of a system that recorded messages directly on paper. An electromagnetic relay was used to regenerate the signals over long distances to compensate for degradation, and an electromagnet was used at the receiving end to move a pen to record the coded message on a strip of paper. The Morse telegraph system was patented in 1840, and operators gradually found that they could read the sound of the pen as easily as from the paper. The pen was eventually replaced by a sounder.

Morse had considerable difficulty in obtaining financial backing to demonstrate his invention but eventually obtained a $30,000 grant from Congress to build a 40-mile telegraph line between Washington, D.C., and Baltimore. On May 14, 1844, he completed the link and succeeded in sending his famous message, "What hath God wrought," between the two cities. Morse subsequently enlisted the help of Amos Kendall, a retired postmaster general, to set about building a nationwide telegraph system. Kendall applied his knowledge about postal services to accomplish this task, raising money to invest in lines connecting cities with drops within cities. Telegraph companies quickly sprouted up in major American cities catering to the exploding demand for person-to-person message communications for individuals, businesses, and governments. Being a written message communications medium, telegraph services grew to rival the national postal service, and railway companies became involved in the business. By 1851 there were fifty companies in the telegraph business in the United States, most licensed under Morse's patent. Many of them merged in 1856 to form the Western Union Company. By 1857, the six leading telegraph companies in the United States had signed a treaty dividing the nation into six regions, but these were subsequently merged into three, and finally into a single company. The Western Union Telegraph Company emerged as the de facto monopoly provider of telegraph services in the United States spanning the nation coast to coast by 1861.

By 1851, Britain had 4,000 miles of internal telegraph lines. In the same year, a telegraph link was inaugurated between Britain and France. Two unsuccessful attempts were made to link Britain and the United States, but it was not until 1867 that the first successful transatlantic telegraph cable was laid. It ushered in the era of instant transatlantic communications.

Besides representing a successful commercial business itself, the telegraph became the basis of a number of important new business ventures. One of these was a printing telegraph invented in 1855 by David Hughes in which messages were typed out at the transmitted and receiving ends. Several decades later, telegraph companies began introducing switched teleprinter services. These evolved into the worldwide telex services in the mid-twentieth century. Telegraphy grew to play an important role in the newspaper industry and the stock exchanges. It provided the incentive for P. J. von Reuter in Aachen, Germany, to form his own company in 1849 to transmit commercial intelligence including stock market information across Europe. His business has since grown into the vast Reuters global information and intelligence empire that is involved today in everything from providing newswire services, corporate and economic information, and securities, foreign currency, and other financial information services. But today it relies on databases and a global computer and communications network to make its services available throughout the world.

A quarter century after its invention, telegraph service had become an essential service for newspapers, journalists, merchants, financiers, stock exchanges, railroads, and businessmen in North America, Europe, and Asia. European governments used it to keep in touch with their vast and growing colonial empires in the late nineteenth and early twentieth centuries. By the turn of the century, nearly 400 million telegrams were being sent annually throughout the world. Europe was connected by 130,000 kilometers of telegraph wire and the United States of America by 80,000 kilometers.

The telegraph had an extraordinary impact on business in the late nineteenth and early twentieth centuries. By making information available instantly across the markets of the world, it integrated local, national, and international markets, thus destroying the monopoly power and control that many business organizations had over local and regional markets. The telegraph transformed the spatial and temporal organization of economic activity throughout the world and came to synchronize the social, economic, and political activities of everyone across space and time. The telegraph "provided the decisive and cumulative break of the identity of communications and transportation," wrote James Carey. It became "a model of and a mechanism for the control of the physical movement of things, specifically for the railroad. . . . [It] . . . brought a decline in arbitrage, [that is,] the buying cheap and selling dear by moving goods around in space . . . [and it affected] the practical consciousness of time through the construction of standard time zones."[2]

The telegraph complemented the railroad, setting off an economic revolution in its own right in the late-nineteenth and early-twentieth centuries, according to the economic historian Alfred Chandler. The railroad and telegraph companies were the first modern business enterprises to appear in the United States, and they became the model for the modern industrial corporation. They provided "the fast, regular and dependable transportation and communications services so essential to high volume production and distribution—the hallmark of large, modern manufacturing or marketing enterprises."[3] The telegraph became strategic for businesses to coordinate their operations on an ever-expanding scale through space and time and enabled them to expand nationally and then internationally. It initiated the first of several waves of technological innovations that resulted in the globalization of business and communications media in the late nineteenth and twentieth century.

TELEPHONY: THE SECOND ELECTRONIC COMMUNICATIONS REVOLUTION

The invention of the telephone precipitated the second electronic communications revolution in the late nineteenth century. Because it was a two-way medium and because it carried voice, the telephone initiated a more socially and economically significant communication revolution than the telegraph. The telephone is a marvel of technical and engineering design and operation, and it became the first true universal, instant, global, personal, information, and communications medium. Today, the telephone system interconnects hundreds of millions of people around the world and provides them with the means to communicate instantly by voice, written message, computer, and facsimile whether they are at home, in the office, or in a car, a truck, or an airplane. The telephone became one of the most important social and economic technologies in history by providing a medium for exchanging personal and business information, coordinating social, economic, and political activities, facilitating decision making, and simply keeping in touch.[4] And, it does this with little or no human intervention.

The telephone was invented by Alexander Graham Bell, a Scotsman, who emigrated to Canada and subsequently moved to Boston as a teacher of the deaf. Bell was a brilliant scientist and inventor interested in everything from the science of speech and hearing to flight and communications, and during his lifetime, he even built a hydrofoil that set a world water-speed record in 1919 that held for a decade, as well as an airplane called the Silver Dart. One of Bell's great interests in life was to find ways to enable the deaf to hear. While in Boston in the mid-1870s, Bell was working on ways to improve the telegraph at the request of the Western Union Telegraph Company. Working with his assistant, Thomas Watson, in his laboratory in Boston on June 2, 1875, the two men apparently made an improper connection in setting up their equipment and succeeded in transmitting not intermittent current, but continuous current so that they actually transmitted sound. Bell began perfecting the apparatus to carry the human voice.

On February 14, 1876, Bell applied to the New York patent office for a patent for the telephone. Two hours later, a rival, Elisha Gray, showed up at the patent office to file a patent for the telephone. Although Bell was awarded the patent, it was not until March 6, 1876, that he succeeded in getting the device to transmit the now-famous words: "Come here Watson, I want you." This was the first recorded electrical transmission of the human voice.

Bell was not a businessman but a humanitarian and visionary who wanted the telephone to develop in a different kind of business than the telegraph. He saw the telephone developing into a business that would enable every individual, home, and business to communicate with one another rather than one that served primarily businesses. In a letter to a group of British investors, Bell wrote that the telephone would enable "a man in one part of the country [to] communicate by word of mouth with another in a distant place."

Instead of running the telephone business himself, Bell relied on Gardiner Hubbard, a lawyer and businessman (and subsequently his business partner and father-in-law), to commercialize his invention. Hubbard tried selling the Bell patents to Western Union for a sum of $100,000, but Western Union executives balked at the idea that anyone would ever want to talk to one another over great distances. Western Union would soon regret this decision. Hubbard decided to proceed by forming the Bell Telephone Company to concentrate on the New York business and the New England Telephone Company to locate franchises in local areas throughout the country. He then formed National Bell to concentrate on long distance service. In 1878, Hubbard hired Theodore N. Vail (a distant relative of Alfred Vail) and made him general manager of National Bell. Vail was a unique individual because of his training and experience in the communications business. Vail came from the U.S. Postal Service, having risen to general superintendent of the United States Rail Mail Service, so he was very familiar with the challenges and the management practices of building and operating a national communications business. It was Vail who devised a strategy to unite and integrate the Bell companies into one of the greatest corporate enterprises in the world, and, whether he intended it or not, he turned Bell's vision of the telephone into a working reality.

Telephone service developed rapidly in the United States. In 1878, the first exchange was opened in New Haven, Connecticut, with twenty-one subscribers. By January 1884, Boston had been linked to New York, a distance of 480 kilometers. By 1900, there were over one million telephones in the United States and local systems were linked into national systems, and the telephone business had become established in all industrialized countries. In 1878, the first telephone company was formed in Britain. Telephone service was adopted in Germany as a state monopoly in 1877. In April 1880, National Bell formed a subsidiary called Bell Canada to set up and operate a telephone service in Canada. In 1897, telephone service became a state monopoly in Britain and France, Italy, Germany, and other countries followed by adopting the same state monopoly model.

THE TRIUMPH OF VAIL, AT&T, AND THE BELL SYSTEM

The telephone business was a lucrative one in the United States right from the beginning, and it was not long before it attracted competitors, the biggest and most formidable of which was Western Union. Not long after telephone service was inaugurated, Western Union bought the Gray patents, formed the American Speaking Telephone Company, and entered into an agreement with

Thomas Edison to supply it with new telephone technology. It then began establishing local exchanges in major cities in competition with Bell. By 1878, Western Union had 56,000 telephones in twenty-six cities and was doing its best to prevent Bell from expanding its local and long-distance network. Western Union pressured Bell to sell out, but Vail responded by threatening to enter the telegraph business. Under the threat of competition, Western Union backed down. In 1879, Vail negotiated a deal whereby the two companies agreed to divide the market. Western Union agreed to sell its telephone business as well as control over the competing telephone patents to Bell in return for 20 percent of Bell's licensing fees. Each company agreed to stay out of the other's business. Free from competition from Western, Vail could then concentrate on expanding long-distance telephone service and selling local exchange franchises. He also extended his control over the industry by licensing other manufacturers to make equipment for the growing Bell empire. This generated another important source of revenue, and it assured Bell control over the manufacturing of telephone equipment.

But Vail was also planning for the time when the patents owned by the National Bell would run out. In 1880, National Bell became the American Bell Telephone Company and began issuing permanent licenses to local franchise companies permitting them to use all of Bell's patented equipment in return for signing over between 35 and 50 percent of their common shares to American Bell and agreeing to pay twenty dollars per telephone per year. In this way, Vail was able to ensure that American Bell would have a permanent interest in as many local operating companies as possible together with a permanent stream of revenue when the patents expired. These local operating companies would eventually become subsidiaries of Bell.

At the same time, William Forbes, American Bell's president, and Vail continued emphasizing horizontal expansion and began building the American Bell empire vertically by expanding into equipment manufacturing and eventually into research and development. Vail convinced Western Union to sell its interest in Western Electric and, once this transaction was concluded, he began expanding its capacity. In 1885, American Bell created the American Telephone and Telegraph Company (AT&T) as a subsidiary to concentrate on developing the long-distance market. With the creation of a tricorporate structure engaged in local and long-distance services as well as manufacturing, Vail began building a company so powerful that competitors would find it impossible to beat. AT&T-Western Electric set up joint ventures not only in Canada but in other countries as well. One was a joint venture with Nippon Electric Company (NEC) in Japan to manufacture telephone equipment for the Japanese market.

But competition did make great inroads into the Bell empire after the Bell patents expired in 1894 and, some have argued, because of the departure of Vail who retired as president of AT&T in frustration over the way the business was being run. Bell executives, according to Robert Sobel and David Sicilia, authors of the book *The Entrepreneurs*, did not share Vail's vision of creating a national telephone utility that provided the best possible local and long-distance service. Independents had grown to equal the size of AT&T and many were growing more rapidly. In 1902, J. P. Morgan gained control of AT&T and put Vail on its board of directors. In 1907, Morgan invited Vail to come out of retirement at the age of sixty-two to accept the position as president of AT&T. One of the changes Vail made was to change AT&T into the parent company which owned the Bell patents and the stock of the local companies. Vail also changed the philosophy and the strategy of the company.

Rather than managing the telephone business for its cash flow and profit potential, Vail set about to create the affordable universal telephone service. The 1910 annual report of AT&T set out Vail's vision for the telephone industry and the role that AT&T and the Bell System and the concept of universal service should play in it:

The Bell system was founded on broad lines of "One System, One Policy, Universal Service," on the idea that no aggregation of isolated independent systems not under common control, however built or equipped, could give the country the service. One system with a common policy, common purpose and common action; comprehensive, universal, interdependent, intercommunicating like the highway system of the country, extending from every door to every other door, affording electrical communication of every kind, from every one at every place to every one at every other place.

Vail was a master strategist, and he used his exceptional wit and skill to build such a universal telephone system in just a few decades, and, in the process, he created an industrial enterprise that was able to monopolize the telephone industry in the United States for almost three-quarters of a century. Vail's strategy was to strengthen AT&T vertically and horizontally and use the power of the Bell Telephone System to squeeze out the independent telephone companies and force them to sell out to AT&T. And he could use a variety of strategies and tactics to achieve his purpose. He could refuse to grant local independents access to AT&T's long-distance lines or charge very high fees for such interconnection. Since competitors depended on Western Electric for equipment, he could charge them high prices or refuse to sell them the equipment outright. AT&T also controlled the standards by which equipment could be interconnected to the network so this too could be used to preclude competition. If all else failed, he could simply move into the local area and undercut his competitors in price. He could use any of these strategies to force independents to sell out. These strategies together with Vail's emphasis of offering superior service at lower rates worked wonders and, within five years, Vail had succeeded in outstripping the independents in growth and profitability and restoring the Bell system to its former glory.

Vail's strategy also enabled AT&T to extend the company's monopoly into equipment manufacturing. AT&T even succeeded in purchasing 30 percent of its former biggest rival, Western Union, in 1909, and Vail became president of the company the following year. With Western Union under its wing and the battle against independents going well, AT&T came under investigation in 1912 by both the Interstate Commerce Commission for its monopoly practices and the Justice Department for violating the country's antitrust laws. This was just one of the many attempts by a U.S. agency to break up the Bell empire, and it failed in large part due to the negotiating tactics of Vail.

Vail argued that an affordable, universal, high-quality telephone service was in the best interest of the nation and that the telephone business constituted a natural monopoly and should be administered as such. Vail's arguments won the day for AT&T, and the Justice Department reached a settlement in 1913 with AT&T agreeing to divest itself of its stock in Western Union, abandon efforts to purchase more independents, and allow independents to interconnect with its long-distance network. AT&T was able to keep Western Electric and all of its local operating companies as well as the freedom to take over other local companies. The natural monopoly doctrine was effectively enshrined as the public interest.

In 1925, another element was added to the growing AT&T empire and the Bell Telephone System. In that year, Vail merged the research and development staff of Western Electric and AT&T to create Bell Telephone Laboratories with the responsibility to conduct basic and applied research into new telecommunications technologies. In the decades that followed, Bell Telephone Laboratories or BTL as it came to be known, built up one of the most impressive records of research and development ever achieved by any company in the world. Manley Irwin at the Whitmore School of Business in New Hampshire, who conducted extensive research into the history of the Bell Telephone System, wrote,

BTL thus institutionalized research, and the laboratory became essentially a patent factory. By the early 1930s, BTL was producing 6,000 patents a year and enjoyed a portfolio of 6,000 patents and licenses to 9,000 others. By the start of the World War II, the preeminence of Bell Telephone Laboratries was well established. Funded by a license contract upon operating company revenues, the breadth and range of BTL married basic development to applied product development. Western Electric, AT&T's manufacturing affiliate, paid for product development, and Bell's operating companies paid for basic development. In short, Vail had constructed a process to supersede an event. Research was institutionalized as an ongoing endeavor. It was to be a model later replicated by other American industries.[5]

Over the next half century, scientists and engineers at Bell Telephone Laboratories ran up an impressive record of innovations and inventions in every branch of electronics, including radio, telecommunications, and computers. The most notable included microwave radio, mobile radio, and cellular radio telephony, coaxial cable, semiconductor technology including the transistor, and optical fibers, electronic switching, and computer software. Scientists from Bell Telephone Laboratories received more Nobel Prizes than any other organization in the world, and it was the strength of Bell Telephone Laboratories that enabled AT&T to continue dominating the telephone industry for over a half a century. Like AT&T and the Bell system, Bell Telephone Laboratories effectively became an American institution.

Telecommunications steadily grew and became more and more important to business and the public throughout the 1920s, and it was in recognition of this that Congress passed the Communications Act of 1934. The act created the FCC, the Federal Communications Commission, to regulate all federal telegraph and telephone matters. It cast into stone the fundamental structure of the telephone industry that existed at that time when AT&T and its affiliated local operating companies generated 94.3 percent of all local exchange messages. It also institutionalized vertical integration in the industry by recognizing that the monopoly over local and long-distance service also extended to the manufacture of equipment and the provision of facilities. The act recognized telephone service as an essential public service and a natural monopoly that would be regulated as a public utility. Regulation would also serve to protect AT&T from competition. The Communications Act effectively enshrined into legislation the fundamental public policy goal of universal, affordable public telephone service. This public policy goal has withstood the test of changing times and circumstances, and it represents a fundamental pillar of telecommunications policy and public utility regulation in every nation in the world today.

There is a body of opinion that the Communications Act was the work of Theodore Vail because it incorporated his vision of how the telephone and the telephone industry should serve society and the role that AT&T and the Bell system should play in it. It is nevertheless a testimony to the extraordinary management, leadership, and vision of Theodore Vail. Vail had achieved what Bell had set out to achieve but could not—the goal of creating a universal, national, public telephone service run by AT&T and the Bell system as a monopoly.

WIRELESS RADIO AND THE THIRD ELECTRONIC COMMUNICATIONS REVOLUTION

The third electronic communications revolution was launched with the invention of radio, or what was called "wireless" in the early days. Wireless communications developed from one of the most theoretical fields of science. James Clerk Maxwell, while working with Michael Faraday to develop and apply the principles of electromagnetic induction, hypothesized the existence of electric radiation of which light, he deduced, was but one manifestation. Although Maxwell did not prove that these waves actually existed, his theory set off a race among scientists to prove that they did.

It was the German physicist Heinrich Hertz who actually proved that electromagnetic waves did exist, and this gave him the distinction as the discoverer of radio waves. In 1988, Hertz showed that an electric spark generated across two electrodes would induce a spark in two similar electrodes connected by a coil at a distance of twenty meters. He concluded that energy was transferred between the two at the speed of light and he called this medium of energy transfer "electromagnetic radiation." It was in recognition of Hertz's contributions to the science of electromagnetic radiation that such waves have become known as "hertzian waves," and the "hertz" has become the fundamental unit for the measurement of frequency.

A number of other scientists contributed to the development of radio. In 1988, the Frenchman Edouard Branly discovered the radioconductor which worked on the principle that it became a conductor of electricity in the presence of an electromagnetic wave. It was actually a receiving antennae. Branly was able to demonstrate that the device could detect waves at a distance of several dozen meters even through solid objects and could even set off electric bells and telegraph relays. In 1894, Oliver Lodge, an Englishman, introduced "tuning," an improvement on the ideas of Branly. By adjusting the receiver to the frequency of the transmitter, reception of the signal and the quality of the communications could be improved enormously.

In the United States, Nikola Tesla successfully carried out much of the pioneering work in the areas of alternating current, high voltage transformers, and the transmission of electric energy by waves. Another contributor to the development of radio communications was the Russian, A. S. Popov, who demonstrated in 1895 that a long vertical wire significantly improved the reception of electromagnetic waves. The antenna was thus born. The next year, he succeeded in transmitting the words "Heinrich Hertz" over 250 meters using the first radio-electric Morse connection. In the same year, an Italian aristocrat by the name of Guglielmo Marconi succeeded in transmitting a radio signal a distance of 2400 kilometers using Morse code. But Marconi had to go to England to gain support for his work from the British Post Office (BPO). The British Post Office was interested in the application of wireless to postal services because it was about to take over most of the British telephone system. In 1897, Marconi founded his own company, which became the now-famous Marconi Wireless Telegraph and Signal Company, in the year 1900. On December 12, 1901, he succeeded in completing his famous wireless communications across the Atlantic between Poldhu in Cornwall, England, and St. John's, Newfoundland, a distance of 3400 kilometers. In reward for his work, Marconi received the Nobel Prize in physics in 1909.

Before the wireless became the important form of communications that it is today, a number of other inventions beyond that of a receiving antennae had to take place. One was the discovery by two Americans scientists, Dunwoody and Pickard, in 1910 that galena (lead sulphur crystals) had properties that made it serve as a natural frequency oscillator. This discovery led to the invention of the crystal receiving set which made it possible for thousands of amateurs to build their own wireless sets so they could receive the first radio broadcast transmissions.

But the most important and lasting contributions to radio communications occurred as a result of developments in electric valves or cathode ray tubes in the late nineteenth century. A cathode ray tube works on the principle that rays or beams of electrons are emitted from a heated electron source or cathode in a vacuum in an outward (radial) direction. Other electrodes can be inserted in the tube and used to control the electron beam to create a amplifier. In 1897, the German scientist Karl Braun perfected the cathode ray tube or cathode ray oscilloscope which led directly to developments in a number of key areas including television. In 1909, Braun was awarded the Nobel Prize in Physics for his pioneering work. In 1904, John Ambrose Fleming, professor of electrical engineering at London University, invented a diode, the essential component of the rectifier circuit, which was also critical to the development of radio because it converted alternating current to direct current in radio receiving sets. Two years later, in 1906, the American Lee de Forest discovered that an electrified grid placed across the path of the electron beam in a diode, that is, between the cathode and the anode, had the effect of amplifying the electrical signal on the grid. The triode or "Audion," as de Forest called it, made it possible to amplify incoming radio signals so they could be heard with the naked ear. The invention of the triode set off some of the most important and lasting developments in modern electronic communications. One of these was the oscillator circuit, which generated a powerful radio signal at a given set of frequencies depending on the size of the various capacitors and resistors in the circuit so it led naturally to the development of radio broadcasting.

Cathode ray tubes soon replaced spark-gap radio transmitters because they gave off a broad spectrum of radiation and could be tuned to a narrow wave band. They also made it possible to build more powerful transmitters and receivers so signals could be more clearly and loudly received. Headphones could then be replaced by loudspeakers, and by using a microphone to modulate the amplitude of the transmitted wave, audio sounds could be transmitted and received directly between individuals and groups over long distances. This was the basis of radio as we know it today. The invention of the triode became not only the basis of radio but of television, radar, and even the first computers.

Technological developments such as these sparked the first transmission of the human voice by radio in the early twentieth century. On Christmas eve in 1906, Reginald Fessenden, operating from an experimental transmitting station at Brant Rock, Massachusetts, broadcast a spoken Christmas message and played "O Holy Night." Merchants and American navy ships at sea off the coast who were expecting the dots and dashes of Morse code were astonished to hear the human voice and Christmas music. In 1908, Lee de Forest broadcast phonograph music from the Eiffel Tower in Paris, and in 1919 he broadcast arias sung by Enrico Caruso from New York's Metropolitan Opera. In 1915, speech was transmitted across the Atlantic from Virginia to Paris for the first time.

Developments in radio communications ushered in the era of commercial public broadcasting after the First World War. For nine months commencing on

February 23, 1920, Marconi broadcast a regular news service from his transmitter at Chelmsford in England. On November 2 of the same year, Westinghouse Company began regular radio transmissions of music, news, and entertainment on station KDKA in Pittsburgh.

Developments in radio spawned new industries including a rapidly growing entertainment industry. By 1922, there were 600 commercial radio broadcasting stations and a million listeners in the United States of America alone. In 1924, an estimated twenty million Americans listened to the national election returns from more than 400 stations. In London, the famous 2LO station came on the air in 1922 and, in 1927, the British Broadcasting Corporation was founded as a public corporation. By then, Britain had about two million radio receiving sets in operation. In the same year, a fight between Jack Dempsey and Gene Tunny was broadcast allegedly causing ten fans to die of excitement. Between 1922 and 1932, the number of radio sets in America increased from less than 1 percent to 60 percent, and radio broadcasting was having a profound effect on American life and American business.

AT&T, Westinghouse Electric Corporation, General Electric, and Radio Corporation of America (RCA) played important roles in the development of radio in America not only as manufacturers of equipment but as broadcasters as well. In the early years of radio, these companies entered into a series of alliances to divide the market for equipment and facilities up among themselves and each set up its own radio stations. Westinghouse set up KDKA in Wilkingburg, Pennsylvania, and WTZ in Newark, New Jersey. AT&T set out to control the radio business from the very beginning through the many patents it owned on radio equipment, including the patent on the triode tube which it purchased from de Forest in 1913. In 1921, AT&T established station WEAF in New York and, in 1923, it linked seven radio stations into a network. AT&T also controlled long-distance circuits which were required to form radio networks, and it began using its control over both telephony and radio to exclude other station operators. It was in these early years that RCA began playing a dominant role in the development not only of radio broadcasting, but in entertainment, including motion pictures, theater, and phonograph recording and music production as well. These developments are important in retrospect because they are not unlike the wave of mergers and acquisition and strategic alliances that leading manufacturers, network operators, and suppliers of software, content and services are adopting today in an all-out effort to create and dominate the electronic super-highways of the future.

RCA has its origins in events that took place during the First World War and its aftermath. During the war, the United States government determined that it was in America's national interest that the British domination of radio through the Marconi Wireless Telegraph and Signal Company should be broken and that an American company should be created to control radio facilities. So in 1917, it seized the American assets of American Marconi (which Marconi created in 1899), and the company was run by the U.S. Navy until it was taken over by a consortium consisting of General Electric and Westinghouse Electric. In 1919, American Marconi became the Radio Corporation of America, or RCA, specializing in the development of wireless radio and wireless telephony. AT&T was excluded from the RCA consortium by the United States government because of its control over both the radio and telephone industries. Nevertheless, AT&T did succeed in purchasing stock in RCA and RCA became part of the General Electric, AT&T, Westinghouse alliance under which GE and Westinghouse produced receivers and parts, RCA marketed them, and AT&T sold transmitters and leased circuits.

In 1925, the Federal Trade Commission began investigating the relationships between RCA, AT&T, Westinghouse, and GE for possible trade restriction violations. AT&T was not doing well in the broadcasting business at the time in part because it did not provide any programming, but its transmission business was very profitable. RCA, on the other hand, provided programming and its radio stations were doing well. It was partly due to the threat of the Federal Trade Commission's investigation and partly to AT&T's relative lack of success in radio broadcasting that AT&T and RCA came to a new agreement in 1926 whereby AT&T agreed to abandon the broadcasting business in return for RCA's commitment to use AT&T's long-distance transmission facilities. AT&T's Washington radio station was sold to RCA along with its WEAF station in New York, which became WNBC, the flagship for the National Broadcasting Company (NBC).

David Sarnoff, RCA's chief strategist, subsequently transformed RCA into an integrated entertainment company to complement its radio broadcasting and manufacturing operations. In 1928, he took RCA into the theater business with the formation of Radio-Keith-Orpheum (RKO). RCA also went into the phonograph business with the purchase of the Victor Talking Machine Company and into phonograph production through another of its many subsidiary companies. To these were added several large music publishers, including Leo Feist and Carl Fisher and, subsequently, a talent agency was started. By then, RCA had become an integrated entertainment company to complement its radio operations. Sarnoff was working toward a vision of creating an RCA whereby artists appearing on RCA's National Broadcasting Company could be heard on RCA radios; motion pictures made by RKO could be exhibited at RKO theaters equipped with RCA sound systems; and musical recordings published by Feist or Fisher for Victor could be played on Victrolas. Even the artists working for these companies could be represented by an RCA agent. (In many respects, the giant conglomerate mergers that are taking place today in the world film production, telecommunications, cable television, broadcasting and publishing industries are a re-enactment of these same dynamics.) They illustrate the dynamic nature and the synergism between the interaction of technology, corporate strategy, and the structure and organization of society.

It was as a result of the rapid growth of radio and its importance to American business and American society that the U.S. Congress passed the Radio Act in

1927. It created the Federal Radio Commission to regulate the industry. The Columbia Broadcasting System (CBS) was formed in the same year. In 1930, the United States government initiated further action against the so-called Radio Trust, in part as a result of the success of RCA and Sarnoff, and, two years later, it forced General Electric and Westinghouse to divest themselves of their RCA holdings. Subsequently, Congress passed the Communications Act of 1934 which created the FCC to oversee and regulate the telephone and radio industries.

Radio also played a critical role in the Second World War both directly as a broadcast medium as well as indirectly through its effects on the development of radar. In 1935, with a war with Germany looking increasingly likely, the British Air Ministry accepted a proposal by Robert Watson-Watt to develop equipment that would use radio signals to detect and track flying aircraft in what became known as "radar" (an acronym for radio detection and ranging). Within weeks, a team of British scientists led by Watson-Watt were tracking aircraft miles off shore, and plans were underway to build five radar stations. Within two years, the radar equipment was reduced to the size of a two-foot box so it could be squeezed into a two-engine plane. Airborne radar had been developed. Radar was so successful in the war that Germany's top ace blamed the defeat of the Luftwaffe on Britain's "radar-and-fighter-control network." Radar has been credited with having been strategic to winning the Battle of Britain.

TELEVISION: THE FOURTH ELECTRONIC COMMUNICATIONS REVOLUTION

Until the mid-twentieth century, the only practical means of communicating moving or motion pictures was by using cameras to capture images, storing them on celluloid tape, and projecting them onto a screen in a movie theater, that is, through the use of chemical, electrical, and mechanical technologies. The communication of moving pictures by electronic means was a scientific and technological dream even though Alexander Graham Bell proposed a new means for communicating images using light as early as 1880. He called his invention the photophone but he was not able to develop a practical working model. Although considerable experimentation was underway in the late nineteenth century, it was not until the years leading up to the Second World War that television became practical, feasible, and economical. It was after World War II that the fourth electronic communications revolution really took off and television became the universally popular and powerful medium that it is today.

The concept of television inspired scientists and engineers in the early twentieth century and initiated a race to develop a working experimental device. Scientists in Japan, Russia, Britain, Germany, and the United States were experimenting with television in one form or another. The most successful early technique was based on photomechanical technology developed by the Scottish inventor John Logie Baird. In 1929, the newly created British Broadcasting Company (BBC) licensed Baird to start a regular public television service. The venture was not successful because the apparatus was clumsy and expensive and the picture quality was poor. It was taken over by the BBC in 1932 and subsequently abandoned in 1937 because it was clearly far inferior to an all-electronic system invented by Philo Farnsworth and Vladimir Zworykin in the United States.

Both Farnsworth and Zworykin were leading figures in the invention of television but Zworykin and David Sarnoff at RCA played key roles in its commercial development. While working at Westinghouse, Zworykin, a Russian electrical engineer, developed the iconoscope, a rudimentary camera in 1923, and the kinescope, or television tube in 1926, the two basic components for capturing and displaying television signals. Zworykin's television worked on the principle that a stream of electrons scanned across each of the light-sensitive dots of the mosaic in the camera, creating an electronically coded signal which was then transmitted. Upon reception at the television set, the signal was decoded in the television's picture tube and the original image was created by means of a stream of glowing dots on the television screen. Replenishing or refreshing the screen was done faster than the eye could detect giving the sensation of a moving picture.

David Sarnoff at RCA became intrigued with the potential of television and subsequently hired Zworykin to lead RCA's effort to develop a commercial television system. RCA, AT&T, and GE poured millions into the development of television. But it was Philo Farnsworth who demonstrated the world's first all-electronic television system in 1928. In 1929, RCA demonstrated the Zworykin television and in 1933, RCA made the world's first experimental transmission of electronic television from the top of the Empire State Building in New York with a picture resolution of 240 lines.

Before RCA was able to manufacture a television set commercially, Sarnoff had to obtain the patent rights from Farnsworth. Once these were acquired, RCA demonstrated its first television set at the 1939–1940 New York World's Fair. By that time, the British company, Electrical and Musical Industries (EMI), had produced its own version of the iconoscope which it called the emitron. The British Broadcasting Company scrubbed the Baird system, and on November 2, 1936, it began operating the world's first public, regular television service, based on a new standard 405-line transmission system.

NBC, RCA's broadcasting subsidiary, began its own television broadcasting service on April 30, 1939, just before the outbreak of the Second World War, but the picture quality was still poor and sets were expensive. By 1942, there were only 20,000 television sets in Britain and half that number in the United States. The television revolution had to await the end of the Second World War. Public television service resumed in Britain in June of 1946 with an estimated 12,000 viewers. Within ten years, the number of American families having a television set jumped from a fraction of 1 percent to 72 percent. Viewers were watching such classic sitcoms as "I Love Lucy" and "The Honeymooners" and popular game shows like "The $64,000 Question."

By 1960, an estimated ten million homes in Britain had television sets and eighty-five million in the United States. And about 720 million viewers around the world watched the first moon landing in 1969. By 1970, the world had a quarter million television sets, and television was having a most powerful cultural, economic, and political influence on industrial societies the world over. Rising employment levels were recorded in the production of television equipment and television programs and in broadcast services throughout the fifties and into the sixties when the Japanese began making more successful inroads in television manufacturing. Color television was developed both by RCA and CBS in the fifties, and by the end of the sixties, most American homes had color television sets. By then, television had transformed America through its effects on advertising, news, and entertainment. It became a medium for shaping public opinion and an important political force in its own right. It played important roles in the birth of rock music and the civil rights movement, in the election of John F. Kennedy in 1960, and in coalescing opposition to the Vietnam War. It also became one of the most important means for exporting American programs and American culture around the world.

THE EXPANDING NATIONAL AND INTERNATIONAL TELECOMMUNICATION INFRASTRUCTURE

The postwar period witnessed the spread of telephone networks into the rural and remote regions of industrialized countries and the linking of all of them into a national telecommunications infrastructure. At the same time, this infrastructure was continuing to undergo transformations as a result of major innovations in switching and transmission systems, many of which were developed by the Bell System.

One of the biggest technological breakthroughs was the introduction of automatic, electromechanical switching. Because it was automatic, it was faster and more efficient than manual switching, and it transformed the telephone business from an incredibly labor-intensive to a highly capital-intensive one. One of the results was drastic cuts of telephone operators. Electromechanical switching gradually gave way to fully electronic switching in the sixties and seventies, and these eventually to the computerized switching systems of today with their highly automated, software features that give them the ability to process voice, data, and image communications; to route traffic optimally throughout the network; and to monitor, detect, diagnose and repair problems as they arise.

Both local and long-distance communications were further revolutionized as a result of innovations in multiplexing and microwave radio and coaxial cable transmission systems. Both developments increased transmission capacity and improved economics by orders of magnitude, resulting in major reductions in the price of long-distance telephone service and stimulating a corresponding increase in the demand for service. Multiplexing, invented by Bell Telephone Laboratories in 1927, was a way of modulating higher frequency transmission signals with lower frequency voice signals so that copper, for example, could carry several voice conversations simultaneously. This meant a reduction in the use of copper and in the cost of local and long-distance services.

The second invention was microwave radio communications which, combined with multiplexing, resulted in further reductions in the cost of long-distance service. In 1947, the Bell Telephone system inaugurated the first commercial microwave link between New York and Boston. It consisted of ten towers and carried both telephone and television signals. New York was linked to San Francisco in 1948 by 109 microwave towers allowing the nation to watch the signing of the U.S.-Japan peace treaty on commercial television. By the 1950s, transcontinental microwave systems covered the nation, routinely handling 2000 or more voice channels on hops averaging twenty-five miles. Hops could be extended on some of these to over 100 miles. Microwave communications changed the economics of telecommunications by another order of magnitude, increasing transmission capacity particularly in long-distance communications and the economies of scale of the entire telephone network.

The third technological breakthrough was coaxial cable developed at Bell Telephone Laboratories in 1940, and it laid the foundations for the cable television industry in the sixties and seventies. Because they operated efficiently at very high frequencies, coaxial cables could carry many voice or television signals simultaneously using multiplexing techniques, and, because an outer shield protected the signal from interference, it could carry better quality signals more reliably and securely than any other transmission system. It was these quality, economic, and broadband capabilities that made coax the natural transmission medium for the local distribution of television signals. By the late fifties, coaxial cables were being used to link homes that were too far from a television transmitter to a much bigger, more powerful, and expensive community antenna that picked up television signals and relayed them to households. This gave birth to community antenna television or CATV, now the cable television industry. By 1960, there were about 640 CATV systems serving 650,000 subscribers in the United States. By 1971, the number had exploded to 2,500 systems serving 4.9 million subscribers.[6]

An international telecommunications infrastructure was also being developed to complement and extend those at the national level. In 1891, England became linked to the Continent by submarine cables. But because of the effects of distance on the strength and quality of telephone signals, New York was not linked to San Francisco until 1915. A radio link was introduced across the Atlantic in 1927, but it had very limited capacity and was subject to atmospheric interference. Similar radio-telephone links were established with Australia and South America. The first transatlantic radio-telephone link was installed by AT&T between the United States and England in 1929, and radio-telephone links were also established between North and South America. In 1933, European engineers began using microwave communications to transmit telephone signals across the English Channel, a distance of a dozen miles. But radio-telephone communications were not very reliable, and the quality of the signal was often poor for very long-distance transatlantic or transoceanic communications.

In 1956, the first transatlantic telephone cable, called TAT-1, came into service linking the United Kingdom, Canada, and the United States. It was 3600 kilometers long and had a capacity of forty-eight voice channels. Fifty repeaters were installed to enable Americans and Europeans to talk directly with one another across the Atlantic without any interference. In 1963, another transatlantic cable called TAT-2 was completed. It had a capacity of 138 simultaneous voice conversations and linked England and the United States. These links became the vanguard of a series of new transatlantic and transpacific telecommunications links that expanded the number of voice circuits between the continents of the world. They played a critical role in building a global telecommunications infrastructure which would ultimately be complemented by a network of satellite and optical fibers in the sixties, seventies, and eighties.

By the latter half of the twentieth century, every country—developed, developing, and many less developed—had come to depend on its telecommunications infrastructure in one way or another for its day-to-day operations but they chose different means and institutions to organize, operate, and control their industries and their infrastructures. Telecommunications had either evolved into a monopoly or was set up as a monopoly in every country, but two models had evolved to administer, manage, and control telecommunications undertakings. In the United States and Canada, the companies were primarily privately owned but controlled by a public regulatory authority or commission. In all the other countries, telecommunication undertakings were owned, managed, and operated by national governments.

In the United Kingdom, France, Germany, and Japan, for example, telecommunications constituted a state-owned and state-run monopoly operated by the posts, telephone, and telegraph companies or PTTs, which enjoyed a monopoly not only on telephone and telegraph services but postal services as well. In some countries this even extended to banking services. It was the job of these PTTs to build and operate their nation's telephone and telecommunications infrastructure.

Other countries also adopted the model of vertical integration developed by AT&T in the United States so the PTT monopoly also extended into equipment manufacturing. Consequently, there was little or no competition either at the national or international levels. Western Electric and General Telephone and Electric (GTE) enjoyed a monopoly on equipment supply in certain parts of the United States, Siemens in Germany, Cable and Wireless (C&W), Plessey Telecommunications, and General Electric (GEC) in the United Kingdom, Compagnie Générale d'Electricité (CGE) and Thompson-CSF in France, Northern Electric (now Northern Telecom) in Canada, Philips in the Netherlands, L. M. Ericsson in Sweden, and Nippon Telegraph and Telephone (NTT) in Japan.

International Telegraph and Telephone (ITT) had operations in several countries as well.

The structure of the telecommunications industry, the ownership of telephone companies, and the linkages between the PTTs and manufacturers were characteristic of the industrial age. That was an age when individual nation states had a great deal of autonomy and sovereignty, when nations were defined in terms of geography and land masses, when technology and economics gave legitimacy to national institutions and control over geographic land masses and all of the economic activities taking place within them. As we shall see in later chapters, these have given way to new realities made possible by technology and globalization.

At the international level, several key organizations were created to coordinate international telecommunications undertakings and maintain cooperation among nations. One of the most important was the International Telecommunications Union or ITU, now a special agency of the United Nations. Formed in 1865 by a small group of European nations, its role was to assist nations in defining and establishing a modus operandi for telegraphic communications extending across their borders. Since then the organization has gradually evolved to take on an increasingly more cooperative role in every aspect of international telecommunications developments, including developing standards for the interconnection of facilities and networks as well as the principles for pricing international services and sharing revenues among member countries. The role and status of the International Telecommunications Union is also rapidly changing today as a result of rapid technological change, globalization, and competition.

THE MATURE (GOLDEN) AGE OF INDUSTRIAL-INFORMATION CAPITALISM

It was the diffusion of electromechanical and electronic technologies and the development of national and international electronic communications infrastructures, along with public policies and economic institutions, I would argue, that played central roles in creating the mature "golden" age of industrial capitalism in the postwar period. Stable, continuous economic growth combined with price stability and growing productivity and efficiency to accelerate wealth creation characterized this period. Between 1945 and 1960, America's GNP increased by 52 percent and the nation's per capita GNP rose by 19 percent. In the 1960s, GNP climbed 46 percent and per capita GNP grew by 29 percent. By 1970, 99 percent of American households had a refrigerator and a television set and 70 percent had a washing machine.[7] This growth was propelled by the expanding consumer society and the growth of export markets. Industrial society had also become permeated by various physical infrastructures, including transportation, communications, hydroelectric and oil and gas pipelines, as well as soft economic infrastructures, like banking and finance and these too contributed to its growth. Complementing these were massive investments in education, medicine, and health care. Each of these contributed in its own way to raising the material (and nonmaterial) standard of living of the masses. But it was the synergy between all of these technological, economic, and infrastructure and institutional factors, I would argue, that were responsible for raising the standard of living of ordinary people by orders of magnitude.

A mass production, mass consumption society, however, could not have developed without the development of mass communications. Radio, television, newspapers and magazines, and advertising brought information, news, and entertainment and cultural content to an information-starved society, but each played fundamental roles in creating a mass consumption and mass production society. One of their most important effects was through advertising. In the book *Communications in History*, William Leiss, Stephen Kline, and Sut Jhally wrote,

The developed phase of the market industrial society is the consumer society. . . . What marketers had realized was that, with the population as a whole having far greater discretionary income, leisure time, and employment security than ever before, work was no longer the focus of everyday life. The sphere of consumption could take its place. By linking consumption through electronic media to popular entertainment and sports, marketers and advertisers eventually fashioned a richly decorated setting for an elaborate play of messages, increasingly in imagistic or iconic form, about the way to happiness and social success.[8]

To keep their factories operating at maximum capacity and efficiency, in effect, to "move the goods" cascading off their assembly lines, business had to intensify its selling efforts, and this meant tremendous investment and expenditures on advertising. Advertising played a big role in creating a consumer society in the early twentieth century. According to Daniel Pope, as early as 1920, "the lead in advertising had passed to manufacturers of nationally distributed brand-named goods. . . . it was in the formation of the national consumer market that the advertising industry as we know it today was born and nurtured."[9]

Industrial society had changed in other ways, as well, in particular, from one dominated by agriculture and manufacturing to one dominated by services, according to Heilbroner and Singer.

In 1620 everyone in America was in immediate touch with nature. In 1820 70 percent of all working persons were still farmers or farm employees. By 1900 fewer than 40 percent were engaged in agriculture. Today perhaps 3 percent of the labor force works in farming . . . approximately 30 percent . . . labors in manufacturing of some kind and full 70 [percent] in services.[10]

An equally notable development in the evolution of the industrial and information economy and a unique characteristic of the mature stage of industrial capitalism was the supplanting of the institution of the market as the coordinator of economic activity by the professional manager and the multiunit business enterprise. In his landmark book, *The Invisible Hand: The Managerial Revolution in American Business*, Alfred Chandler observed that the institution of the market became superseded by the institution of managerial capitalism. Chandler described this transformation in the following way:

What the new enterprises did do was take over from the market the coordination and integration of the flow of goods and services from the production of raw materials through the several processes of production to the sale to the ultimate consumer. Where they did so, production became concentrated in the hands of a few large enterprises. At first, this occurred in only a few sectors or industries where technological innovation and market growth created high-speed and high-volume throughput. As technology became more sophisticated and as markets expanded, administrative coordination replaced market coordination in an increasingly large portion of the economy. By the middle of the twentieth century the salaried managers of a relatively small number of large mass producing, large mass retailing, and large mass transporting enterprises coordinated current flows of goods through the processes of production and distribution and allocated the resources to be used for future production and distribution in major sectors of the American economy. By then, the managerial revolution in American business had been carried out.[11]

John Kenneth Galbraith acknowledged in the sixties that a new kind of industrial state had evolved in step with a new kind of industrial corporation that had taken on a more important central planning, central control, and strategic intelligence role. In his 1967 book, *The New Industrial State*, he wrote:

In an economy where organized intelligence is the decisive factor of production, the selection of the intelligence so organized is of central importance. . . . In the past, leadership in business organization was identified with the entrepreneur—the individual who united ownership or control of capital with the capacity for organizing the other factors of production for innovation. With the rise of the modern corporation, . . . the guiding intelligence—the brain—of the enterprise . . . [has passed to] a collective and imperfectly defined entity . . . [which includes] senior officials, . . . white- and blue-collar workers . . . [and] embraces all who bring specialized knowledge, talent, or experience to group decision making. I propose to call this organization the Technostructure.[12]

We will see in subsequent chapters that these same technological, managerial, and economic forces are still at work today, but now they are changing and transforming the world economic system in equally significant ways. Managerial capitalism and consumer capitalism have gone global in their search for competitive advantage, opportunity, and profit.

NOTES

1. For an entrepreneurial perspective on the industrial revolution in the United States, see Robert Sobel and David B. Sicilia, *The Entrepreneurs: An American Adventure Story* (Boston: Houghton-Mifflin Co., 1986).

2. James Carey, "Time, Space and the Telegraph," *Communications in History: Technology, Culture and Society*, ed. David Crowley and Paul Heyer (New York: Longman, 1991), pp. 133–137.

3. Alfred Chandler, *The Invisible Hand: The Managerial Revolution in American Business* (Cambridge: Harvard University Press, 1977), p. 79.

4. Ithiel de Sola Pool, *The Social Impact of the Telephone* (Cambridge: MIT Press, 1977).

5. Manley Rutherford Irwin, *Telecommunications America: Markets Without Boundaries* (Westport, Conn.: Quorum, 1984), pp. 18–19.

6. Report of the Sloan Commission on Cable Communications, *On the Cable: The Television of Abundance* (New York: McGraw-Hill, 1971), p. 30.

7. In Western Europe, the figures were slightly less. See Stanley Lebergott, *The American Economy: Income, Wealth, and Want* (Princeton: Princeton University Press, 1976), p. 102.

8. William Leiss, Stephen Kline, and Sut Jhally, "Advertising, Consumers and Culture," in *Communications in History*, p. 176.

9. Daniel Pope, *The Making of Modern Advertising* (New York: Basic Books, 1983), pp. 30 and 180.

10. Robert Heilbroner and Aaron Singer, *The Economic Transformation of America: 1600 to the Present* (New York: Harcourt Brace Jovanovich, 1984), pp. 338–339.

11. Chandler, *The Invisible Hand*, p. 11.

12. John Kenneth Galbraith, *The New Industrial State*, 4th ed. (Boston: Houghton Mifflin, 1985), pp. 73–74.

Chapter 3 _____

The Microchip and the Computer: Technological Underpinnings of the Postindustrial Society

It was in the postwar period that capitalism began sewing the seeds of its own destruction in true Schumpeterian style. For it was during these years that a new intellectual revolution was incubating in the minds of scientists and engineers in universities and private research laboratories throughout the world. It would quickly grow and spread to initiate the microchip and computer and telecommunications revolutions of the fifties, sixties, and seventies. This revolution would make obsolete the vast electrical and electromechanical machinery and equipment that constituted the technological foundations of industrial society. It would also make obsolete some of its most basic infrastructures and many of its social, economic, and political institutions. And it would transform work, management, and organization as well as capitalism itself.

The intellectual foundations of this technological revolution were laid by mathematicians who applied scientific principles to build electronic computing machines. One of these was the English mathematician George Boole whose concepts of Boolean algebra became the basis of computation in the modern-day digital computer. Problems, according to Boole, could be analyzed by representing them as a series of propositions or statements and solved by performing a series of operations—AND, NOT, and OR. In 1937, Claude Shannon, a mathematician and engineer, showed how electromechanical circuits containing relays (or switches) could be designed based on Boole's systems of logic to perform mathematical calculations, comparisons, and logical and conditional branching operations. This is why the computer can best be considered a logic machine rather than a calculator or electronic machine. Shannon's paper set off a race in leading private and university institutions throughout the world in the forties and fifties to develop the first general purpose digital computer based on the principles that he established.

Alan Turing, a British mathematician, conceptualized a kind of automatic computer, called a Turing Machine, in a paper published in the Proceedings of the London Mathematical Society in 1936. In it, he set out the conditions under which mathematical problems could be solved using automatic computers and also described what the computer might look like. Turing showed that as long as the problem could be restated in the form of an algorithm of coded instructions or a program, it could be solved by a computer. The computer would read the instructions on punched paper tape by means of an optical device and write its results on punched paper tape. Turing became involved in the British War effort in 1943, building the famous code-breaking computer called the Colossus. It was the Colossus that enabled the British to crack the German Enigma code and gain access to Hitler's war plans throughout the remainder of the war. This development was of such strategic importance that it is considered by many to have been as important as radar, for example, in contributing to the defeat of Nazi Germany.

The name John von Neumann is synonymous with the electronic digital computer. Von Neumann was a brilliant scientist and mathematician of Hungarian origin who made pioneering contributions to everything from quantum physics, game theory, and mathematical logic, to probability and statistics, and economics. He also laid the foundations of the theory of cellular automata which is the basis of the new flourishing science of artificial life. In a paper written in 1945, von Neumann conceived the design of the modern high-speed digital computer with memory. By storing both instructions and data in memory in binary form, von Neumann was able to design a computer capable of operating almost automatically in an unattended fashion with a minimum of human manual intervention and relatively independent of clumsy electromechanical memory and input and output devices. And, by making its internal components fully electronic rather than electromechanical, its speed was limited only by the state-of-the-art electronics.

In John von Neumann's computer design, instructions were fed into the central processing unit (CPU) from memory and executed in a sequential manner thus making the performance of the computer completely dependent on the speed of the CPU. Von Neumann's concepts were regarded as so important to the development of the modern-day computer that a computer that operates in this way is called a "von Neumann computer." From that day to the present, scientists have been trying to overcome this "von Neumann bottleneck." They have made significant progress by developing what are known as parallel computers which use tens, hundreds, or thousands of central processing units operating in parallel and in cooperation with one another to solve complex computational problems. These became commercially available in the late eighties and early nineties and are on the leading edge in the development of supercomputers which are capable of operating at terabit speeds, that is, trillions of instructions per second. These few basic principles are all on which the millions of computers that are used in offices, factories, aircraft, automobiles, and robots throughout the world operate, and there are some who believe to this day that nothing fundamentally new has been developed in the design of digital computers since the von Neumann contribution of the forties.

The explosion of knowledge and science and technology after the war triggered an intense interest in developing computers that had the power of the human brain, and it spawned in particular the new field of science called artificial intelligence, the term used by John McCarthy at Massachusetts Institute of Technology in 1956. McCarthy and other computer scientists such as Claude Shannon, Alan Turing, Marvin Minsky, Allen Newall, and Herbert Simon, for example, tried building artificial intelligence machines by writing computer programs to simulate in one way or another the internal working of the brain. It was largely the work of Edward Feigenbaum that led to the development and commercialization of expert systems in the eighties.

A second approach was to build machines based on the analogue control and feedback principles developed by MIT scientist and mathematician Norbert Wiener, who founded the science of cybernetics, the Greek word for helmsman, which Wiener defined as the science of "control and communications in the animal and the machine." In 1948, Wiener and John von Neumann collaborated on a book entitled *Cybernetics: Or Control and Communications in the Animal and the Machine* which described the possibilities and problems of building a brain that could take over human tasks. Others who pursued this approach included Warren McCulloch and Frank Rosenblatt. Rosenblatt incorporated his ideas into a computer called the Perceptron in 1956. It was the result of efforts such as these that Joseph Engelberger and George Devol founded Unimation in the late fifties. Unimation became a world leader in the development of robots for industrial uses.

Once the conceptualizers and theoreticians had laid the groundwork for the computer, the practical men, primarily the electrical and electronic engineers, followed them by actually building the machines that previously existed only on paper and in the minds of a very few leaders in the field. They were followed by business professionals who had them designed for practical day-to-day commercialized applications and for profit.

THE AGE OF EXPERIMENTAL MACHINES

The forties and early fifties are considered the age of experimental computers. John Atanasoff developed many of the principles of the modern computer and is regarded by some as the inventor of the digital computer. Howard Aitken was another computer pioneer who completed the Mark I computer in 1944 at Harvard University with the financial assistance of IBM. IBM dominated the business machine industry under its leader Thomas J. Watson who became intent on dominating the computer industry as well. In 1947, IBM unveiled the powerful and flexible Selective Sequence Electronic Calculator or SSEC but it did not have a memory.

In 1946, J. Presper Eckert and John Mauchly at the Moore School of Electrical Engineering at the University of Pennsylvania built the Electronic Numerical Integrator and Computer or ENIAC, the first fully electronic digital computer based on vacuum tube (valve) technology but it too did not have a memory. The ENIAC had 19,000 vacuum tubes, weighed thirty tons, and took up 1500 square feet of floor space.

In 1949, a German inventor by the name of Konrad Zuse completed the Z3 computer, now recognized as the first fully functional, program-controlled, general purpose digital computer in the world. Zuse pioneered such innovations as the use of binary and floating point decimals and an algorithmic language called Plankalkul. Professor Maurice Wilkes at Cambridge University completed the development of an electronic stored-program, general-purpose digital computer also in 1949. Alan Turing built the ACE computer at the National Physical Laboratory in Britain. Meanwhile, John von Neumann and his team at the Institute of Advanced Studies at Princeton University were incorporating von Neumann's designs into Electronic Discrete Variable Automatic Computer (EDVAC). Completed in 1952, it incorporated a memory for storing both the data and programs in memory in binary or digital form. It had 4,000 vacuum tubes and over 10,000 crystal diodes.

The age of experimental computers lasted into the fifties when all of the basic ideas and technological inventions became available to create the first generation of commercial general purpose computers. Concepts such as the stored program control, binary representation of data and programs and the use of punched cards were becoming standard in the fifties. Electromechanical and fully electronic and magnetic storage technologies were also becoming commercially available. The triode became a natural means of fast switching in the central processing unit. It was a significant improvement over electromechanical relays in terms of speed and reliability, and it reduced the switching time from seconds to milliseconds. But the real computer revolution had to wait until the end of the World War II when a much faster and a more reliable solid-state device known as the transistor was invented.

THE STRATEGIC ROLE OF TRANSISTOR/ SEMICONDUCTOR TECHNOLOGY

The effects of the digital computer on society have been nothing short of revolutionary, but the computer revolution would not have occurred without an equally pervasive semiconductor or microchip revolution. Developments in solid-state physics and semiconductor technology led to the invention of the transistor, then the integrated circuit, followed by the microchip and the microprocessor and, eventually, the microcomputer and personal computer. The transistor and the integrated circuit must, therefore, rank among the most important developments in history, having possibly greater significance and impact as the invention of the printing press, the telephone, the radio and television set, the internal combustion engine, and the atom bomb.[1] Without the semiconductor, there would be no revolution in robotics, satellite communications, personal computers, and no word processing systems. There would be no cruise missile and no such thing as Star Wars, and the automobile would not operate as efficiently as it does today. There would be no such thing as electronic banking, no flexible manufacturing revolution, and no such thing as speech recognition or voice synthesis systems.

The transistor, the integrated circuit, and the microchip transformed the computer (and all of the many machines and devices that would incorporate them) from a huge, bulky, slow, material-intensive and energy-intensive machine into a single miniature solid-state device and into the domain of electrons and photons operating inside crystals where it could operate unencumbered by the physical laws and barriers of Newtonian physics. In this subatomic world—this hyperspace—knowledge and ideas and theories can be created, simulated, and tested dynamically and stored, manipulated, and communicated throughout space at or near the speed of light. The only long-term limits or constraints of this new medium are knowledge, imagination, and organization. Mankind has only just begun to explore and feel comfortable working (and living) in this new-found cyberspace, as it has come to be known.

The transistor was invented at Bell Telephone Laboratories by a group of scientists who were trying to develop solid-state devices to replace the bulky, inefficient, and unreliable electromechanical relays or switches in telephones. In 1947, William Shockley, Walter Braittain, and John Bardeen came up with a very crude device consisting of a small piece of germanium with two wires placed closely together, but it had switching and amplification properties much like the diode and the triode. They called the device the point contact transistor, and the trio was awarded the Nobel Prize in physics in 1956 for its invention. It was succeeded by the junction transistor, a much improved design over its predecessor, but still made from germanium.

Texas Instruments announced commercial production runs of the first silicon transistors in 1954, and before the year was out, it had produced the first transistor radio. Sony Corporation of Japan subsequently produced the world's first handheld transistor radio. Silicon quickly replaced germanium as the core component in transistors because it was more stable and cheaper to produce, and it set off what we now know as the transistor and semiconductor or microchip revolution. Silicon became the critical ingredient in the development of metal oxide semiconductor (MOS) technology which continues to be the basis of the semiconductor industry today. But other kinds of materials such as gallium are being used today because of the ability of gallium arsenide semiconductors to switch circuits many times faster than those made of silicon. Speed is critical in image-and signal-processing applications in defense, industry, and medicine, for example, as well as speech processing.

The transistor constituted the foundation for the second generation of commercial computers in the fifties. Transistors meant that computers could operate thousands of times faster and operate much more reliably and efficiently and use much less energy than those that used vacuum tubes. They were also the first in a series of many continuous steps that resulted in the miniaturization of computers and communications equipment and made possible such developments as the personal computer, the cellular telephone and the videocassette recorder, to name a few of the many hundreds of new devices that now incorporate them.

The transistor was followed in 1959 by a new kind of device containing several transistors connected by circuitry which became known as the integrated circuit, or IC. The patent for inventing the integrated circuit is shared between Jack Kilby of Texas Instruments and Robert Noyce of Fairchild Semiconductor. It became the basis of the third generation of computers. IC devices operate on the same principles as the transistor only they have many other kinds of discrete components including resistors and capacitors in addition to transistors.

Most of the integrated circuits used today are based on MOS technology and the planar technique for producing them. The planar process uses a photolithographic technique consisting of three consecutive processes—oxidation, photoetching, and diffusion.[2] These are used repeatedly to build up intricate patterns of diverse conducting layers that constitute the circuits of a semiconductor chip. Two other promising techniques—X-ray lithography and electron-beam lithography—are currently under development to manufacture the extremely high density semiconductors for the late twentieth and early twenty-first century.

By 1965, manufacturers were turning out chips with ten transistors in what was known as small-scale integration (SSI). Between 1963 and 1971, the price of integrated circuits fell from over $30 to $1 and the number of discrete components on a chip increased from twenty-four to sixty-four. By 1969, the challenge was to put 1,000 circuits on a chip, and by 1975, the number had jumped to 32,000. Small-scale and medium-scale integration gave way to large-scale integration (LSI) and eventually to very large-scale integration (VLSI).

The design and manufacture of semiconductors and their operation and application illustrate both the intellectualization and dematerialization processes described in chapter 1 and the enormous synergies that are the product of these dual processes. The engineering techniques used to design, test, and produce integrated circuits ensure that the greater the number of discrete components that are fabricated into a single wafer, the lower are the costs of production and the greater their performance. This translates into enormous economies of scale in their production and enormous synergies in their operation and applications. The greater the density of the circuitry, the greater the savings in materials, energy, and human effort in their fabrication and, therefore, lower costs and the greater the efficiency, speed, and functionality (and built-in intelligence) in their operation. These synergies are inherent in the intellectualization and dematerialization processes, and they are collapsing more and more materials and hardware into microchips and increasing the density, speed, efficiency, and functionality of microchips and all of the machines that contain them. The economies were described by Robert Noyce in the following way:

First, the integrated circuit contains many of the interconnections that were previously required and that saves labor and materials. The interconnections of the integrated circuits are much more reliable than solder joints or connectors, which makes for savings in maintenance. Since integrated circuits are much smaller and consume much less power than the components they replace, they make savings possible in such support structures as cabinets and racks as well as in power transformers and cooling fans. Less intermediate testing is needed in the course of production because the correct functioning of the complex integrated circuits has already been ensured. Finally, the end user needs to provide less floor space, less operating power and less air conditioning for the equipment.[3]

The principles of what I have called the intellectualization and dematerialization processes are exhibited in what have been termed the ''learning curve'' or ''experience curve'' and Moore's Law. The learning curve expresses a relationship between the reduction in the costs of components (and an increase in their functionality) in relation to production output. According to Noyce, for the electronics industry of the seventies, this translates into a 28 percent decline in costs with each doubling of the output or experience of the industry or, equivalently, an annual decline in costs of about 25 percent. No other industry has been able to match this standard of performance record consistently over such a long period of time. These learning curve economics are still at work in the semiconductor today. Gordon Moore, Intel Corporation's cofounder, postulated in 1960 that chip densities would double every two years but had to revise this because technological progress had actually accelerated. In 1976, he estimated that chip densities would double every eighteen months. This means a quadrupling in three years instead of four. Over a period of thirty years, this represents an increase in chip densities by a factor of over one million. According to Moore's Law, we should anticipate memories with capacities of 1,000 megabits to become common by the year 2000. This is looking like a highly accurate forecast.

The explosion in the performance, speed, and functionality of microchips and their declining cost led quite directly to the revolutions in mainframe computers, minicomputers, and microcomputers and the synergies are being experienced in ever-widening business and socioeconomic circles, first in the corporate organization, then the marketplace, and finally in national economies of the world.

SOCIOCULTURAL AND INSTITUTIONAL SYNERGIES

A number of key sociocultural and institutional factors were also behind the computer and microchip revolutions in the early years and they created a synergy of a different kind—a synergy of cultures—which complemented and reinforced the intellectual, scientific, and industrial production synergies. One was the unique mix of scientific, engineering, and educational and industrial cultures in the states of Massachusetts and California, for example, where some of the most advanced scientific research and development institutions in the world were located. These included the Massachusetts Institute of Technology in Cambridge as well as Stanford University in California and the Bell Telephone Laboratories where the transistor was invented. These cultures created a climate where scientists and engineers in universities and private research laboratories could create and experiment with innovative ideas and circulate that knowledge between universities and industry. Many of them formed their own companies while others worked for former colleagues who preceded them. Their industrial culture was an essential part of the process of invention and the diffusion of ideas and technology throughout America and throughout the world and many of them made great fortunes for themselves. Dozens of countries, including Japan, France, and Britain, have since tried to replicate and duplicate this sociocultural process of industrial innovation.

This was the age when American military and economic power was at its peak, when high technology was strategic to America's military efforts, and developers and manufacturers could be guaranteed hundreds of millions of dollars for participating in such ventures as the ICBM Minuteman program, the Apollo lunar mission, and the Vietnam War. According to Michael Borrus and John Sysman of the Berkeley Roundtable on the International Economy, for a time in the fifties, about one half of the research budgets of IBM and AT&T were paid for by defense contracts, and from 1962 to 1965, military and space procurement for integrated circuits accounted for more than 75 percent of total industry sales.[4] It was this cultural and institutional setting in combination that enabled America to gain a leadership role in high technology and maintain it over the decades until the late eighties when other countries, especially Japan, would begin to seriously challenge this leadership in key segments of the industry.

THREE GENERATIONS OF COMPUTERS AND THE RISE OF IBM

Three generations of commercial computers followed the development of experimental computers of the fifties, each delivering greater functionality and performance in ever-smaller size and operating with ever-greater efficiency and reliability. Each took the computer further into the invisible domain of software and intelligence, and independent of materials, energy, transportation, geographic location, and human physical effort.

The first commercial computer, called the Univac I, was built by the Eckert Mauchly Corporation. The two men received a contract from the U.S. Census Department to build a computer to process census data, and they had left the Moore School at the University of Pennsylvania in 1950 to form their own company. But they soon experienced a shortage of cash and turned to Remington Rand for assistance to complete the project. Remington Rand bought them out and turned the company into its Univac division. Univac delivered its first computer, the Univac I, to the Census Department in 1951. It employed vacuum tube technology together with an electrostatic drum memory system and a magnetic tape storage system along with paper tape and punched card input and output devices. The Univac I was a spectacular success. But IBM, having lost its long-standing Census Bureau contract, immediately launched an ambitious development program to catch up in the computer industry.[5] Univac had a determined and formidable foe on its hands. IBM dominated the punched card tabulating machine industry, and Thomas Watson, IBM's president, resolved to dominate the emerging computer industry as well.

There was little real effective competition in the card tabulating card machine market and computer markets in the early fifties with IBM enjoying about 90 percent and Remington Rand the remaining 10 percent. IBM's domination was so complete that the Department of Justice filed an antitrust suit against the company in 1952 charging it with monopolizing the tabulating machine business. The case was eventually wound up in 1956 (the same year as AT&T's consent decree) with a consent decree with IBM agreeing to sell as well as lease its equipment and to make some of its patents available to Remington Rand.

But IBM had many strategic advantages that Remington Rand did not have. It enjoyed the advantages of vertical integration and economies of scale in research and development, manufacturing and marketing. It had by far the biggest national and international installed base of punched card tabulating equipment in the world, and this would prove to be a tremendous asset in IBM's effort to dominate the computer industry both in the United States and worldwide. IBM could design and manufacture the card punch equipment it needed for its new computers in factories already set up to produce its tabulating card machines and to use its international marketing and sales force to market its lines of computers as well. Remington Rand had none of these advantages. IBM was thus able to use its economies of scale and scope, its tremendous marketing muscle, its financial strength, and its prowess in technology to strategic advantage in the fifties and sixties to launch generation after generation of computers that enabled it to consolidate its hold on the computer industry worldwide.

In 1953, IBM delivered the 701 scientific computer, and the next year it announced the 650 for the business market. The 650 series was an astounding success. Even IBM management was astonished. By 1956, when computers were coming into their own, IBM dominated the market with about 85 percent of shipments. Remington Rand on the other hand had only about 9.7 percent. The booming market for computers also attracted new entrants. NCR came into the market in 1953, Burroughs in 1956, and General Electric in 1959. In 1957, a group of employees including William Norris left Univac to form a new company called Control Data Corporation (CDC) and Norris became its first president. CDC became a leader in the manufacture of extremely fast large-scale scientific computers.

Second-generation computers based on transistors became available in 1959. Magnetic core memory developed by Jay Forrester at MIT was becoming available on most computers by then. By storing bits of information in miniature magnetic cores, it was possible to store and retrieve data and program instructions electronically extremely rapidly, efficiently, and reliably in a random access manner. Univac, IBM, Burroughs, and Control Data Corporation all launched second-generation computers. The top-of-the-line IBM computer was the 7000 series computers, but IBM brought out smaller versions called the 1401 and the 1620 computers. NCR and RCA also launched new computers. General Electric launched a completely solid-state computer. As a result of growing competition, IBM's market share had dwindled to 65.3 percent by 1965.

The development of third-generation computers represented a milestone in the history of the computer because of its use of semiconductor and magnetic storage technology and its innovative software. The introduction of third-generation computers was marked by the announcement by IBM on April 7, 1964, of the new 360 series in a dramatic public relations exercise which included simultaneous press conferences in sixty-two U.S. cities and fourteen countries. The 360 was also extremely successful for IBM, and by 1967, it accounted for nearly 50 percent of IBM's installed base of computers. It also increased IBM's market share to 68 percent in spite of the fact that its competitors in some cases had much more innovative designs.

The Control Data Corporation 6600 computer, delivered in 1964, had fifteen times the performance of the fastest alternative computer at the time, and CDC dominated this niche for over a decade. CDC also became a leader in the computer service bureau industry as well as a pioneer in the application of computers in education with the development of its Plato System. Burroughs was the leader in a technique called multiprocessing which enabled several computers to work together under a single operating system to achieve much higher degrees of reliability and performance than any other machine. Burroughs also developed virtual memory which IBM used in its 360 series. General Electric became the leader in time-sharing, and MIT chose the GE 635 for developing its special time-sharing operating system (Project MAC). IBM was forced by the competition to incorporate time-sharing in its 360/Model 67 computer.

But the IBM 360 series was innovative in its own way in spite of making use of many of the innovations developed by its competitors. One of its most important features was that it was both a scientific and a commercial computer. Until 1964, computer manufacturers developed and marketed separate scientific and commercial machines. By designing both the hardware and software appropriately, it was possible for the 360 series to be configured either as a scientific or commercial computer. This made a big difference to its costs of production. Since IBM no longer had to go through the trouble and expense of designing and manufacturing two completely separate scientific and commercial computers, it was able to gain important economies of scale in its manufacturing operations which gave it a competitive edge over its rivals. The 360 series also used many new developments and inventions that became standard in the computer industry including the use of the 8-bit byte character representation, 9-track magnetic tapes, and removable (magnetic) disk packs.

SOFTWARE SYNERGIES: ECONOMICS OF THE THIRD GENERATION

The 360 series was perhaps most typical of third-generation computers. These employed medium-scale integration technology to increase the speed of the CPU and the speed and capacity of memory, and these together with other innovations, especially software innovations, made other advances possible. One of these was virtual memory which tremendously improved the economics of computers. Virtual memory is a technique for mapping the very high speed but small memory of the computer onto lower speed, high-capacity magnetic disk storage devices to increase throughput. Virtual memory made it possible for the computer to store many programs in memory at once and to schedule and execute them when the time and resources were available. These and other innovations were instrumental in creating the multiprogramming, multiuser, on-line, and time-sharing computer systems that are common today.

All of these innovations increased the throughput and the efficiency of the computer but also its complexity. But this also meant that the operating system would have to take much greater control over the operation of the entire computer, taking responsibility for controlling, scheduling, and executing all input and output as well as allocating all of the equipment and software resources needed to satisfy user demands. The computer had to be designed to operate more or less automatically with little or no operator intervention. Most computers today, including those used in telephone exchanges, automobiles, and robots and in offices and factories, banks and stock exchanges use these same techniques. All of them derive their unique features from these same automatic operating system control principles.

The third generation also witnessed the first big shift from hardware to software.[6] Indeed, it was the cost of developing the software for its time-sharing computer that forced General Electric to eventually withdraw from the computer market. Software development was the most significant cost in bringing the 360 to market, and it took years for IBM to recoup its investment in spite of the immediate success of the 360. It was developments in operating systems software to support virtual memory, multiprogramming and multiuser applications, and on-line, time-sharing and real-time processing in particular that made the third-generation computers so unique. But the development of high-level languages was equally important. The most important high-level languages were FORTRAN, developed by John Backus while at IBM in 1956 and used primarily for scientific applications; COBOL, developed by Grace Hopper and Charles Phillips primarily for business applications; and BASIC, developed by John Kemeny and Thomas Kurtz at Dartmouth College and designed for interactive use.

High-level languages were strategic to the success of third-generation machines and the 360 series in particular because they gave individual users the ability to quickly and easily write customized programs for their own use and, because these were supported by most manufacturers, programs written in these languages were portable across different makes of computers. This made it possible to create portable libraries of applications software that could be shared by communities of interest groups throughout the world in the sixties and seventies. High-level languages thus led to major increases in programmer productivity which made the computer an increasingly indispensable tool to scientists, engineers, and businesses throughout the sixties and seventies.

It was all of these unique developments in hardware, software, especially operating systems software and high-level languages, communications networks, and database applications, for example, and the synergies of all of them in combination that contributed to the evolution of the computer into a dynamically efficient information-processing, computational and resource allocation, and decision-making entity which led in turn to its widespread adoption in large- and medium-sized businesses. Operating in an increasingly network-intensive environment, these features enabled the computer to dynamically manage all of the hardware, software, and information resources on the computer and on the network and to dedicate these to each user as required, and as they become available in such a way that it appears as if each had all of its resources to his or her unique use. These same features also enabled each user to create, contribute to, and access and share enormous libraries and databanks of software, information, engineering designs, simulation models, and decision support and administrative applications with every other member on the network. And they contributed to the creation of entirely new industries, the most notable of which were the commercial computer processing, database and digital communications services industries. Computers, computer networks, and software applications thus enabled entire communities of scientists, engineers, and business people throughout the world to communicate, collaborate, and cooperate with one another and share their own unique software, information, talents, ideas, and experience. This process is still going on today but it is developments in enterprisewide networks, collaborative computing, workgroup technologies, and multimedia applications that promise to deliver ever-more power systems and intellectual synergies to organizations and individuals.

DEVELOPMENTS IN SEMICONDUCTOR TECHNOLOGY
INITIATE THE MINICOMPUTER REVOLUTION

Developments in small-scale integrated circuits launched the minicomputer age in the sixties. Minicomputers were smaller and less powerful but also less expensive than mainframe computers. They were designed to appeal to small-to-medium-size corporations which could not afford to purchase a mainframe computer or did not have the volume of information processing to justify the expense of a mainframe. The key distinctions between minicomputers and mainframes made them just right for a new market of scientific and engineering users waiting eagerly for their debut.

The minicomputer revolution was launched in 1960 when a new company, Digital Equipment Corporation (DEC), launched the PDP-1 minicomputer. It weighed 250 pounds and had a price tag of $120,000, a fraction of the weight, size, and price of computers at that time. Digital Equipment Corporation was formed three years earlier by Ken Olsen, a graduate from MIT who had worked with Jay Forrester on the development of core memory. Under the leadership of Olsen and its chief designer, Gordon Bell, DEC pioneered many key developments in minicomputers and went on to build successors to the PDP-1. In 1968, it announced its most successful and famous PDP-8 series of minicomputers which created the market niche for minicomputers.

The success of DEC attracted other new entrants to the rapidly growing minicomputer market. In 1968 Edson de Castro, DEC's chief designer, left the company to form Data General. Varian, Wang, Interdata, and Hewlett-Packard also brought out minicomputers. Driven by competition and rapid technological innovation, the speed and performance of minicomputers increased over the years until they began to compete with small mainframe computers and the definitions and performance features that were used to distinguish mainframe computers from minicomputers became blurred along with the distinctions between their customers and their markets. The growing number and success of minicomputer makers put increasing pressure on the manufacturers of mainframe computers, thus accelerating product innovation and development throughout the entire industry.

IBM'S INNOVATIONS IN COMPETITIVE STRATEGIES
AND TACTICS

By the early seventies, IBM dominated most segments of the computer industry worldwide despite the tremendous efforts by the ''seven dwarfs,'' as its mainframe competitors were called, to match or exceed its performance in innovation and marketing. IBM's success could not be attributed to any single strength but to its enormous technological, financial, marketing, and management strengths in combination. The company was vertically and horizontally integrated, and it had huge in-house expertise in hardware and software as well as in marketing and sales. It was also a global corporation. IBM was in fact one of the first companies to actually set up research and development, manufacturing and services and marketing arms in Europe and Asia and other continents. One of its biggest assets by far was its huge installed customer base worldwide. Another was its captive market of loyal customers. The company also had deeper pockets than any other computer company derived from its diverse activities so it could afford to pursue multiple research and development strategies while its competitors were forced to stick to one. It was big enough to internalize market risk that other companies could not, and it could protect itself from market uncertainty and set the pace of development and commercialization across the entire spectrum of computer products. No other computer company in the world could match it.

In their study of the computer industry, Barbara Katz and Almarin Phillips identified four critical characteristics that manufacturers had to have to excel in the computer industry in the first ten years. They included the involvement of top management in decision making, the coordination of finance, marketing, and technology, the ability to resolve conflicts in the business and the perceived importance of commercial segments of the business. IBM, CDC, DEC, and Scientific Data Systems scored high on all four counts. All four attributes were important in the decision of IBM to develop the IBM 360 series. The authors concluded:

It is literally inconceivable that the sequence of decisions relating . . . [to the scrapping of an entire computer development after spending many millions of dollars on it in favor of the new 360 series] would have been made and the results would have been successful in the absence of a vertically integrated structure with coordinated management of the several functions. IBM literally "bet the company" on its 360 decision.[7]

But much of IBM's success was also due to its unique corporate strategy which it crafted and applied like no other company. According to Gerald Brock, author of *The U.S. Computer Industry: A Study of Market Power*, the dominance of IBM can be attributed to an integrated, multipronged strategy which included leasing its computers and refusing to sell them to its customers and bundling its software and hardware together with consulting and other services. Teams of IBM experts would analyze the complete needs of its customers and advise on the best way of applying IBM's computer technology to solve problems. This was an important way of stimulating customer demands for more IBM products. These, combined with sophisticated pricing strategies, were used to control technological obsolescence, to make customers more dependent on IBM and prevent them from using equipment from other suppliers.

All of these strategies were wrapped under what IBM called its "unique product" philosophy which, according to Gerald Brock, was derived from "the need to prevent easy switching between IBM and its competitors and to hold customers with IBM even when competitors appear to have a superior product.'' Brock wrote,

IBM's approach to developing a unique product has been to tie together consulting help, software packages, education, and hardware into a single price package. [Before 1970,] the user paid a single price based upon the hardware and received all the other software ''free.'' This changed the focus of the IBM product from a specific piece of hardware to an entire company's capabilities and reputation and consequently made IBM's product unique in the computer market.[8]

IBM developed many other tactics to combat competition—tactics which leading competitors like Microsoft Corporation, for example, use today. One was the practice of selling computers to universities and educational institutions at deep discount prices. This was a way of initiating and educating the younger generations of students of science and business to the IBM world, gaining their trust and confidence and grooming and training them for the outside world where they would feed the growing number of companies with IBM computers. Many of these loyal IBMers would eventually make decisions to purchase IBM computers. Another strategy was the practice of announcing ''phantom machines.'' These were machines that never saw the light of day but were intended to hold onto customers or delay others from purchasing competing machines.

IBM also made various attempts to dominate standards in the computer industry but was not always successful. It tried unsuccessfully to have its FORTRAN standard adopted as the national standard in the fifties, and in the sixties, it failed to have its 8-bit Extended Binary Coded Decimal International Code (EBCDIC) recognized as the national standard. The American Standards association adopted instead the ASCII (American Standard Code for Information Interchange) code as the standard in 1968.

In the late sixties, IBM began fighting an onslaught of competition from manufacturers of plug-compatible peripheral equipment and it was the target of a number of antitrust suits. In 1968, for example, Memorex, which manufactured memory devices, and Telex, which manufactured disk drives, launched antitrust suits against IBM. Greyhound in the computer services business was another.

In 1969, the Department of Justice filed an antitrust suit against IBM charging it with monopolizing the general purpose computer industry and seeking to break up the company. It cited IBM's practice of bundling software, hardware, and support under one price, its tactics for dominating the educational market, its practice of prematurely announcing new computers and the pricing of computers in market segments where competition was greatest, and its practice of using accumulated software and support to preclude competitors from customer accounts. IBM responded in 1970 by unbundling the prices it charged for programming support, educational services, and applications programs from its hardware. Unbundling, according to Brock, ''dramatically reduced customer dependence on IBM consultants and . . . increased user independence.''[9]

In 1973, IBM and CDC settled out of court an antitrust suit filed by CDC's subsidiary Commercial Credit against IBM in 1968. Under the settlement, IBM agreed to sell its Service Bureau Corporation subsidiary to CDC and stay out of the service bureau business. CDC also received a $101 million cash settlement. One of the provisions of the settlement was that CDC would destroy its computerized index of IBM documents created for its case against IBM. The index of millions of IBM documents could have considerably strengthened the Justice Department's case against IBM which dragged on until 1982 when circumstances had changed considerably and the Department of Justice withdrew its case.

THE FIRST GREAT SHAKEOUT IN THE COMPUTER INDUSTRY

By the early seventies, the entire computer industry was undergoing a dramatic upheaval as a result of changing semiconductor, mainframe, and microcomputer technologies and product markets as well as fierce competition, and a shakeout was in progress. IBM announced the 370 series computers as the successor to the 360 series but there was nothing revolutionary about it, unlike the announcement of the 360. MOS memory completely replaced core memory in the 370 series because it was faster, cheaper, smaller, and more efficient. Cheaper, faster, higher capacity magnetic disks and semiconductor memory also became standard on all computers in the seventies. Paper tape and punched cards gave way to small magnetic disks and tapes and eventually to floppy disks as the microcomputer and personal computer revolutions gained momentum. Although the 360 series killed off much of IBM's competition, new entry was also taking place.

In 1970, Gene Amdahl, principal architect for IBM's 360 series, left IBM to form his own company, Amdahl Computers. Amdahl was dissatisfied with IBM's inability (actually, it was IBM's refusal) to incorporate LSI logic in its computers. In October 1971, Amdahl announced the first high-performance large-scale integrated chip, and, four years and $40 million later, it shipped its first Amdahl 470 V/6 computer. The V/6 was faster and less expensive than the top-of-the-line IBM 370, and it challenged IBM, forcing the giant corporation to speed up the introduction of new products.

Amdahl Computers was one of the few companies that was able to successfully compete with IBM during this period, and it did so by building so-called plug-compatible mainframe computers. These were computers whose hardware was so much like that of IBM that they could use the same software and peripheral equipment. This way, they could run all of the software that users had written for their IBM computers. The same cloning techniques would also prove successful in competing with IBM in the personal computer industry a decade later.

At the same time, opportunities were developing to build even more powerful computers. Seymore Cray, one of the original team members who left Univac to form CDC, eventually left the company in 1972 to form his own company, Cray Research. Cray became a world leader in the design and manufacturing of a new generation of superfast computers, called naturally "supercomputers."

Control Data, Univac, Burroughs, Honeywell, RCA, General Electric, and even Xerox, all members of the group of seven dwarfs, developed third-generation machines. Several of these were innovative in their own designs. CDC launched the Cyber 70 series of very fast computers and Burroughs the Illiac IV computer, a very fast parallel processing computer which used multiple CPUs but it was a generation or more ahead of its time. None of these was strong enough to challenge IBM's dominance of the mainframe computer industry. Even the strategy of manufacturing plug-compatible computers failed to dent IBM's growth or market share. Mainframe manufacturers also had to contend with growing competition from the minicomputer manufacturers led by Digital Equipment as well as Amdahl Computers which produced more superior, high performance computers than even IBM produced.

All of these developments in combination led to a major shakeout in the computer industry in the seventies—a shakeout that is still in progress today. Still suffering from the cost of developing the software for its time-sharing computer system, General Electric sold its computer operations to Honeywell in 1970. RCA failed to win customers from IBM with its strategy of cloning IBM computers in its Spectra 70 series, and RCA chairman, David Sarnoff, announced in 1971 that RCA was leaving the computer business. It sold its computer division to Sperry Rand/Univac. In 1976 Xerox which had entered the computer business only seven years earlier with the purchase of Scientific Data Systems sold its subsidiary Xerox Data Systems to Honeywell. Even Amdahl Computers was suffering. In 1980 its founder, Gene Amdahl, sold a large block of stock to Fujitsu Corporation but lost control of the corporation in the process. Subsequently, Amdahl left to found Trilogy Corporation to design, manufacture, and market large-scale, high-performance mainframe computers. Several years later, in 1986, Burroughs and Sperry agreed to combine their minicomputer and mainframe efforts and form Unisys Corporation.

THE MICROPROCESSOR INITIATES THE PERSONAL COMPUTER REVOLUTION

It was innovations in microelectronics and efforts to cram more and more circuitry and functionality on a single chip that has led to one of the greatest industrial transformations in history. These led to the creation of the microprocessor and microcomputer in the seventies and precipitated the personal computer revolution in the eighties. These were landmark developments that challenged IBM's dominance over the computer industry and eventually forced it to scrap all of its old strategies and devise entirely new ones to compete in the new and transformed computer industry.

The history of the microchip, the microprocessor, and the personal computer (PC) revolution goes back to the late fifties to the Palo Alto area of California.[10] William Shockley, feeling he had outgrown Bell Laboratories and wanting to strike out on his own, decided to go back to his home in Palo Alto, California, where he set up his own company, Shockley Semiconductor, in 1955. Shockley attracted many bright young minds but was unable to keep them happy. Bank-rolled by Fairchild Camera, a well-known supplier of camera equipment, a group of them (subsequently called the Fairchildren) left Shockley to start up their own company called Fairchild Semiconductor in 1957. Two of the men who joined Fairchild Semiconductor, Robert Noyce and Gordon Moore, eventually left in 1968 to form the now-famous Intel Corporation, which launched the microcomputer revolution and owns the patents to most of the computers that are based on the IBM PC. The Palo Alto area of California, where all of the action took place, became known as "silicon valley," and it is still the heart of the American and the world semiconductor and computer industries. Silicon valley developed its own unique culture of scientists, venture capitalists, soft-ware specialists, and the myriads of other kinds of businesses and business professional that cater to the unique needs of the high-tech world we live in today. And other countries have attempted to copy its success.

In 1971, Intel Corporation announced the first microprocessor called the Intel 4004. It was designed by a team led by Ted Hoff for a Japanese company called Bussicom which had contracted Intel to produce components for a program-mable desktop calculator.[11] Hoff had to find some way of reducing the enormous number of components required to synthesize the calculator. To solve the prob-lem, he designed a general purpose microprocessor with the entire CPU on a single chip. The instructions for making it operate and perform the various functions were stored in a read-only memory chip (ROM). Another chip was added for input and output. Intel also invented the erasable programmable read-only memory (EPROM) which made it possible to reuse memory by dynami-cally erasing and overwriting it as required.

The Hoff team had given birth to the microprocessor although no one rec-ognized it for some time. It contained 2,300 transistors and had the computa-tional power of the ENIAC. It also performed as well as the $300,000 IBM machines of the early 1960s and its CPU measured just one-eighth inch by one-sixth inch. It took Hoff and Intel Corporation some time to realize that the variety of applications of the microprocessor were limitless in theory and pos-sibly in practice. In 1972, Intel Corporation followed up with an 8-bit successor to the 4004, called the Intel 8008. It had 20,000 transistors. In 1973, National Semiconductor launched a circuit board with processor and memory chips for control applications. In 1974, Motorola announced the 6800 microprocessor. By 1974, Intel had developed the Intel 8080 chip, the first true general-purpose microprocessor. A complete computer was now available on a single printed circuit board. It was capable of executing 290,000 instructions a second and it became the industry standard for the 8-bit market. In 1977, Robert Noyce summarized the progress made in the development of the microcomputer in a *Scientific American* article on microelectronics in the following way:

Today's microcomputer, at a cost of perhaps $300 has more computing capacity than the first large electronic computer, ENIAC. It is 20 times faster, has a larger memory, is thousands of times more reliable, consumes the power of a light bulb rather than of a locomotive, occupies 1/30,000 the volume and costs 1/10,000 as much. It is available by mail order or at your local hobby shop.[12]

In 1979, Intel announced the 64-kilobit random access memory (RAM) chip. All of the hardware was ready for the personal computer revolution.

The first commercially available microcomputer in kit form was launched by a company called MITS in 1974. The new computer, called the Altair, named after the mythical planet in the Star Trek series, was advertised in the January 1975 issue of *Popular Electronics* for $350. It was powered by the Intel 8080 chip. Apple, Commodore, and Tandy brought out ready-made computers built with their own software in the next two years. Apple introduced the Apple I computer, its first mass-market computer, in April 1976, and, a year later, it introduced the Apple II. Commodore announced the Personal Executive Terminal (PET) in April 1977 and Tandy, the TRS-80, in August of the same year.

These were revolutionary developments because they put individuals as users as well as producers instead of large corporations in control of the computer revolution. The *New Scientist* summed up the significance of these early machines in the following way:

Until 1974, computing was the preserve of large corporations, hedged around with rules and regulations designed to share out an expensive resource. The Altair and more refined machines such as the Commodore PET and the Tandy TRS-80 which followed it turned that notion on its head. Individuals, those with a technical bent anyway, could please themselves about how and where they used a computer. In this sense microcomputers were subversive. They spawned an underground culture in California with its own heroes, myths, and shibboleths. Insiders knew they had gotten one over the establishment. Unlike the development of the minicomputer closely associated with the American space effort of the 1960s or the mainframe which grew out of war time weapons and code cracking research, microcomputer development took place outside the mainstream of computer science.[13]

THE STORY OF APPLE COMPUTER

No history of the personal computer revolution is complete without at least a brief description of the role that Apple Computer, one of the great legends of silicon valley, played in it. In the mid-seventies, Steven Wozniak and Stephen Jobs, members of the Homebrew Computer Club at Hewlett-Packard, the company where Wozniak worked, became interested in building their own computer.

Wozniak designed a personal computer called the Apple I and set up shop in 1975 in his garage to produce them for sale. The local Byte Shop agreed to purchase fifty machines, and the duo was in business. In 1976, Wozniak and Jobs formed the now-famous Apple Computer company to produce personal computers for the commercial market. In 1977, Apple Computer brought out an improved personal computer called the Apple II at a price of $1,298. The Apple II along with the launching of the Lisa computer in January 1983 and its successor, the Apple Macintosh introduced in 1984, led to Apple becoming the undisputed leader in the personal computer industry. The Macintosh had 128K of memory and a retail price of $2,495, and it used the Motorola 68000 microprocessor instead of Intel's 8080 or successor microprocessors. This machine revolutionized the personal computer industry and set the standard by which all personal computers are judged today.

IBM LAUNCHES THE PC REVOLUTION

By 1980, IBM was coming under tremendous pressure from inside and outside the company to develop a more effective strategy for the rapidly growing personal computer marketplace. But everything about the new market was different from IBM's traditional mainframe and minicomputer businesses. Its client base consisted of individuals primarily, that is, programmers, engineers, scientists, financial experts, and very small businesses, instead of corporate Management Information Systems (MIS) people. Its distribution channels were different. Its competitors were small but very innovative and nimble. IBM dominated no part of the hardware and software segments of the new market like it did in the mainframe industry. To catch up with Apple Computer and take the lead quickly, IBM devised a radically different strategy from any that it had ever previously executed. Instead of trying to produce all of the hardware and software in-house, it turned to outside suppliers. It chose to purchase the microprocessor from Intel Corporation, its operating system, the programming language from a small company called Microsoft Corporation, and it chose retailers such as ComputerLand and Sears, Roebuck to sell its machines to the public. Actually the strategy was not innovative at all for IBM effectively copied much of Apple Computer's strategy which, after all, worked very well for Apple Computer. Why would the same strategy not work for IBM? The strategy did work very well at first, but in hindsight, it turned out to be one of the biggest mistakes in IBM's history. In June 1980, IBM set up the "Acorn Project" to bring out a desktop personal computer in one year.

New York, August 12, 1981! IBM issued a press release announcing "its smallest, lowest-priced computer system—the IBM Personal Computer . . . designed for business, school, and home, the easy-to-use system sells for as little as $1,565." The IBM PC came standard with 64K of memory and was priced at $2,665. It was powered by the Intel 8088 microchip running at 4.77 MHz and an "advanced operating system" which IBM called PC-DOS, supplied by a start-up company called Microsoft Corporation. With this announcement, the personal computer revolution was officially launched. The debut of the PC was chosen as the 1982 "machine of the year" by *Time Magazine*, and its picture appeared on the front page of the January 3, 1983 issue. By 1991, more than 125 million PCs or PC-compatible computers were in operation around the world, far more than any other computer and they put the personal industry on a road that would transform the world.

Other manufacturers announced personal computers in the same year as IBM. Hewlett-Packard and Xerox brought out their own personal computers. Commodore announced the Commodore 64, one of the most popular home computers ever made. In 1982 the first 32-bit microcomputers appeared on the market effectively making it possible to put the power of a mainframe computer into a desktop personal computer.

The personal computer revolution was also a software revolution. Several key software packages were instrumental in marketing the personal computer as a productivity-enhancing device and winning over the business community and the public generally to the merits of personal computing. One of these was the BASIC programming language for personal computers developed by Microsoft, which made it possible for users to write programs in high-level languages rather than machine code. Another was the CP/M (control program for microprocessors) operating system developed specifically for microcomputers by Gary Kildall in the late seventies. CP/M was the first general-purpose (floppy) disk-based operating system for 8-bit microcomputers, and it provided a standard for both manufacturers and software producers to create a big market for personal computer products.

A third major advance came in 1979 with the introduction of a spreadsheet program called VisiCalc for the Apple II by two MIT graduates, Daniel Bricklin and Bob Frankston. VisiCalc was a very special product at a very special time for it made it possible for a whole new community of professional users who were not programmers to easily create their own programs to perform complex mathematical calculations and simulate various hypotheses to aid decision making. VisiCalc became an instant hit and made personal computers indispensable to the business world. The development of a word processing package called WordStar also played an important role in the personal computer revolution in its early days. By 1983, the personal computer revolution had become unstoppable and second-generation and third-generation software was coming onto the market. In that year, Mich Kapor, founder of Lotus Development Corporation released the spreadsheet program Lotus 1–2–3 which quickly became the best selling PC program.

By the mid-eighties, software companies were beginning to offer more robust "integrated software" products which incorporated word processing, spreadsheet, database, graphics, and communications software. Lotus Development Corporation introduced Symphony in July 1984. Vicicorp introduced Vision. Apple Computer introduced Appleworks, and Ashton-Tate introduced All-in-one. The next stage in the personal computer revolution was desktop publishing which was pioneered by new and innovative software applications from Apple Computer. By the late eighties, the desktop publishing revolution was in full swing.

THE CONTRIBUTIONS OF XEROX PARC TO THE COMPUTER REVOLUTION

In some respects, it was Xerox Corporation indirectly that made some of the greatest contributions to the early development of the personal computer in its now-famous Palo Alto Research Center (PARC) located in silicon valley. Between 1971 and 1976, Xerox bankrolled some of the youngest and brightest computer scientists, engineers, and software developers it could find and gave them the opportunity to define the paperless office-of-the-future.[14] Xerox PARC pioneered many hardware and software innovations that were subsequently developed and commercialized by other companies. These included chip-making technology, portable computing, bit-mapped screen displays, laser printers, drawing tablets, the Ethernet local area network, mouse- and icon-based computing, desktop publishing and typesetting, and WYSIWYG (what you see is what you get) word processing. Graduates of PARC went on to make contributions in their own right and many created their own companies. They included Bob Metcalfe, the inventor of Ethernet and founder of 3Com Corporation; John Ellenby, a key designer of Grid's Compass microcomputer; and Larry Tesler who joined the Apple team in 1980 to direct the Lisa project. Other graduates from PARC went to Microsoft Corporation, DEC, and Convergent Technologies and made their mark on these companies.

One of the greatest contributions of the PARC team was the development of the graphical user interface (or GUI, pronounced "gooey," a screen-based, icon-windowing system) which has since become a standard by which all other personal computer software and user interfaces are judged. Among its most outstanding features are its use of icons, graphs, and windows on the computer screen to enable users to simply and easily communicate and interact with the computer in a "user friendly" manner without the need for complex instructions, combinations of key strokes, or user manuals. The graphical user interface designed at PARC used icons to represent files and programs, pull-down menus to access instructions, commands, split screens, and overlay windows to present information in an easily readable and managed manner. Another of its most important contributions was the use of a handheld mouse to represent a pointer system for selecting information and scrolling and zooming in on information displayed on the screen. Most of these innovations were incorporated into Apple's Lisa and Macintosh computers, and they were key to giving Apple and its Macintosh computer the success they enjoy today. All personal computers and workstations today are based on the innovations made by PARC and Apple

Computer, including Microsoft Windows, IBM's Presentation Manager, and X-Windows developed by MIT.

THE RISE OF MICROSOFT CORPORATION

Another of the legends of the microcomputer revolution is Microsoft and William Gates, its cofounder who, like Jobs, was a university drop-out. While at Harvard, Gates became enthusiastic about the prospects for the Altair computer when it was announced in 1975. With the assistance of Paul Allen, his partner, Gates set about to develop an interpreter for the new computer, and, in 1975, he and Allen founded Microsoft Corporation. The result was Microsoft BASIC, which subsequently became the first universal programming language for the personal computer. But the really big break for Microsoft Corporation came when IBM invited the company to jointly develop the MS/DOS operating system for the IBM PC. Gates hired Tim Patterson, a programmer from Seattle who had written a rudimentary operating system called Q-DOS (for Quick and Dirty Operating System), and adapted it for the IBM PC; then Microsoft went on to conquer the world.

Microsoft also developed a great deal of software for the Apple Macintosh computer which undoubtedly contributed to the success of both companies, and it contributed to the development of IBM's Presentation Manager which IBM brought to market in 1989 for its PS/2 computer. The success of Microsoft made Gates the first PC billionaire by 1986. By 1990, Microsoft had revenues of $1.1 billion making it the biggest software company in the world. By then, it had a virtual monopoly on DOS operating system having sold over forty million copies.

THE PC EMERGES AS THE DOMINANT FORCE IN COMPUTING AND THE WORLD

IBM's PC strategy worked well until the mid-eighties when it began encountering fierce competition from clone makers, and its share of the PC market was in sharp decline. By then, the weaknesses of its PC strategy were becoming increasingly evident. By turning to outsiders for its critical hardware and software components—to Intel for its microprocessors, Microsoft for its operating system, and retailers for its distribution—IBM had created an industry that was for all intent and purposes beyond its control. For the first time in history, by 1985, the hottest and highest growth segment of the computer industry no longer needed IBM.

IBM was being hurt in particular by clone manufacturers such as Tandy and upstarts like Compaq, founded in February 1982 by Rod Carrion and two other engineers from Texas Instruments. These companies were able to purchase PC chips readily from Intel, and they were developing machines more rapidly than IBM and selling them at a lower price. It was in response to its declining market share that IBM introduced the faster and more advanced 8-bit XT personal computer in 1983. The next year it introduced a more advanced machine called the AT. The AT used the new 16-bit Intel 286 microprocessor and came with a hard disk. IBM also entered the home-computer market in October 1983 with the IBM PCjr but it was a marketing disaster. By 1985, the XT and AT models were being cloned by the competition as well. By 1987, the price of the personal computer had dropped to less than $1,000 as a result of these price wars.

Compaq was an example of the competition that IBM had to face in the eighties. Compaq's initial success was due to its luggable IBM-compatible PC, introduced in November 1982, but the company followed on with further innovations, outperforming IBM in the PC market by offering IBM PC compatibility combined with portability, fancy graphics, and better performance than IBM. Compaq's sales exploded from $111 million by the end of its first year of operation in 1983 to over $1 billion in 1987, a feat that no other startup has been able to match. In 1989, Compaq's sales exceeded $3 billion. Its market share was achieved primarily at the expense of IBM.

The success of the clone manufacturers in gaining market share subsequently forced IBM to announce a successor to the PC in April 1987. Called the PS/2, the new personal computer was based on one of the most powerful new chips in the industry—the Intel 386. The high-end model came with one megabyte of internal memory and was priced at $6,995. It was also fast—operating at a speed of three MIPS (three million operating instructions per second). This time, however, IBM resorted to a strategy that it had successfully used time and time again in the mainframe business. It designed its new computer around a new proprietary Micro Channel Architecture, which was intended in part to correct certain design deficiencies in its PC but primarily to slow the growth of clone manufacturers. In the same year, IBM and Microsoft announced a joint venture to develop a new operating system, called OS/2, to replace MS/DOS for new computers. It would have much more powerful features, including Mac-like graphics as well as communications and networking features. On the competition front, Apple Computer announced the Macintosh SE and Macintosh II computers in 1987. The Mac II came with one megabyte of internal memory and was priced at $5,498. The next year, Apple introduced the Macintosh FX which used the Motorola 68030 microchip.

At the same time, a new generation of companies was developing the specialized high-performance RISC-based workstations market by harnessing the growing speed and sophistication of microprocessors for the use of engineers, architects, designers, graphic artists, and publishers. Reduced instruction set computers (RISC) used fewer instructions than traditional PC systems which were based on complex instruction set computer (CISC) architectures. This gave RISC computers a speed advantage over PC-based computers. Sun Microsystems and Apollo Computer were among the first to introduce RISC workstations in the mid-eighties. The Sun 4/100 RISC-based workstation, introduced in 1984, came with 8 MB of internal memory and a price tag of $18,900. Its speed was 7 MIPS, and it used a new operating system called UNIX which was rapidly becoming the standard for the workstation market.

UNIX was developed in 1969 by Kenneth Thompson at AT&T's Bell Telephone Laboratories and Dennis Richie who invented the programming language called C. Since C was being used by many microcomputer manufacturers, once UNIX was written in C, it had the potential of becoming a de facto operating system, and this is the strategy AT&T settled on to turn it into a universal operating system for all computers. Certain features of UNIX, including its multitasking and multiuser capabilities, and its portability across many kinds of computers systems made it a dominant player in the workstation and telecommunications markets. AT&T adopted a nonproprietary, open systems strategy as a means to encourage suppliers to develop software that was could run on any computer that used the UNIX operating system.

By 1988, all of the leading computer manufacturers were producing workstations, and the Japanese were making inroads into the industry. By then, IBM had purchased an interest in Intel Corporation which was designing an even more powerful chip called the Intel 486 which it introduced in 1989. The 486 was designed to bring the power of the early-1980 mainframe computers to personal computer users in the early nineties. Motorola introduced the 8030 and 8040 microprocessors to match those of Intel.

By 1990, the personal computer revolution had hit the home, stimulated by domestic and international cutthroat competition, a rapidly declining price, and ever more attractive software applications. IBM introduced the PS/1 computer in 1990 expressly for the home market. Based on the Intel 286 microchip, the PS/1 came with its own GUI, an integrated word processing, spreadsheet, and communications software package; a built-in modem to allow connection to on-line database services; and a program to connect with Prodigy, the IBM-Sears computer service providing banking, shopping, and airline reservations services. The low end of the PS/1 was priced under the magic $1,000 barrier. In response, Apple Computer introduced the Apple Classic in October 1990 at the rock-bottom price of $999. Home owners began snapping up these and other computers manufactured by Commodore and Atari, for example, in growing numbers. Microsoft launched Windows 3.0 for the IBM PC in the fall of 1990, and it became an instant hit. By the end of 1991, Microsoft was enjoying a monopoly position not only for MS/DOS software but windowing software for PCs as well, and it had displaced IBM as leader in the personal computer industry.

By 1992, the transformation of the entire computer industry worldwide was well underway with powerful 386, 486, 68030, and 68040 microchips and personal computers containing them. The computer industry worldwide had developed into a $93 billion industry with personal computer hardware and software its largest and fastest growing segment. Literally everything was changing—not only hardware and software—but the leaders as well. Microsoft and Intel were spectacularly successful in 1992. Their stocks soared on the New York Stock Exchange, and they were taking the lead away from IBM as the pace-setter in the computer industry. IBM's share of the PC market fell to 16.4 percent by September 1992, and both IBM and DEC were fighting for their lives. Ken Olson was ousted from the head of DEC, and the company was split into smaller units. IBM announced that it would shed a further 25,000 staff in addition to the 40,000 it had shed in the previous two years and split itself up into thirteen separate companies.

A new race began heating up in the early nineties to develop the next generation of multimedia computers that could handle video and voice as well as data and text. IBM, Apple, and Motorola announced a joint venture in 1991 to develop the new generation of PowerPC computers based on IBM's fast RISC-based chip designs and IBM and Apple operating systems platforms. Intel introduced the Pentium as the successor to the 486 in March 1993. Microsoft announced its new operating system Windows NT in May 1993. IBM and Apple announced their first PowerPC computers in March 1994. The computer industry had also entered the mature mass market stage of its evolution. Mass marketers like Dell and Packard Bell and giant retail distributors were taking over and a massive shakeout was in progress in the computer industry. The center of gravity of the industry was shifting dramatically to client server systems, wireless computers, and personal communications devices, and multimedia computing and electronic publishing were becoming big growth areas. And telecommunications and cable television companies, broadcasters, publishers, and entertainment companies along with Japanese consumer electronics companies were entering into joint ventures to develop new mass market service applications based on the new generations of microchips and personal computers for the emerging electronic superhighways that all were trying to create.

COMPUTER TIDE: A CAPSULE SUMMARY OF THE IMPACTS OF THE COMPUTER AND THE MICROCHIP ON BUSINESS AND SOCIETY

It is now widely accepted that it was developments in computers and microchips that set off the information revolution of the sixties, seventies, and eighties.[15] They created new industries, destroyed old ones, and transformed others. They also transformed the nature of work and management and set off an organizational revolution. Until the late eighties, however, the uses of computers in organizations were primarily technology-driven and applications-driven with no major impact on the way companies were organized or operated. Organizations customized mainframe computers, minicomputers, and personal computers to serve the specialized needs of individual departments and every level of the corporate hierarchy.

As the personal computer revolution gained momentum in the eighties, local area networks (LANs) were developed to interconnect and integrate these various islands of automation that existed in organizations.[16] LANs gave individuals the capability to communicate with one another, share information, software, and systems resources, and to work together to make decisions in myriads of ways that were never before possible with mainframes and minicomputers. By the early nineties, developments in both computers and telecommunications were facilitating the creation of enterprisewide networks and fully distributed computing and bringing computer and communications power to every individual in the organization. In these and other ways, the momentum was building up and initiating the real revolution—the revolution in work, management, and organization that companies are experiencing today.[17]

Computerization has also been changing the basis of competition in many industries, and this added further momentum to the revolution.[18] Many corporations in the eighties began to realize that information technology could be used as a source of strategic competitive advantage, for example, to generate new products and services, to add value to existing products and services and build barriers to entry and change the balance of power in supplier relationships.[19] As we shall see in later chapters, computerization was also having dramatic effects on the structure of entire industries and sectors of the economy, and, through its effects on developments in electronic commerce, it was also changing the way markets and the economic system itself were organized and operated.[20]

CREATING AN "INFORMATION ECONOMY"

It was not until the early sixties that the impacts of the microchip and computer and communications revolutions were subjected to a rigorous and thorough quantitative analysis. The work was carried out by Fritz Machlup, an economist at Princeton University, who was interested in quantifying the growing proportion of knowledge-related activities in the economy and their contribution to economic growth. Machlup published his results in 1962 in a book entitled *The Production and Distribution of Knowledge in the United States.* According to Machlup's calculations, the knowledge economy accounted for roughly 29 percent of gross national product (GNP) and 31 percent of the nonfarm labor force of the United States in 1958 and it was growing at an average annual rate double that of GNP. The Department of Commerce in the United States and the Organization for Economic Cooperation and Development (OECD) subsequently funded research into the knowledge economy and corroborated the work of Machlup.[21]

The impacts of the information revolution on the economy can be best summarized by the a 1989 report by the OECD entitled *Information Technology and New Growth Opportunities.* It stated:

Information Technology (IT) is arguably the most pervasive technology of our time. It not only comprises a major, growing branch of economic activity in its own right—a branch which has been a major ''driver'' of economic growth in the postwar period— but also generates a flow of product and process innovation in other branches. These encompass both rationalizing (productivity-enhancing) innovations and growth-promoting ones which enable new types of economic activity. Their impact spans manufacturing, services and government (including defence). More broadly, IT enables structural changes to take place in the economy. Rapid growth in IT alters the relative size of industrial branches. Improved computational capabilities allow larger organizational entities to be managed and permit management to span more complex portfolios. Improved communications capabilities permit centralized control of multinational corporations. Thus, IT helps firms grow larger, more complex and to operate globally—tending to undermine the power of individual nation-states and to increase the need for new forms of international organization on the side of the government. Further, the growing opportunities for information-handling generated by IT permits these to develop into separate industrial sectors. New service sectors thus appear, leading some economic activity (classically, the writing of computer software) to be reclassified from "manufacturing" to "services."[22]

NOTES

1. For a history of the microelectronics revolution, see Tom Forrester, Ed., *The Microelectronics Revolution: The Complete Guide to the New Technology and Its Impact on Society* (Oxford: Basil Blackwell, 1980).

2. William Oldam, "The Fabrication of Microelectronic Circuits," *Scientific American*, Special Issue on Microelectronics 237, no. 3 (1977).

3. Robert Noyce, "Microelectronics," *Scientific American*, Special Issue on Microelectronics 237, no. 3 (1977), p. 67.

4. Michael Borrus and John Zysman, "Alliances, Networks, and International Competition," *Datamation*, 1 June 1985, p. 18.

5. IBM had held the U.S. Census Bureau contract since 1896, through its predecessor company, the Computing-Tabulating-Recording (CTR) Company. Thomas J. Watson became CTR's CEO in 1924 and changed its name to the International Business Machine Corporation.

6. For an good overview of computer software, see *Scientific American*, Special Issue on Computer Software 251, no. 3 (1984).

7. Barbara Goody Katz and Almarin Phillips, "The Computer Industry," *Government and Technical Change: A Cross-Industry Analysis*, ed. R.R. Nelson (New York: Pergamon Press, 1982), p. 218.

8. Gerald Brock, *The U.S. Computer Industry: A Study of Market Power* (Cambridge: Ballinger, 1975), p. 98.

9. Gerald Brock, *The U.S. Computer Industry*, p. 99.

10. For excellent descriptions of the history of the micro revolution, I strongly recommend Robert Slater, *Portraits in Silicon* (Cambridge: MIT Press, 1987); and Everett M. Rogers and Judith K. Larsen, *Silicon Valley Fever: Growth of High-Technology Culture* (New York: Basic Books, 1984).

11. Masatoshi Shima and Federico Gaggin also played key roles in designing the Intel 4004, the world's first microprocessor, its successor, the Intel 8008, as well as the Zilog Z80, the microprocessor that powered the first generation of business microcomputers worldwide. See Federico Faggin, "The Birth of the Microprocessor," *BYTE*, March 1992, pp. 145–150. *BYTE* reported on July 17, 1990, that after a 20-year battle with U.S.

Patent Office, Gilbert Hyatt, systems designer, electronics engineer, and aerospace consultant, was granted the patent for a "Single Chip Integrated Circuit Computer Architecture," giving him the distinction of inventor of the microprocessor. See "Micro, Micro, Who Made the Micro?" *BYTE*, January 1991.

12. Robert Noyce, "Microelectronics," *Scientific American*, Special Issue on Microelectronics 237, no. 3, 1977.

13. John Banks, "The Ten-Year Trek from Altair," *New Scientist*, Microcomputers in Science Supplement, 18 October 1984, p. 2.

14. "Xerox Park—Heroes of the Micro Revolution," *Computers & Electronics*, September 1984, p. 76. Also an interview with John Seely Brown, *Computerworld*, 17 August 1992, p. 79.

15. For an assessment of the impacts of the Information Revolution, see Tom Forrester, *High-Tech Society: The Story of the Information Technology Revolution* (Cambridge: MIT Press, 1987).

16. F. Warren McFarlan and James J. McKenney, "The Information Archipelago—Maps and Bridges," *Harvard Business Review*, September-October 1982.

17. For a description of the effects of information technology on organizations, see D. Quinn Mills, *Rebirth of the Corporation* (New York: John Wiley, 1991); Shoshana Zuboff, *In the Age of the Smart Machine: The Transformation of Work and Power* (New York: Basic Books, 1988). Also by Peter Drucker, "The Coming of the New Organization," *Harvard Business Review*, January-February 1988, pp. 45–53; Rosabeth Moss Kanter, "The New Managerial Work," *Harvard Business Review*, November-December 1989, pp. 85–92; and Robert H. Hayes and Ramchandran Jaikumar, "Manufacturing's Crisis: New Technologies, Obsolete Organizations," *Harvard Business Review*, September-October 1988, pp. 77–85.

18. There are at least two classic cases where corporations have used information technology to create strategic competitive advantage. One is the case of American Hospital Supply which put computer terminals on the desks of its clients so they could access information and order drugs automatically. The other example is American Airlines which developed the Sabre airlines reservations system. Sabre became so important that agents could not do without it, and it established itself as a virtual monopoly in the airlines reservations industry in the United States. The government eventually had to step in and regulate the industry. For other examples, refer to F. Warren McFarlan, "Information Technology Changes the Way You Compete," *Harvard Business Review*, May-June 1984, pp. 98–103; Michael E. Porter and Victor E. Miller, "How Information Gives You Competitive Advantage," *Harvard Business Review*, July-August 1985, pp. 149–160.

19. *Revolution in Real Time: Managing Information Technology in the 1990s* (Boston: Harvard University Press, 1990); and Michael S. Scott Morton, ed., *The Corporation in the Nineties: Information Technology and Organizational Transformation* (New York: Oxford University Press, 1991).

20. Thomas W. Malone, Joanne Yates, and Robert I. Benjamin, "The Logic of Electronic Markets: Is Your Company Ready for Computer-Aided Buying and Selling?" *Harvard Business Review*, May-June 1989, pp. 166–170.

21. The Department of Commerce funded a major project to quantify the concept of the knowledge economy. The results were published in a report by Marc U. Porat and Michael R. Rubin, *The Information Economy* (Washington, D.C.: Department of Commerce, 1977). The authors reported that the information sector contributed over 46 per-

cent to GNP and 53 percent of total national income of the United States in 1967. The OECD subsequently replicated this work for its member countries. See *Information Activities, Electronics and Telecommunications Technologies* (Paris: OECD, 1981). The studies showed that the information sector contributed 29.6 percent and 32.2 percent respectively to the GNP of Japan and Austria, while those of the United States and Canada contributed respectively 41.1 percent and 39.9 percent.

22. *Information Technology and New Growth Opportunities*, Information, Computer and Communications Policy Committee (Paris: OECD, 1989), p. 137.

Chapter 4

Growth, Expansion, Convergence, and Creative Destruction

The information revolution was complemented by innovations in satellites and coaxial and microwave communications systems as well as digital switching and transmission systems which precipitated the telecommunications revolutions of the sixties and seventies. Together, these led to the fusion or convergence of computers and communications technologies and initiated the office and factory revolutions in the seventies. They also set off revolutions in cable television, broadcasting, publishing, and entertainment as well as retailing and banking and financial services. The forces of competition and technological innovation grew and gained momentum until they began to transform the technological and economic underpinnings of Western societies and they had far-reaching structural, legal, and institutional implications in the regulated sectors of the economy, especially in the telecommunications, cable television, broadcasting, and banking and financial services industries. The information and telecommunications revolutions also became inextricably linked to international trade in services and international competitiveness as well as deindustrialization and unemployment. They challenged the economic and political sovereignty of every nation, forcing them to make dramatic changes in their industrial and information and trade policies to accommodate a new world information order that had emerged.

By the end of the eighties, when some of the legal, institutional, and other contradictions were resolved, the telecommunications industry in the United

States, Britain, Japan, and other industrialized countries were substantially de-regulated. AT&T and the Bell system in the United States were broken up, and seven regional holding companies were created in its place. A process of pri-vatizing state-owned enterprises was underway worldwide which is still going on today. The world economy and world society had become a much smaller and interdependent entity. This chapter will briefly describe this transformation, beginning with the problems created by developments in satellite communica-tions and the interdependence of computers and telecommunications in the fifties and sixties and the new industrial and economic order they created.

SPAWNING A REVOLUTION IN SATELLITE COMMUNICATIONS

Along with the transistor, the microprocessor, the laser, and the optical fiber, the communications satellite must rate as one of the most important technolog-ical developments in the postwar period. Because it can carry telephone and television signals as well as information and news and because a single satellite can cover an entire hemisphere, it had dramatic military as well as economic, industrial, cultural, and political implications. The satellite communications rev-olution began with the launching of Sputnik I by the Soviet Union in 1957, and it launched both the United States and the Soviet Union into a race to exploit space and space technology for military as well as commercial purposes. In July 1958, the U.S. Congress passed the National Aeronautics and Space Act estab-lishing NASA as a civilian agency to lead America's space development activ-ities. But it was the leadership of the United States in microelectronics and computer technology that proved critical to eventually surpassing the Soviet Union in the development of satellite technology and led to its landing a man on the moon in 1969.

In the late fifties, the United States tested several scientific communications satellites including Explorer I, launched in 1958, and various military satellites as well as passive communications satellites, including ECHO I and ECHO II which simply reflected radio signals. (Those that followed were active in the sense that they had electronics on board to amplify signals.) The age of com-mercial satellites communications began in 1962 with the launching of Telstar I which was built by AT&T's Bell Laboratories. It had a capacity of only 600 two-way telephone circuits but that was plenty in those days. Most importantly, it provided a means for an entire continent to communicate instantaneously.

These early communications satellites had a serious drawback, however. Be-cause they were continually moving with respect to the earth, they provided only intermittent service. Only when a satellite is in a stationary position with respect to the earth can it serve as a reliable communications station. This occurs when the satellite is located at a distance of about 23,000 miles or 36,000 kilometers from the center of the earth and orbits it in the plane of the equator. These so-called geostationary satellites thus appear stationary with respect to positions on the earth's surface. It was the British science-fiction writer Arthur C. Clarke who in 1945 in the Journal *Wireless World* proposed using geostationary satellites as a means of overcoming the problem of intermittent service. Clarke concluded that three geostationary satellites appropriately located around the earth could be made to serve the entire world with instant communications. Each satellite would broadcast programs to about one-third of the planet thereby providing the entire globe with instant television coverage. One satellite would have to cover Africa and Europe, another the Americas, and a third China and Oceania. The technical problems were eventually overcome by scientists and engineers at MIT and the age of the geosynchronous satellite began in 1964 with the launching of the SYNCOM III satellite. It was used for the first live transpacific television broadcast of the 1964 Olympic Games in Japan.

Political and commercial developments paralleled technological developments in the satellites business. In 1962, the Federal Communications Act was passed giving the FCC the power to regulate the operation of all communications satellites. The Communications Satellite Corporation (Comsat) was created by a special act of Congress in 1962 and incorporated in 1963. It became America's "chosen instrument" for developing and operating its national satellite communications facilities as well as to serving the world. Comsat was given a monopoly on all American international satellite communications, but its activities were restricted to providing bulk circuits to other common carriers for resale purposes. Its first satellite, called Early Bird, was built by Hughes Aircraft and launched in April 1965. It almost doubled the number of voice circuits across the Atlantic.

A landmark agreement was signed on August 20, 1964, by seven countries to establish a global commercial satellite system called the International Telecommunications Satellite Organization (Intelsat). The new organization had a mandate to develop and operate satellite systems for providing international telecommunications and broadcasting services. Intelsat took over the Early Bird satellite and renamed it Intelsat I. Intelsat II was launched in 1967. With the launching of Intelsat III in 1969, satellites were stationed over the Atlantic, and the Pacific and Indian oceans, thus making Arthur C. Clarke's dream of global satellite communications a reality. Intelsat III effectively created the "global village," the term coined by Marshall McLuhan to describe the instantaneous, globalization effects of telecommunications. On July 20, 1969, Intelsat broadcast live television coverage of the mission of Apollo II to the world, bringing moving pictures of man's first steps on the moon into the living rooms of millions of people around the globe.

It did not take long for industrialized countries to recognize that satellites had strategic economic and sociocultural implications in addition to defense. These included domestic and international communications, remote sensing of the environment, search and rescue, and weather forecasting. For these reasons, satellites became the focus of the industrial strategies of the European community, Japan, Canada, as well as the United States.

Western European nations established the European Space Research Organization (ESRO) and the European Launcher Development Organization in 1964 to coordinate research into and development of Europe's aerospace and telecommunications industries. In 1973, these two organizations were merged to form the European Space Agency (ESA) which has carried out much of Europe's space research and development activities, including the Ariene launch program, which now aggressively markets its services and dominates the commercial space launching industry worldwide. In 1977, the European Conference of Posts and Telecommunications Administrations (CEPT) formed the European Telecommunications Satellite Organization (Eutelsat), modelled on Intelsat, to establish, operate, and maintain the space-segment satellite services in Europe. In 1969, the Japanese government created the National Space Development Agency (NASDA), Japan's equivalent of NASA in the United States and ESA in Europe. Canada created a new satellite communications organization called Telesat Canada by a special act of Parliament in 1969 to develop and operate a satellite communications system to serve its national needs. In 1972, Telesat launched the first world's first domestic geostationary communications satellite, called "Anik," the Eskimo word for "little brother."

The first big commercial users of communications satellites were telephone companies which used them for very long-distance domestic and international telephone services. Private companies with very large volumes of national and international voice and computer traffic also became big users. But satellites became the subject of heated national debates in many countries arising from the fact that they are a natural medium for distributing national and international television signals to the head ends of cable television companies for delivery to the home. Television broadcasters regarded them as a serious competitive threat for this reason. But satellites were a potential threat to cable television companies as well. By increasing the transmission power of the satellite itself, much smaller, inexpensive earth receiving dishes (TVROs or receive-only earth stations) could be manufactured. Home owners could use these to receive television signals directly thereby bypassing established broadcasters and cable television operators. Satellites, therefore, threatened both established television broadcasters everywhere in the world and cable television companies in the United States and Canada which were among the most wired countries in the world.

But it has been the international, "transborder" effects of satellites that caused so many problems in the sixties and seventies in spite of the fact that many social scientists and futurists perceived them as having the potential to unify the nations of the world and create a better world. Because they carried news, drama, cultural, commercial, and advertising information independently of national borders, most governments have perceived communications satellites as a serious threat to their cultural, economic, and political sovereignty over the years and most still do today. The broadcasting of transmission signals by satellite is a highly regulated business in almost every country in the world.

PROBLEMS CREATED BY THE GROWING
INTERDEPENDENCE OF COMPUTERS AND
TELECOMMUNICATIONS

Another set of public policy problems arose in the sixties and seventies as a result of the growing interdependence of computers and telecommunications. Early batch processing systems were highly capital-intensive undertakings that required highly skilled operators so they were most cost-effectively used when operated in a high-volume, shared-user environment. A demand, therefore, arose for high-quality digital data communications facilities to interconnect remote batch terminals with the central computer. With the advent of time-sharing in the sixties, the demand also grew for lower speed telecommunications facilities and services to permit individual users to access mainframe computers from remote terminals in an on-line fashion.

Not all organizations could afford to buy expensive mainframe computers or hire trained personnel to run them in-house, however. Even large- and medium-size businesses often did not always have sufficient processing capacity to meet their peak demands but could not justify buying another computer. It was situations like these that created an opportunity for companies to establish themselves as suppliers of raw computer processing power as well as specialized applications software to meet the needs of large, medium, and small businesses on a commercial basis. Companies like Control Data, IBM, General Electric, Electronic Data Systems (EDS), Automatic Data Processing (ADP), Tymshare, and others set up computer service bureaus to supply computer processing services to businesses, universities, and governments. This new industry also depended on access to efficient and economical digital data communications facilities and services to reach customers. Their growth, profit, and competitiveness depended on it.

Besides making it possible to sell computer processing services commercially, the mainframe computer also created opportunities to sell information outright through the use of computerized databanks. The commercial databank services industry was created to cater to the demands of businesses and governments requiring access to scientific, economic, financial, and demographic information and reports as well as news. Information such as this is important for conducting research and development, market research, economic forecasting, and investment and political risk analysis. Early suppliers of databank services included companies such as Mead Corporation, which provided legal information services via its LEXIS databank; Lockheed, which began offering a databank service called the DIALOG in 1972; and others, including Dun & Bradstreet in the corporate information business and Medline in the medical information services business. Newspaper publishers such as *The New York Times* and manufacturing companies like TRW also set up databank service operations. Like the commercial computer services bureau industry and governments and private companies, the databank industry relied on telecommunications facilities and the regulated telephone companies to provide services and, therefore, its growth and profitability.

The introduction of minicomputers in the early sixties also had a manifold impact on both the computer and telecommunications industries. Minicomputers ushered in the age of distributed processing which, more than any application or use, depended on access to efficient digital data communications services to connect minicomputer and mainframe computers into a network. Computer-to-computer communications and networking became ever more important with the evolution of distributed processing and the emergence of the microcomputer age.

It was through a marriage of minicomputers and communications that a new kind of digital communications service was developed in the sixties to meet the growing demands of these computer services bureaus and databank services companies as well as the business community of users in general. The new technology, called packet-switching, used time-division multiplexing (TDM) techniques to enable individual users to share the same transmission channels on a time-sharing basis in a similar way as they share time-shared computers. Because the facility was shared, it was less expensive to use, and because the service was based on digital technology, its quality, reliability, and security was superior to that of leased line analogue channels available from telephone companies. As their data traffic requirements grew, commercial packet-switching services provided an important source of efficiency and productivity improvement for a growing number of businesses.

Packet-switching was pioneered by the Defence Research Projects Agency (DARPA). In 1969, DARPA financed the development of a network, appropriately called ARPANET, to test the feasibility and economics of the new technology. ARPANET grew to connect hundreds of universities and military establishments across the United States and eventually overseas in the seventies, and it subsequently came to constitute the backbone foundation for the Internet, the network of networks that connects millions of users around the world today. Once packet-switching proved to be technologically feasible and economically attractive, it was commercialized by companies like Tymnet and Telenet which leased bulk transmission facilities from the carriers. Because it combined both computers and telecommunications in new and unique ways, packet-switching defied the traditional definitions of telecommunications services. On the one hand, companies that supplied these services constituted data processing service organizations. On the other hand, they could be regarded as legitimate telecommunications common carriers. Telephone companies regarded these suppliers as a competitive threat and lobbied the FCC to curtail their expansion. The FCC, on the other hand, was in a quandary as to what they constituted under the Communications Act and whether or not the act required it to regulate them.

Microelectronics and minicomputers had a big impact on the telecommunications industry in another way as well. Many large companies with a great deal of telephone traffic relied on private leased-line transmission facilities and small privately owned telephone switches called private branch exchanges (PBXs) to manage their corporate telephone networks instead of relying on the services of the telephone companies. Semiconductor and computer technology made it feasible and economical to build computerized switches called private automatic branch exchanges (or PABXs). Because these were computers, they could be programmed to process and switch both voice and data and to perform network control and other functions. Both telecommunications and computer equipment manufacturers began producing these new products which enabled big companies to make much more efficient use of and better manage their corporate computer, telecommunications and information resources. The result was competition between the telecommunications and computer industries opened up on yet another front.

THE FIRST COMPUTER INQUIRY

It was in response to growing complaints by businesses, telephone companies, and their competitors that the FCC launched what has become known as the "First Computer Inquiry" (Computer I) on November 9, 1966, to address what it called the "regulatory and policy problems raised by the interdependence of computer technology, its market applications, and communications common carrier services" (Docket 16979). The biggest issue by far that the FCC had to deal with was whether or not the computer services industry should be regulated like the telecommunications services industry or whether the telecommunications industry should be deregulated like the computer industry. The FCC took an intermediate position when, in 1971, five years after launching its proceeding, it tabled its report.[1] The new policy recognized the existence of "hybrid" communications and data processing services. Where message switching was offered as an incidental feature of a hybrid integrated service offering which is primarily of a data processing nature, the commission ruled that the service should not be regulated. However, where the service was oriented toward satisfying the communications or message-switching requirements of the subscriber and data processing was incidental, it proposed to regulate the entire service as a communications service.

To guard against discriminatory pricing and other kinds of anticompetitive behavior and to prevent common carriers from subsidizing their competitive services with revenues derived from their monopoly services, the commission adopted a "maximum separation" policy which required communications common carriers to furnish data processing services through a separate corporate subsidiary. The FCC would invoke this so-called "structural separations" policy time and time again in subsequent decisions to ensure fair competition in the supply of telecommunications and other related but unregulated services.

The FCC began applying its new public philosophy even before its final report was submitted. To satisfy the growing number of businesses wanting to attach non-Bell Telephone equipment to the telephone network, it gave a new company called Carterfone permission to attach its own telephone set to the telephone network in 1968. In 1975, after a lengthy public inquiry, it ruled that all terminal equipment, from modems, computer terminals, and PBXs to messaging and answering devices, independent of the manufacturer, could be attached to the telephone network as long as it satisfied certain technical standards. The commission set up a registration program to ensure that all new equipment met the new standards.

BREAKING THE MONOPOLY ON COMMON CARRIAGE: THE SPECIALIZED COMMON CARRIER, DOMESTIC SATELLITE, AND VALUE-ADDED NETWORK DECISIONS

While the First Computer Inquiry was in progress, the FCC was forced to deal with issues relating to the whole question of competition in the long-distance market among other reasons as a result of the commercialization of microwave communications transmission technology. Microwave was a high-capacity radio-based transmission system that used relay stations at 20- to 30-mile intervals and, therefore, relied less on public rights-of-way than wires. It represented a relatively inexpensive way for new entrants to break into AT&T's long-distance monopoly. In its "Above 890 Decision" in 1959, the FCC allocated the necessary frequency bands for the introduction of point-to-point microwave systems and introduced rules allowing individual companies to set up private microwave communications systems to satisfy their own internal transmission needs. Broadcasters and big companies responded positively to the new ruling, but AT&T countered with an aggressive strategy of segmenting the market and introducing a special (Telpak) tariff which discounted the price of leased private lines by as much as 85 percent. The Telpak tariffs effectively killed what had become a thriving business.

The economics of microwave technology improved as a result of developments in microelectronics until it was only a matter of time before several start-up companies became interested in supplying intercity services on a common carrier basis using microwave technology. In 1969, the commission granted a license to Microwave Communications Incorporated (MCI) to begin offering private line services between Chicago and St. Louis using the newest generation of microwave transmission systems. William McGowan, who cofounded MCI in 1968 with an investment of $50,000, is now widely credited with breaking AT&T's telephone monopoly. AT&T fought the MCI application. In his book on the telecommunications industry, Gerald Brock wrote, "It was over seven years from the initial filing of the MCI applications in late 1963 to the final approval of the application in early 1971. The chairman of the board of MCI testified that MCI had spent $10 million in regulatory and legal costs to secure approval for its network. The estimated cost for the actual facilities . . . was under $2 million."[2]

MCI succeeded in doing what most people in the industry thought was impossible. It quickly became AT&T's biggest competitor in the lucrative intercity market. By the end of 1973, another new intercity competitor, Southern Pacific Communications, completed a coast-to-coast microwave system.

By 1971, the FCC had completed a lengthy public inquiry into the whole issue of competition in the common carriage industry.[3] The commission noted that the computer revolution was stimulating a growing demand for specialized common carrier services and that computer users and computer processing service organizations were relying on specialized telecommunications facilities for their day-to-day operations, but that common carriers were not supplying the facilities and services needed to meet their demands. It also observed that specialized telecommunications facilities and services were becoming crucial to the social and economic development of the nation and that public policies were necessary to ensure their efficient and timely development. It concluded that entry into the specialized common carrier segment would not jeopardize the provision of universal public telephone services.

The commission, therefore, adopted a new policy of encouraging entry into the new segment of the industry thereby creating a new class of common carrier, called the Specialized Common Carriers (SCCs). To spare new entrants the expense of a regulatory proceeding before entering the new segments, it ruled that the established carriers should shoulder the burden of proof that such entry would not harm the provision of universal telephone service. Because the local telephone network represented the most serious impediment to the development of specialized common carriers services, the FCC ordered the Bell operating companies (BOCs) to provide specialized common carriers with adequate local facilities on a just and reasonable basis.

The Specialized Common Carrier decision was another milestone in the deregulation of the United States telecommunications industry. It became the foundation upon which the FCC would make a series of decisions opening up to competition various specialized segments of the common carrier industry. Among them were the Domestic Satellite Services (DOMSAT) decision in 1972, the Value-Added Networks (VAN) decision in 1973, and the Resale and Sharing decision in 1976.

Rapid developments were also taking place in satellite communications with advances in microelectronics driven by NASA's growing budget and the space race. Satellite technology had matured to the point in the early seventies where a number of companies had applied to the FCC for permission to launch and operate satellites for providing commercial domestic communications services. In keeping with its recently announced Specialized Common Carrier philosophy that competition in these new segments did not threaten the maintenance of universal service, the FCC opened the domestic satellite communications business to competition in 1972 in what is known as its "open skies" or DOMSAT decision. In that year, the commission approved applications to establish satellite carriage facilities from Western Union, RCA, and Satellite Business Systems (SBS), a consortium comprising IBM, Comsat General, and Aetna Life and Casualty Insurance Corporation. But it prohibited AT&T from entering this new market for a period of three years in order to allow the new carriers time to establish themselves in the industry and prevent AT&T from using its enormous power to dominate the new industry.

By the early seventies as well, digital data communications technology had reached the stage of commercialization. Datran was the first company to enter the market with a fully digital communications service but the company went bankrupt because it could not obtain access to the local telephone network. Several other new entrants subsequently applied to the FCC for permission to supply packet-switching services on a commercial basis. The Commission at that time was attempting to change its regulations to eliminate obstacles that might hamper the development of competition in the growing market for data communications services. The high capital-investment costs and the need to obtain the necessary rights-of-way for installing local and intercity transmission facilities in particular represented major barriers to the introduction of such services.

To overcome these obstacles, the FCC created a new class of service providers supplying what it called value-added network services (VANS). This new class of supplier would lease transmission facilities from the traditional common carriers and interconnect their computers, databanks, terminal and switching equipment, and develop the necessary software to provide processing, transactions, information, and other services to the public. Packet-switching service was particularly attractive to low-volume data communications users because it provided them with an efficient, low-cost and high-quality digital data delivery system which only large corporations until then could afford. But it was critical for such growing industries as the databank, computer processing, and transactions services industries.

Two of the first companies to obtain a license under the FCC's new VANS policy were Graphnet and Telenet in 1974. Telenet, a spin-off from the ARPANET project, became the first company in the world to offer commercial packet-switching services in 1975. Subsequently, another company called Tymnet received permission to offer a value-added network service as well.

But there were still problems, particularly for medium and small companies which did not have the traffic volume or the financial muscle to make full use of leased private-line facilities. Large companies which did could derive important benefits through economies of scale in their private networks. In order to make these same benefits available to medium and small companies, the FCC ruled in 1976 that companies individually or as a group could lease common carriage facilities from the carriers for their shared-use and resell excess capacity on the free market. This so-called ''sharing and resale'' decision was the commission's way of further expanding the scope of competition and extending the economic benefits of new technology to smaller companies.

BREAKING THE MONOPOLY ON LONG-DISTANCE TELEPHONE SERVICE

In all of its decisions, the FCC had taken great pains to protect public telephone service from competition in order to ensure its integrity as a universal, affordable service, an obligation and an objective it was responsible for under the Communications Act. The commission recognized in its 1974 Specialized Common Carrier decision, however, that the local telephone network was an effective barrier to entry so it ordered the Bell operating companies to provide SSCs with local facilities including access to the local telephone network. One of the first companies to gain access was MCI which had established a beachhead in the intercity microwave market by the mid-seventies and was eager and ready to expand into other markets. Once it had gained access, it introduced a new service in 1976, called Execunet, which was priced on a per-call basis. The new service was essentially a message toll service and, therefore, competed directly with AT&T's long-distance telephone service. MCI had effectively penetrated the public telephone monopoly in violation of the FCC's rules. Fears were expressed that, unless the FCC forced MCI to terminate its service, local rates could otherwise be forced up by as much as 100 percent or more. The FCC did order MCI to discontinue the service but subsequently lost an appeals court decision which overturned its order. The Supreme Court also ruled in favor of MCI. Southern Pacific Communications began offering a similar service through its subsidiary, called Sprint shortly thereafter. Competition in long-distance telephone services had become a "fait accompli."

But other far more powerful technological, industrial, and political forces were at work along an increasingly broad front to transform the telecommunications industry and no single body or legislative or regulatory authority was in control or capable of controlling events any longer.

THE GLOBAL ECONOMIC IMPLICATIONS OF THE INFORMATION REVOLUTION

Every nation was experiencing the fallout from the information revolution in the seventies. The capacities of international satellite and transoceanic telecommunications linkages were growing rapidly. The Intelsat IV, launched in 1971, had a capacity of 4,000 telephone circuits and two television channels. The Intelsat IV-A series, launched in 1976, had a capacity of 6,000 circuits and two television channels. In addition, the sixth transatlantic undersea cable (TAT-6) was completed in 1976. These constituted a cause of great concern for many governments because they were being used to export a growing variety of databank and computer-based processing services from the United States. A computer processing network called CYBERNET, for example, owned by Control Data Corporation, operated in six European centers. The General Electric Information Services supplied services in Europe from the United States by satellite. Another on-line computer service, called SWITCH, connected thirty major processing centers. And a worldwide interbank financial transactions (SWIFT) network was in operation which provided computer processing and telecommunications transmission services for its 400 or so member countries. Governments perceived these as having important trade, employment, and economic development implications for many nations, especially in Europe. If their industrial economies were evolving into information economies as many social scientists were predicting, the fear was they would become increasingly dominated by U.S. companies that already controlled most of the manufacturing and information-related services business worldwide. Information technology, therefore, became strategic to every nation.

Developments in information and communications technologies raised many other cultural, economic, and political concerns. Direct broadcast satellites (DBS), for example, raised concerns about the domination of the world by American culture. Earth resources satellites were another source of conflict. NASA launched the environmental and meterological satellite (ERTS) in 1966 and the remote sensing satellites Landsat I and II in 1972 and 1973. In 1974, the U.S. government established the Earth Resources Observation Satellite (EROS) data center in 1974 to disseminate the data from remote-sensing satellites. Because remote-sensing satellites could be used in an undetectable manner to survey the land masses of other countries extraterritorially, they were perceived to be a vehicle for invading and violating the economic, legal, and political sovereignty of nation-states. Like DBS and the transborder flows of data through computer networks (TBDF), there were no international laws governing remote-sensing satellites, and many nations began pressuring international bodies including the United Nations and UNESCO to develop rules to regulate and control these international activities. Satellites became so important that they initiated an international race among developed and less-developed nations for their share of scarce orbital positions.

It was in response to these concerns that efforts were made in a number of international fora including the United Nations, UNESCO, and the OECD to impose restrictions on the "transborder data flows" of information. They also culminated in calls in the late seventies for the creation of a "new world information order."[4] The publication in 1980 of the book *The World Challenge* by the French journalist Jean-Jacques Servan-Schreiber drew international attention to the domination of the world information economy by the United States and the threat it posed to the world.[5]

All of the leading industrialized countries were challenged by the information revolution in the seventies, and most developed national industrial and information and communications policies to better prepare themselves for the coming information age. The Japanese government recognized the economic significance of the information revolution as far back as the sixties. In 1972, it made public a report entitled *The Plan for Information Society: A National Goal toward the Year 2000* (Japan Computer Usage Development Institute). The report articulated a clear long-range plan for developing the country's information technology and information industries and turning Japan into an information society. Included in it were national goals for the development of a world-scale manufacturing capability for producing semiconductor chips and office and factory automation equipment, including robots as well as a mass education program to create a computer-literate Japanese society. The strategy also called for initiatives for creating and upgrading scientific and technical databanks and an extensive network of libraries. Almost a decade later in 1980, an advisory committee to Ministry of International Trade and Industry (MITI) published a report in which it proposed that Japan launch a ten-year research and development program to develop a "Fifth Generation of Computer" based on knowledge information processing systems (KIPS) concepts. Two years later in 1982, MITI followed up on its proposal by creating the Institute for New Generation Computer Technology (ICOT) with annual funding of 7 billion yen per year. The initiative created a sensation in scientific, industry and political circles around the world. Leading artificial intelligence (AI) experts in the United States warned that "The Fifth Generation Project is Japan's ambitious plan to seize worldwide leadership in the computer industry."[6] Edward Feigenbaum and Pamala McCorduck warned that the initiative "could give Japan the lead in this race to become a postindustrial society."[7] Governments in the United States, Europe, and other countries responded to the challenge.

Information technology became a central focus of France's industrial strategy in the sixties under its president, Charles de Gaulle, who transformed the country into a national showcase of French technology. In 1976, President Giscard d'Estaing commissioned a national study to assess the effects of computerization on French society and how France should respond. In their report, published in 1978, authors Simon Nora and Alain Minc predicted that "mass computing will take hold, becoming as indispensable to society as electricity."[8] The report emphasized the threats as well as the opportunities of computerization and the convergence of computers and telecommunications, which the authors called "télématique," or "telematics," for French industry and French society. The report called for a telematics network linking all parts of the country with one another and with other countries and a standards policy to enable European manufacturers and data network suppliers to create an indigenous European market for information technology products and services. It also proposed the creation of an European satellite system to deny the United States a monopoly over European satellite communications and broadcasting industries and a program to promote the development and regulation of database services. National programs were also advocated for promoting the use of computers and telecommunications in schools and preparing teachers to educate and train the new generation of students for the information society.

Britain, West Germany, and other European nations developed similar industrial strategies. A 1978 British report called for government action to promote the development and diffusion of information technology through awareness programs and education and training programs. The report also advocated generous support for research and development, the provision of risk capital to developers and producers of information technology products and services, as well as regulations and standards to support these objectives. The recommendations became the basis of a $140 million industrial strategy to support its microelectronics industry and $110 million to support an applications development program. Funds were also allocated to set up an Office of the Future program, a Microelectronics Applications program, and a Fifth-Generation Computers program called "ALVEY." The British government also created a Ministry of Information Technology (IT) to oversee and manage its IT programs, and it designated the year 1981 "Information Technology Year" as a big public awareness exercise to demonstrate its commitment to IT.

THE INFORMATION REVOLUTION CHALLENGES AMERICAN INDUSTRIAL POLICY

The subject of industrial policy and the challenges facing American companies in the information age were reaching a climax in the United States in the late seventies and early eighties as a result of the international debate on transborder data flows and the establishment of a new world information order as well as the concern over the effects of the declining economic power of the United States internationally. Many Americans were convinced that the country was becoming "deindustrialized" and that government had to do something both to protect American industry as well as make it more competitive. By then, international trade, information technology, and national security issues had become interwoven with domestic regulatory and industrial policy issues in telecommunications, broadcasting, and banking and financial services. All had become strategic to the future of America as the leading international economic power.

The subjects of deindustrialization, industrial strategy, and deregulation were widely debated in the 1975 and 1979 national elections which brought Jimmy Carter and Ronald Reagan to power. A 1976 report entitled *National Information Policy: A Report to the President of the United States* recommended that the United States develop a comprehensive national information policy and prepare legislation governing the dissemination of government-held information as well as privacy and copyright guidelines, and establish an office of information policy in the White House to advise on information policy issues. Information policy issues were at the top of the agenda of the Carter administration, and in response, President Carter reorganized his government by phasing out the Office of Telecommunications Policy (OTP) in 1977. In 1978 he created the National Telecommunications and Information Administration (NTIA) in the Department of Commerce. The NTIA became responsible for advising the president on both domestic and international information and communications policy matters.

American businesses and the U.S. government also became increasingly alarmed about the industrial effects of the national industrial strategies of governments in Europe and Japan, specifically their protectionist policies and the creation of trade barriers to the import of American goods and services. These national industrial policies together with the targeting of specific sectors for massive investment and subsidies programs were beginning to have an effect on America's trade position in the world information economy. Japan was beginning to challenge America's domination particularly in the semiconductor industry, and a few leading information technology products, including France's Minitel and Britain's Prestel videotext services, were beginning to show up in Europe and Japan that were not available in the United States, and this alarmed some Americans. In the late seventies a growing number of American academics, politicians, and business leaders began calling for a national industrial strategy to counteract and retaliate against those of other countries.

Central to the American debate on industrial policy in the early eighties was the concept of "deindustrialization," which became synonymous with the declining competitiveness of old-line manufacturing industries and the consequent job loss caused by moving plants to overseas locations and foreign competitors entering these markets. But some Americans saw an upside of the changing economic environment. The real strength of the American economy, they asserted, was in its high-technology sector, particularly information technology and services. America could continue being the greatest economic power on earth as long as it continued to innovate and use high-technology, and this, many argued, called for an industrial strategy that focused on research and development, investment, and trade and educational policies. As the world economy made the transition from one based on low-value industrial goods and services to one based on high-value information goods and services, that is, to an information and knowledge-based economy, America would have to develop specific policies to enable it to better compete, that is, to "reindustrialize."

Reindustrialization meant devising specific policies for declining, or "sunset," industries of the industrial age, and other policies for its rising, dynamic, high-growth, "sunrise" industries of the information economy. Leading theorists argued that special industrial policies and programs should serve to accelerate this transition and transformation of America's economy to an information society and facilitate the necessary industrial restructuring that would accompany it.[9] One set of support policies should target sunrise industries while another should address the problems of declining industrial sectors which would eventually be abandoned to off-shore producing countries. But the subject of an explicit industrial strategy was cut short by the election of Ronald Reagan as president in 1979. Reagan adopted a strong militaristic posture, including the Stars Wars Defense Initiative (SDI), which served as a negotiating strategy with the Soviet Union, and he also accelerated Carter's policy of deregulating key sectors of the economy.

THE SECOND COMPUTER INQUIRY REDEFINES THE BOUNDARIES

By the late seventies, the computer revolution and its interdependence and integration with telecommunications had reached a new and more advanced stage. The development of microprocessors had led to the widespread use of distributed processing and personal computers promised to bring processing power to the desktops of workers everywhere. Both developments fueled growing demands for data communications services to interconnect their personal computers, minicomputers, and mainframe computers both within and between companies. At the same time, computer chips were being integrated into every conceivable type of telecommunications equipment—into telephone switches, PBXs, and into old and new varieties of terminal equipment. And both IBM and AT&T were invading the territory of the other to capitalize on this convergence.

IBM announced a growing number of new telecommunications products in the mid-to-late seventies including the PABX 3750, and it entered the telecommunications services business in 1977 through its partnership in Satellite Business Systems to provide private voice, data, and video communications services to business customers. These services competed directly with those offered by AT&T. On another front, Xerox, the giant office copier company, was readying a new communications service called XTEN which combined computer processing and microwave radio and satellite communications to distribute documents around the country. AT&T was also busy announcing new products and services for the data communications and data processing marketplace. Through a technique known as data under voice (DUV) AT&T was able to adapt its analogue network to provide a nationwide digital data communications service called Dataphone Digital Service (DDS) in fifty cities by 1978. It also introduced the Transaction Network Service (TNS) designed especially for the electronic funds transfer marketplace. Another AT&T service (CCSII) was designed for the voice store-and-forward market. AT&T also brought to market a new terminal device called the Dataspeed 40/4 which embodied both data processing as well as communications features, and in 1976 it announced a new computer communications service called Advance Communications Service (ACS) which would permit computer users to talk to one another directly. Each of these products and services involved computer processing and, therefore, violated the provisions of either Computer I or the Consent Decree of 1956, both of which prohibited the company from engaging in the manufacture of computer equipment or supplying competitive data processing services.[10]

In 1976, the FCC's Common Carrier Bureau ruled that the Dataspeed 40/4 was a data processing device and, therefore, not a legal telecommunications tariff offering so it prohibited AT&T from offering it. But the next year, after AT&T appealed the bureau's decision, the commission reversed its own decision, ruling that the new product was a communications device. Competitors in the computer industry became alarmed at the new ruling because it would enable AT&T to extend its power across the combined computer and communications sector. Manufacturers and suppliers of terminal equipment appealed to both the FCC and the Department of Justice to prohibit these offering. Pressures were mounting on a number of other fronts for major changes in regulatory and industrial policy in both the telecommunications and the computer industries. Both IBM and AT&T were the target of a growing number of antitrust suits accusing them of unfair trade practices. Meanwhile, the Department of Justice was still attempting to break up both IBM and AT&T. Pressures were also mounting to deregulate the telecommunications industry and let AT&T go head-to-head against IBM.

By 1977, it had become clear that the provisions of the Computer I, which made a distinction between regulated and unregulated communications and data processing services, were obsolete and unenforceable. Recognizing this, the FCC launched the Second Computer Inquiry to rethink the whole question of whether to continue its policy of separating the computer and communications industries. The commission wound up its inquiry in 1980 with a report embodying a new framework for regulating the telecommunications industry.[11]

Computer II established a new regulatory framework for the telecommunications industry by dividing common carrier communications services into three classes: "Voice" communications services related to the transmission of the human voice constituted a basic communications service. "Basic nonvoice" services related to the pure transmission of computer-related information. "Enhanced nonvoice" services referred to any service where computer processing altered the content of the information or messages of the user. The decision also recognized the futility of making distinctions between computer and communications equipment and deregulated the terminal equipment market. To pave the way for the convergence of computers and communications, Computer II allowed regulated common carriers to provide communications services involving substantial data processing but under structural separation and other conditions that would prevent them from using their monopoly power unfairly.

AT&T immediately formed a new subsidiary called American Bell to exploit the new opportunities opened up in the competitive services market. But, in allowing AT&T to enter these competitive markets, the FCC determined that it was no longer bound by the 1956 Consent Decree. In effect, it revoked the provisions of the Consent Decree but this gave the Department of Justice the ammunition it needed to demand the breakup of AT&T. But other developments were taking place in parallel that were dramatically transforming the industrial and regulatory structure of the U.S. telecommunications industry.

THE NEW (ELECTRONIC) MEDIA REVOLUTION

Developments in satellites and cable television and the convergence of computers and telecommunications, in particular, had set off a cable television and broadcasting revolution by the late seventies. The FCC's 1972 Open Skies decision did what many economists had predicted. It stimulated investment, speeded up technological innovation, multiplied satellite capacity, lowered transmission costs, brought the price of earth stations down significantly, and stimulated demand by businesses, broadcasters, and cable television companies. These developments together with the liberalization of ownership restrictions on earth stations made it possible to distribute broadcasting signals very economically to cable television networks across the entire nation. In addition, the broadband nature of coaxial cable made it feasible to carry as many as one hundred channels. Another technology, known as multipoint microwave distribution systems (MMDS), used omnidirectional, low-power microwave radio technology, making it technologically feasible to distribute television signals to high-rise apartments and hotels. Interactive cable was also becoming technologically feasible. All of these innovations fueled the cable television revolution of the seventies.

The FCC was slowly making changes in its regulations to accommodate these innovations. In 1972, it issued new rules that allowed cable companies to import at least two distant signals but it also required them to carry local broadcast signals as well. Those in the top 100 markets were required to provide two-way capability and a minimum of twenty channels. It also required companies to set aside access channels for the use of the general public and for educational institutions and local governments. By 1975, over 10.8 million home owners, or about 16 percent of all households, subscribed to cable television services.

Growth of the cable television industry was further stimulated in 1977 as a result of the FCC authorizing the use of fifteen-foot (4.5-meter) earth stations instead of the 30-foot (9-meter) dishes previously used for television reception. This reduced the cost of earth stations from roughly $100,000 to under $40,000 thus making satellite reception economically feasible for cable systems with more than 1,000 subscribers. Developments in both satellite and microwave communications and a relaxation in regulation enabled broadcasters to expand into regional and national markets, significantly increasing their audiences and their advertising revenues. It also led to the age of pay television.

The first successful national cable television programmer was Home Box Office (HBO), a subsidiary of Time Inc. of New York, which began distributing current Hollywood films and sports events to local cable systems locally and via microwave in 1973. In 1975, HBO launched America's first national delivery of its programming service on RCA's Satcom I satellite and the cable television revolution was underway. By 1977, HBO was broadcasting to 800,000 subscribers on more than 370 cable systems. In 1978, Viacom's Showtime entered the pay cable market giving HBO its first taste of competition. The use of satellites and broadband cable television systems led to the development of specialty channels or ''narrowcasting.'' According to *Satellite Communications*, a monthly publication which reports on satellite developments, by the end of 1978, eight programmers in addition to HBO and Showtime, were transmitting television signals nationally to cable operators. They included the American Satellite Network, the Christian Broadcasting Network, Fanfare Television, Madison Square Garden Sports, PTL Club, and Wold and Turner Communications' WTCG. By 1981, the second television revolution was well under way with close to twenty million households or 25 percent of the American homes subscribing to more than 4,300 cable systems across the country.

The distribution of broadcasting signals by satellite also led to the development of "fourth networks" such as the Public Broadcasting System and National Public Radio which began using satellites in 1978 to attract national audiences. One of the most successful was developed by Ted Turner, owner of television station WTCG in Atlanta. In 1977 Turner transformed WTCG into a "superstation" by using satellites to deliver his programs throughout the country. By 1980, over 800 cable television stations were carrying the WTCG signal. By this time, Turner had also added an entertainment channel of mostly old films. In 1980, he added the now-famous cable news network (CNN) to his operation broadcasting out of Atlanta and other superstations developed throughout the country.[12] By 1981, direct broadcasting satellites were ready for commercial use, and in that year, Satellite Television Corporation, an affiliate of Comsat, was given approval by the FCC to develop a service for beaming to the rooftops of American homes.

The growing choice of programs on cable led to increased penetration and greater competition for franchises as well as a search for a greater variety of content. One of the largest national cable television companies, Warner Cable Corporation of Columbus, Ohio, began offering thirty channels comprising locally produced community programming content, premium sports, arts, educational channels, and new movies over an interactive cable system, called Qube, in 1977. Qube's interactive technology enabled subscribers to participate in referenda, quizzes, and game shows, and it also provided home security services including fire, burglary, and emergency services. By 1980, Warner Cable Corporation was the front-runner in competing for cable franchises in the United States based solely on its experience with its Qube service. Other big media conglomerates including Time Inc., Cox Communications, Westinghouse Corporation, Times Mirror, and Storer Broadcasting fought for franchises throughout the eighties. Outsiders were also active. American Express, for example, purchased 50 percent of Warner Cable in 1980.[13]

Cable television was perceived by many as having an exceptionally bright future in the late seventies and early eighties. "Egalitarians saw in cable the promise of abundant channels with open access for all to television audiences; new mechanisms for participatory democracy were envisioned," wrote author Benno Schmidt, Jr., in 1978. "Futurists saw cable systems as the first step toward elaborate home consoles that would deliver the morning paper, provide access to computer information banks, let people vote from their homes in vast town meetings, as well as provide access to richly varying entertainment possibilities."[14]

Startling developments were taking place across the entire information and communications landscape in the United States by 1980 as a result, in particular, of innovations in a variety of promising new electronic media technologies. One of these was the videocassette recorder introduced by Sony Corporation in 1975. By 1980, the video revolution was underway, and it was beginning to have noticeable effect on broadcasting and cable television. Other new media technologies came into existence through the marriage of computer and telecommunications technologies. One of these was videotext, which made it possible to use ordinary telephone, cable television, and radio networks to deliver news; information; and entertainment, games, and educational content to homes. To many, videotext represented nothing less than a new mass communications medium to the home and a conduit for providing an endless variety of information, entertainment, and educational content. And it initiated an international race involving the governments of France, Britain, Japan, Canada, and Germany to develop a nationwide videotext information service. In 1981 the French government began giving Minitel terminals to telephone subscribers free of charge in 1981 to replace the telephone directory. In the United States, telephone companies, broadcasters, and cable television companies, in addition to banks, retailers, and publishers spent tens of millions of dollars to create markets for videotext in the late seventies and early eighties. Electronic technology was also making its way into printing and publishing.

It was this explosion in the development and use of cable television, satellites, pay-television, videotext, videocassette recorders, and video disks and the promise of much more things to come that occupied the attention of technologists, social scientists, industry people, and politicians in the early eighties. The rise of new information and communications media and the convergence of print and audio and video technologies led to growing demands for more freedom to create and deliver greater varieties of content to consumers. The convergence of technologies was also leading to the convergence of the various information and communications industries and forcing them to compete directly with one another. Satellites provided a means to bypass terrestrial telephone companies, broadcasters, and cable television companies. Videocassette recorders represented a form of bypass of broadcasters and cable television companies. Videotext represented a form of bypass of publishers. Electronic banking represented a means of bypassing banks. On the other hand, this convergence of industries also represented major opportunities for all of them. For all of these reasons, academics, business professionals, and politicians in the United States began calling for deregulation of the entire communications sector in the late seventies and early eighties. A 1981 House of Representatives report, entitled *Telecommunications in Transition: The Status of Competition in the Telecommunications Industry*, described this in the following way:

In the information industry, particularly in its video sector, we are in the midst of a technological revolution which promises true abundance. The evolution of new forms of delivery systems and new program suppliers presents the American public with a momentous opportunity—an opportunity to have unfettered access to a broad diversity of video programming. This diversity will allow the removal of a regulatory scheme that has long imposed content and behavioural rules based on a theory of scarcity. These regulations are definitely no substitute for the competition and diversity that a fully competitive marketplace of abundance can provide. The regulatory regimes which were established to conform to [the] compartmentalized view [of the past] are rapidly approaching obsolescence.[15]

THE MODIFIED FINAL JUDGMENT SECURES DIVESTITURE AND THE BREAKUP OF THE BELL SYSTEM

National economic and political developments were reaching a climax in the United States in 1980 with the issues of industrial strategy, trade policy, and deregulation at center stage of the political decision-making arena. Under President Jimmy Carter, a flurry of bills were tabled in both the Senate and Congress to deregulate across the entire spectrum of telecommunications and broadcasting services and to do a complete rewrite of the Communications Act. In 1976, a pro-Bell Telephone group introduced into Congress a bill called "The Consumer Communications Reform Act," dubbed the "Bell Bill" because it was allegedly written by Bell attorneys. The bill warned that competition threatened the maintenance of universal public telephone service because it would drive local rates through the roof, and it proposed turning the clock back to the preregulation era to prevent this from taking place. It was during this period that Bell launched one of its most intensive lobbying campaigns to combat opposition to its monopoly, and it spent millions in advertising and organizing its three million shareholders to fight the bills that followed.

Between 1976 and 1981, a number of other bills were drafted and introduced into the Senate and Congress to amend or rewrite the Communications Act of 1934. All of them endorsed the use of free markets as the most effective means of achieving industrial development and to use regulation in only those areas where market forces were deficient. Most called for the deregulation of telecommunications, broadcasting, and cable television. They also proposed allowing telecommunications carriers into unregulated businesses under certain conditions and several supported the breakup of AT&T and the Bell System as a prerequisite to deregulating the telecommunications business. Finally, on October 7, 1981, Congress passed the "Telecommunications Competition and Deregulatory Act of 1981," which explicitly favored free markets and competition as the most efficient means of regulating the industry. It recognized that as competition developed, deregulation would ensue. The act also set out several prerequisites for introducing competition while preserving universal service.

Under the Reagan administration and with the policy agenda strictly focusing on deregulation and competitiveness in the world, pressure was mounting in the

Department of Justice to wind up its antitrust cases against both IBM and AT&T. Legislation affirmed the importance of free markets. Computer II had given AT&T the freedom to enter competitive segments of the computer-communications market but the 1956 Consent Decree forbid AT&T from entering competitive markets. But AT&T was already operating in competitive markets. The Justice Department demanded nothing less than the breakup of the Bell System. One possibility was to separate it vertically by splitting off its manufacturing and research and development arms—Western Electric and Bell Telephone Laboratories, respectively. The second was by splitting the mega-corporation horizontally, that is, by separating the twenty-two local operating companies—the source of the real monopoly power—from the parent company. The Department of Justice was seeking the former but would settle for the latter. AT&T considered the latter to be in its own best interest. At least that way a vertically integrated telephone company would still continue to exist in the old Bell System tradition, and it would manufacture everything from telephone equipment to computers as well as supply telephone, digital data, and many other kinds of services. Separating its manufacturing and research arms from the parent company could have destroyed AT&T altogether.

On January 8, 1982, AT&T and the Department of Justice finally came to an historic agreement to replace the 1956 Consent Decree with a new consent decree. However, the presiding judge of the Court in Washington, D.C. Judge Harold Greene, ordered AT&T and the Department of Justice to file their arguments as a revised settlement proposal of the 1956 Consent Decree rather than a replacement of it. He thus combined the antitrust case and modifications of the 1956 Consent Decree into one. After hearings before five congressional groups, Judge Greene issued his decision on August 24, 1982. It was called the Modified Final Judgment or "MFJ," and it secured nothing less than a breakup of the Bell System that the Department of Justice had been seeking for almost a century.[16]

The Modified Final Judgment represents a landmark decision in U.S. antitrust history because it fundamentally reshaped and restructured the U.S. telephone industry. Before divestiture, AT&T was one of the biggest corporations in the world, ranking first in the list of the top 500 largest corporations in America in terms of assets and net income and second in sales. It serviced 146.2 billion telephones in 6,874 exchanges before divestiture accounting for more than 80 percent of the U.S. total. Its 1982 profit exceeded $7 billion, more than any other company in the world. Western Electric accounted for nearly two-thirds of the total manufacturing sales of telecommunications equipment in the United States in 1982 with sales close to $13 billion. Bell Laboratories had a research and development budget of over $2 billion putting it in third place behind General Motors and Ford.

AT&T had to divest itself of its ownership of the twenty-two Bell operating companies (BOCs), thus severing its hold on the local telephone companies. It also had to sever all agreements with the local companies over a period of years but provide them with certain technical and other services until they were capable of providing them themselves. In return for the divestiture of the BOCs, AT&T was permitted to keep its Long Lines Department, Western Electric, and Bell Telephone Laboratories. As important as any of these, it was also permitted to enter any competitive segment of the telecommunications industry except information services from which it was barred for a period of seven years. The MFJ effectively freed AT&T from the regulatory straight jacket that was imposed on it by the FCC's computer rulings as well as the 1956 Consent Decree.

THE CLONING OF AT&T INTO REGIONAL HOLDING COMPANIES

The MFJ reorganized the local telephone exchanges into more than 150 Local Transport Areas or LATAs within which telephone service was provided on a monopoly basis by the Bell operating companies. The twenty-two BOCs were reorganized into seven regional holding companies (RHCs)—Bell Atlantic and NYNEX in the East, Ameritech in the Midwest, Southwestern Bell in the Southwest, and US West Communications and Pacific Telesis in the West. Because of the monopoly power they enjoyed over the local exchange network, they were barred from manufacturing equipment and providing information, enhanced, and interexchange services where they might use their monopoly power unfairly, and they have been lobbying ever since to have these restrictions lifted. To ensure fair and workable competition in interexchange telephone services, the local exchange companies were obliged under the "equal access" provision of the MFJ to provide access to all interexchange carriers, including AT&T, Sprint, and MCI, on a fair and equitable basis.

Each RHC represented a giant in its own right and some were more than half the size of the new AT&T. Each owned several of the former twenty-two BOCs which provided exchange and exchange access services along with an equal share of a central service organization called Bell Communications Research, or BellCore, which performed research for the group. Through subsidiaries, each became involved in supplying such competitive services as cellular telephone services, customer premises equipment, and directory services. But many diversified far beyond the traditional bounds of the telecommunications services industry into such fields as information-processing, real estate, cable television services, and in ventures abroad through joint ventures and acquisitions as described chapter 8.

AT&T was still one of the biggest telecommunications firms in the world, even after divestiture. Its $34 billion in assets ranked it the fourth largest in the United States, behind Exxon, General Motors, and Mobil. It employed 385,000 people, making it the second largest employer in the country. What was left of AT&T was reorganized: ATTIX (AT&T Interexchange) became the successor to AT&T Long Lines and incorporated a new unit called AT&T Communications (ATTCOM). Most of the operations of Western Electric became part of a new organization called AT&T Network Systems which, along with Bell Laboratories, AT&T International, and AT&T Information Systems (formerly American Bell and now ATTIS) were incorporated into a new and completely unregulated operating unit called AT&T Technologies. Other units of the new organization included AT&T Networks, Consumer Products, Government Services, and International Services.

Divestiture brought an end to some of the inconsistencies and conflicts that plagued the telecommunications industry in the United States for over a half a century. It went a long way towards freeing AT&T to enable it to operate in competitive markets and in recognizing the natural monopoly power of the local exchange carriers. In time, divestiture also changed the psychology and the culture of AT&T, and the BOCs to a much lesser extent, making them more attune to the needs of their customers and new opportunities and challenges of the information age.

ACCELERATING CONVERGENCE IN THE POSTDIVESTITURE ERA

The postdivestiture era saw a continued acceleration in technological innovations and competition as the information revolution entered a new phase. Technology became commercialized at a faster rate in the semiconductor and computer industries but especially in the telecommunications industry.[17] The microelectronics revolution changed the direction of both the computer and telecommunications industries by ushering in the age of personal computing, end-user computing, and distributed processing, and it created instant markets for new software and communications and information services. It also created a rapidly growing market for local area networks to connect personal computers with one another and with other corporate information resources, and they began to compete with the PBXs supplied by telecommunications manufacturing companies as the hub of the evolving office- and factory-of-the-future. Telecommunications carriers accelerated the deployment of the new generation of digital switches that could process and switch both voice and data traffic to meet the demands of growing numbers of business computer users. Many of these developments opened up markets for enhanced communications services including electronic banking, finance, and retail services along with publishing, entertainment, and information services to homes and businesses.

By the mid-eighties, it looked as if the showdown between AT&T and IBM, which many had been anticipating for a decade, was about to take place. IBM had become more aggressive in the telecommunications and office equipment markets in the aftermath of the 1982 decision by the Department of Justice to drop its thirteen-year-old antitrust suit, and AT&T was free to enter computer markets as a result of the MFJ. Both AT&T and IBM announced value-added network service (VANS) offerings in the early eighties. AT&T's Net 1000 and IBM's Information Network were direct competitors to one another. Each company designed its service to strategically position itself for the expected growth in national and global markets for computer and enhanced communications services which ranged from software development and database management to data communications services, including electronic mail and funds transfer services.

IBM announced a variety of new communications products for its computers based on its proprietary Systems Network Architecture (SNA), but it also launched a major drive into telecommunications equipment manufacturing and services. In 1982, it announced a $300 million agreement with Motorola for a cellular radio service covering 250 U.S. and Puerto Rican cities. IBM also entered the telecommunications equipment supply business in 1983 with the purchase of 19 percent of Rolm, a manufacturer of PBX equipment. The next year, it moved to purchase the remaining shares of Rolm and initiated development of the 8750/9750 digital PABX for its launch in 1987. In 1984 as well, IBM increased its share of Satellite Business Systems by acquiring all of the shares of Comsat General. The next year Aetna Casualty and Life Insurance withdrew from Satellite Business System selling its interest to IBM, which subsequently sold its share to MCI in return for 16.4 percent interest in MCI. For a while, speculation was rife that IBM was about to use MCI to compete head to head with AT&T. IBM was also responding to developments in the personal computer market. It announced a Token Ring LAN in 1985 in response to the growing use of the Ethernet LAN which was supported by a consortium of suppliers including Xerox, Intel, and Digital Equipment.

AT&T entered the computer and office equipment manufacturing industries in 1983 with the announcement that it was purchasing 25 percent of Olivetti for $253 million. In 1984, it announced its new 3B line of minicomputers and its PC 6300 personal computer workstation along with its Starlan local area network. The following year, it announced its agreement with several computer manufacturers in America and Europe to jointly promote and develop UNIX as the standard for the workstation market. AT&T also forged alliances with Toshiba in Japan, Lucky-Goldstar in South Korea, and companies in Taiwan and Singapore to gain a presence in the Asian market. In 1985, it entered into a joint venture with Mitsui and fifteen other Japanese companies, including Sony and Hitachi, to develop a value-added network service for the enhanced services market in Japan in competition with a joint venture between IBM and Mitsubishi Corporation.

IBM became increasingly active in international computer communications markets as well. It 1984, it formed an alliance with STET, Italy's state-owned manufacturer of factory and telecommunications equipment. In 1985, British banks and retailers chose IBM and British Telecom to set up a nationwide point-of-sale and funds transfer network. IBM entered into a joint venture with Japan's Nippon Telephone and Telegraph (NTT) in the same year to form a new company called Nippon Information and Communications Company (NIC) to develop the software that would enable VANs developed by IBM and Japanese computer companies to communicate with one another. In Europe, IBM's new service offerings included Information Network Services that provided information exchange services for multinational companies and data for trade and transportation companies. It also formed Intercontinental Information Service (ISS) to link IBM value-added networks in the United States, Japan, and Europe.

As the eighties progressed, both AT&T and IBM were working across an increasingly broad front in new and emerging markets with banks, brokerage, and financial service companies to develop value-added and enhanced services. Both were competing in the growing fields of information processing, communications, and office automation. Both were working on their own single-vendor, "one-stop-shopping" strategy for manufacturing and marketing telecommunications, computers, office automation systems and equipment, and software and services world wide through acquisitions, joint ventures, and strategic alliances.

TELECOMMUNICATIONS AND THE GLOBALIZATION OF ECONOMIC ACTIVITY

Every nation was feeling the growing economic impacts of globalization and the information revolution along with the economic and political fallout from deregulation and divestiture in the United States throughout the eighties. Global telecommunications networks were linking computer systems in key sectors of the international economy and creating a global electronic infrastructure and a global services economy which did not recognize any national boundaries or regulatory jurisdictions. These infrastructures were having significant impacts on the growth and development of the services sector and international trade and competitiveness. One of the results was that international trade in services was growing more rapidly than trade in goods. Trade in services was also high on the agenda of international organizations, including the GATT which initiated the Uruguayian round of trade negotiations in 1985. And those countries with more liberal telecommunications policies were attracting an increasing proportion of international investment and experiencing a higher rate of growth in international services. Those countries with more restrictive policies, on the other hand, were losing their share of the international services business.[18]

It was for reasons such as these that governments in Europe, Asia, and elsewhere came under mounting pressure to make drastic changes in the way they managed and administered their Postal, Telephone, and Telegraph administrations (PTTs) to make them better serve the national interest. Business leaders and politicians on the European and Asian continents did not want to be left behind in the race into the information age. The changes that began in the mid-eighties in Britain and Japan spread in a bandwagon effect in late eighties and early nineties throughout every continent as country after country in Asia, Europe, North and South America, and eventually Africa adopted similar policies.[19]

THE TIDE OF CHANGE IN BRITAIN

Britain was one of the first nations to follow the lead established by the United States to deregulate major segments of its telecommunications industry but not before 1979, the year that Margaret Thatcher, the "Iron Lady" of British politics, led the Conservatives to victory over the Labor Party to become the new prime minister. It was Thatcher's conservative government that tried to transform British industry into the information age through the introduction of a wide range of market-oriented industrial and regulatory policies. In 1981, the British Parliament passed the *Telecommunications Act* which split British Telecom from the British Post Office and gave the secretary of state the power to license new carriers. A year later, the secretary of state granted a license to Mercury Communications, owned by Cable and Wireless, to provide basic switched telephone services in competition with British Telecom. In 1983, Mercury was permitted to expand into international services. In 1984, the British government introduced new legislation to privatize British Telecom and create the Office of Telecommunications (Oftel) to regulate the industry and introduce new rules to create a competitive industry and ensure fair competition. New regulations were also introduced that governed the operation of enhanced or value-added services. By 1985, there were 688 VANs operating in the United Kingdom.

The British government followed up in 1985 with the sale of 50.8 percent of its stake in British Telecom to the public. The privatization of British Telecom was a tremendous success and other countries around the world adopted virtually the same privatization strategies for their Posts, Telephone and Telegraph administrations (PTTs). The government subsequently introduced a package of new regulatory reform and industrial policies to accelerate innovation and investment in its telecommunications industry. It introduced price caps, a form of incentive regulation, for British Telecom and took some of the most aggressive steps in the world to encourage competition between its telephone, cable television, and wireless communications industries.

JAPAN'S PLANNED ACCOMMODATIONS

Events in Japan were accelerating in the eighties in parallel with those in the United States and Britain. In 1982, the Japanese government made revisions to the 1971 *Public Telecommunications Law* to allow users greater flexibility in their use of leased lines connected to the public telephone network of NTT. In 1984, the Japanese Diet passed two laws that transformed the telecommunications industry in Japan. The first, called the *NTT Law*, ended the total monopoly that NTT enjoyed over domestic transmission facilities. The second, called the *Telecommunications Business Law*, substantially liberalized the Japanese telecommunications marketplace. It also opened the VAN market to competition. The Ministry of Posts and Telecommunications (MPT) was given the mandate to privatize NTT and subsequently regulate it. The new legislation also divided the telecommunications industry into two classes: those companies that supplied transmission facilities (Class I) that continued to be regulated and those that provided enhanced service (Class II) which were unregulated.

The new legislation stimulated a flurry of industrial activity in the Japanese telecommunications industry with big companies like Sony, Mitsubishi, Kyocera, and the Japanese National Railways entering the intercity market and building satellite, microwave, and optical fiber networks in competition with NTT. By 1987, more than ten Class I carriers were operating in competition with NTT. They included Japan Telecom Company, Teleway Japan Corporation, and Daini-Denden Inc., which began supplying public telephone services in 1986. Japan Communications Satellite Company and Space Communications Corporation were in the business of providing nationwide satellite communications services. Competition also came quickly in the international market dominated by Kokusai Denshin Denwa Corporation (KDD) after 1985. One of the new competitors was a consortium called International Telecom Japan (ITJ) which involved Mitsubishi, Sumitomo, Mitsui, the Bank of Tokyo, and Matsushita. Another consortium, International Digital Communications involved C. Itoh, Toyota, and Cable and Wireless of Britain. By 1987, the VANs marketplace had become a focal point of intense competitive activity with over 200 companies operating by 1987.

In 1987, the Japanese government sold 35 percent of NTT to the public in a $62 billion public offering making it the biggest private securities offering in Japanese history. In the fall of 1989 the Telecommunications Council of Japan, the advisory council of Japan's MPT, fell short of recommending the breakup of NTT, not on the basis of antitrust policy but on the basis of national telecommunications policy.

PERCEPTIONS IN THE EUROPEAN COMMUNITY SLOWLY CHANGE

Nations on the European continent were feeling the pressures of technological change and global competition in the late eighties as well. In a "green paper" issued in 1987, the European Commission proposed the adoption of a number of policies for creating a single Europeanwide marketplace for telecommunications equipment and services by 1992. "Information, exchange of knowledge, and communications," the report noted, "are of vital importance in economic activity and in the balance of power in the world today. . . . [and] telecommunications is the most critical area for influencing the 'nervous system' of [this new] . . . society."[20] The report called for free and unrestricted competition in the manufacturing of equipment and the provision of all computer, value-added, and enhanced telecommunications services and requested individual states to begin setting up appropriate institutions to introduce competition. In December 1988, the commission issued rules to deregulate the equipment manufacturing industry and the data transmission, leased-line, electronic mail, and financial data networks by 1991.

On January 1, 1989, the Netherlands became the first nation on the European continent to privatize its PTT and make way for competition in line with the recommendations of the European Commission. Royal PTT Nederland NV was created as a holding company with five profit centers including those providing postal and telephone services. In West Germany, a new law went into effect in July 1989, splitting the Deutsches Bundespost into separate postal and telecommunications organizations. All basic telephone facilities and services would continue to be owned and operated as a monopoly, but all other facilities and services including value-added services and satellite and cellular radio services are open to competition. In 1992, the German government announced its intention to privatize Deutsches Bundespost Telekom, its state-owned telecommunications company. In France, the government split the postal directorate from the telecommunications directorate, renaming the latter France Telecom, with both reporting to the minister of Postal, Telegraph and Telecommunications. In 1991 the Belgium government privatized its PTT, now called Belgacom. The Swedish Telecom's board of directors voted in early 1991 to convert the government-owned carrier into a corporation on July 1, 1991, and asked the government to consider privatizing the company and listing its stock on the exchange in the future.

DEREGULATION AND PRIVATIZATION TRANSFORMS THE WORLD TELECOMMUNICATIONS INDUSTRY

Deregulation and privatization policies are being pursued in Canada, Latin America, and Asia. In Canada, the Canadian Radio, Television and Telecommunications Commission (CRTC) began liberalizing the resale and sharing of private-line facilities in 1985. In 1987, the federal government began selling all of its shares in the country's telecommunications carriers, including Teleglobe Canada, its international telecommunications carrier. In 1991, the federal government announced the sale of its 49 percent ownership of Telesat Canada, its domestic satellite communications company, to Alouette Communications, a consortium of Canada's major telephone companies. In June of 1992, the CRTC opened the intercity, long-distance market to competition. A new "Telecommunications Act" was also passed in 1993, and in September 1994, the CRTC opened the local exchange to competition.

In 1990, the New Zealand government sold its telephone utility, Telecom Corporation of New Zealand, to Ameritech and Bell Atlantic for $2.5 billion. In 1990, the Australian government announced a series of new policy initiatives to restructure its domestic and international telecommunications industry and open it up to competition. The government first merged its domestic and international carriers, Telecom Australia and the Overseas Telecommunication Corporation (OTC), to form a single integrated supplier of facilities and services called Australian Overseas Telecommunications Corporation (AOTC). It also licensed a second competing carrier called Optus Communications, a consortium with BellSouth and Cable & Wireless, with each holding a 24.5 percent equity, to install and operate national and international telecommunications facilities in competition with AOTC. Next, it sold Aussat, Australia's domestic satellite company to Optus Communications. Optus was also given a license to build and operate a second cellular network throughout Australia. According to the new policy, the duopoly will last to 1997 when the market will be further opened up to competition. Both Optus and AOTC are regulated by the Australian Telecommunications Authority (AUSTEL) created in 1989 to oversee the introduction of competition.

Privatization spread to South America in 1990. In November, after splitting the state-owned telephone company, Entel, into two parts, the Argentine government announced the sale of 60 percent of Entel South to Spain's Telefonica and 60 percent of Entel North to Italy's STET (Italtel) and France Telecom's Cable et Radio. In the same year, Mexico announced the sale of a 56 percent stake in its state-owned telephone company, TelMex (Telefonos de Mexico) to France Telecom along with Southwestern Bell and Grupo Carso S.A. de C.V., a Mexican manufacturing and mining company, for $1.76 billion. TelMex has $7.4 billion in assets and $2.2 billion in revenues in 1989. In November 1991, the Venezuelan government announced the sale of 40 percent of its stake in CANTV, the state-owned telephone company to a consortium, which included GTE Corporation, AT&T, and Spain's Telefonica, for $1.89 billion. The Brazilian government has also become increasingly active in deregulation and privatization. It initiated plans in 1992 to sell 58 percent of Telebras, the government-owned telecommunications holding company. Privatization policies were being actively pursued in other parts of South American, in Uruguay, Paraguay, and Chile, for example, and in South East Asia, where Malaysia and Singapore were considering selling portions of their telephone utility to private interests. Eastern European countries have also become very active in the privatization of their telecommunications carriers.

Countries everywhere have embarked on this new agenda in recognition of the new technological and global competitive realities and because telecommunications infrastructure has become so important to economic growth and competitiveness. Telecommunications policy is now inextricably linked to international trade policy and international competitiveness as well as domestic and international banking and financial services regulation. Telecommunications, in short, has become more than just another industry. It has become a key underpinning and a key infrastructure that is central to the social, economic, and political well-being of every nation. It has become a critical pillar of the evolving postindustrial society.

NOTES

1. "Regulatory and Policy Problems Presented by the Interdependence of Computer and Communications Services and Facilities," 28 FCC 2d 291 (1970), Tentative Decision; 28 FCC 2d 267 (1971), Final Decision.

2. Gerald W. Brock, *The Telecommunications Industry: The Dynamics of Market Structure* (Cambridge: Harvard University Press, 1981), p. 213.

3. Specialized Common Carrier Services, First Report and Order, 29 FCC 2d 870, 920 (1971).

4. The year 1980 is the year that the "New World Information Order" received the most international attention. In that year, the International Commission for the Study of Communications Problems, established by UNESCO, published the results of its investigation into "the totality of the problems of communications in modern society." See Sean MacBride et al., *Many Voices, One World: Communications and Society Today and Tomorrow* (Paris: UNESCO, 1980).

5. Jean-Jacques Servan-Schreiber, *The World Challenge* (New York: Simon and Schuster 1980).

6. Patrick H. Winston and Karen A. Prendergast, eds., *The AI Business: The Commercial Use of Artificial Intelligence* (Cambridge: MIT Press, 1984), p. 288.

7. Edward A. Feigenbaum and Pamala McCorduck, *The Fifth Generation: Artificial Intelligence and Japan's Computer Challenge to the World* (Reading, Mass.: Addison-Wesley, 1983), p. 21.

8. Simon Nora and Alain Minc, *L'Informatisation de la société* (Paris: Documentation Française, 1978). The English version is entitled: *The Computerization of Society: A Report to the President of France* (Cambridge: MIT Press, 1980).

9. The books by Robert Reich, *The Next American Frontier* (New York: Times Books, 1983); and James Botkin, Dan Dimancescu, Ray Stata, and John McClellan, *Global Stakes: The Future of High Technology in America* (New York: Ballinger, 1982) called for a national industrial strategy to help America reindustrialize and meet the international competition challenge.

10. The 1956 Consent Decree settled an antitrust suit brought against AT&T in 1949 alleging that Western Electric monopolized the manufacture and supply of communications equipment and apparatus in violation of the Sherman Antitrust Act. The Justice Department sought the divestiture of Western Electric and its dissolution into three competing firms. In 1956, AT&T and the Justice Department came to an out-of-court settlement in which AT&T agreed to withdraw and abstain from entering competitive markets, including computer manufacturing. Western Electric was prohibited from selling its equipment outside the Bell Telephone System. Bell Telephone Labs was forced to make its patents available to other companies on a royalty-free basis. AT&T was also forced to divest itself of all of its foreign holdings, including those in Northern Electric in Canada.

11. Second Computer Inquiry, Final Decision, 77 FCC 2d 384 (1980), p. 8.

12. CNN was broadcasting to 130 countries by 1992. It made history in January 1991 when it broadcast live television pictures of the Coalition Forces invasion of Iraq to the world from inside Baghdad.

13. For a description of these developments, see Wilson P. Dizard, *The Coming Information Age: An Overview of Technology* (New York: Longman, 1982), pp. 109–114.

14. Benno C. Schmidt, Jr., "Pluralistic Programming and Regulation of Mass Communications Media," in Glen O. Robinson (ed.), *Communications for Tomorrow* (New York: Praeger, 1978), p. 211.

15. U.S. House of Representatives, *Telecommunications in Transition: The Status of Competition in the Telecommunications Industry* (Washington, D.C., November 3, 1981), p. 244.

16. Modification of Final Judgement, *United States v. Western Electric Co. Inc. and American Telephone and Telegraphy Co.*, Civil Action no. 82-0192 (DCC filed August 24, 1982). For a description of the regulatory and other developments surrounding the AT&T divestiture, see Walter Bolter et al., *Telecommunications Policy for the 1980s: The Transition to Competition* (New York: Prentice-Hall, 1984); and the breakup itself, see Steve Coll, *The Deal of the Century: The Breakup of AT&T* (New York: Simon and Schuster, 1988).

17. Robert W. Crandell and Kenneth Flamm, ed., *Changing the Rules: Technological Change, International Competition, and Regulation in Communications* (Washington, D.C.: Brookings Institution, 1989).

18. "Telecommunications: The Global Battle," *Business Week* Special Report, 24 October 1983, pp. 126–132.

19. For a description of the changing telecommunications policy and regulatory environment in the OECD countries in the late eighties, see Robert R. Bruce, Jeffrey P. Cunard, and Mark D. Director, *From Telecommunications to Electronic Services* (London: Butterworths, 1986); *The Telecom Mosaic: Assembling the New International Structure* (London: Butterworths, 1988). See also Rodney Stevenson et al., *International Perspectives on Telecommunications Policy* (London: JAI Press, 1993).

20. *Towards a Dynamic European Economy* (Green Paper on the Development of the Common Market for Telecommunications Services and Equipment), Commission of the European Communities, Com(87), 290 final, Brussels, 30 June 1987, EC(1987), p. 1.

Chapter 5 _____

Network Universe

The pace of technological and economic change accelerated in the world information economy throughout the eighties driven by growing international competition, deregulation, privatization, and the convergence of computers and communications. A new generation of high-powered satellites made it economically attractive for businesses to use very small and relatively inexpensive earth stations to communicate among their geographically dispersed operating offices and branches in ways that were not feasible or economical before. Superefficient, high-capacity optical fibers were deployed to completely wire up buildings and entire cities, span nations, and cross oceans and continents. And telephone and cable television companies became engaged in a great race to rewire their local distribution systems with optical fibers so they can bring interactive television and information and entertainment services on demand to residential subscribers before the decade is out.

Technological innovations also set off the boom in cellular telephony in the eighties which grew to penetrate major urban areas and expand into rural areas. Mobile satellites came to be used to communicate with ships at sea and with aircraft and trucks. A race also began to deploy the new generations of personal communications, direct broadcast satellites, and cellular microwave systems to compete with the services offered by the telephone and cable television companies. And some brave companies bet literally billions that networks of tens or hundreds of satellites could be used to provide the entire world community with a plethora of new voice, video, and information services. This chapter will describe how companies are deploying these transmission technologies to create the basic electronic transport infrastructure of the evolving global network economy.

SATELLITE COMMUNICATIONS: THE CONTINUING REVOLUTION

The satellite communications revolution entered a new phase in the early eighties with the deployment of a new generation of commercial high-powered, high-capacity communications satellites that operated in the high-frequency (14/12 GHz) Ku-band.[1] The higher power made it possible to use inexpensive miniature and micro earth stations with diameters as small as five feet (1.5 meters). The higher frequencies prevented interference from terrestrial microwave transmissions which used the lower frequencies. Another advance was the use of time-division multiple access (TDMA) which made it possible for users to share the same communications channels simultaneously much like users do the operation of a time-sharing computer. Sharing in this way had the effect of lowering the cost for individual users and individual applications and expanding the variety of applications. As a result of these innovations, satellite capacities increased, earth stations became smaller and cheaper, and satellite services, particularly in the United States, became more affordable, accessible, and cost-effective.

The FCC in the United States initiated regulatory action in step with these innovations and developments. In 1979, it deregulated receive-only earth stations and liberalized the sale of transponders in 1982, permitting individual companies to purchase transponders for their own use. In 1983, it announced new regulations to decrease the orbital spacing between satellites to two degrees. This considerably expanded what was until then an internationally scarce resource in fixed supply. The FCC also adopted regulations in 1983 to permit the use of satellite antennas with diameters as low as four feet (1.2 meters). In 1984, it completely deregulated Comsat earth stations. In September 1985, it extended its ''open skies'' policies into the international marketplace by giving five companies provisional authorization to enter the international private satellite communications market. They were Orion Satellite Corporation, International Satellite Incorporated, RCA, Cygnus Corporation, and Pan American Satellite Incorporated (PanAmSat).[2] These decisions had a stimulative effect on the satellite communications industry worldwide. They created the market for new satellite business services that used very small earth stations for their internal operations. They also opened the market for the delivery of information services via satellite or ''datacasting.''

The greatest number of communications satellites in the world are operated for domestic purposes. Most are owned and operated by American companies.

AT&T, RCA, GE, GTE, and SBS became active in the market within five years of the FCC's 1972 Domsat decision. But the number dwindled in the eighties through mergers and acquisitions, reflecting rapid technological advances, high investment costs as well as the maturing of the market and growing competition, especially from terrestrial optical fiber communications systems. In 1985, MCI purchased SBS from IBM, Continental Telephone (Contel) purchased American Satellite Corporation (AMSAT), and GE purchased RCA including its subsidiary, RCA Americom Communications Incorporated. In the same year, Hughes Communications, created as a subsidiary to Hughes Aircraft in 1978, purchased Western Union's satellites and several of those owned by SBS. (General Motors purchased Hughes Aircraft in the same year.) GTE became the owner of RCA Astronautics Spacenet satellite system.

By 1988, thirty-two U.S. Domsats were in operation. Eighteen operated in the C-band, ten in the Ku-band, and four were hybrid, that is, they had transponders that operated in the both the C-band and Ku-bands. These were owned or operated by nine companies. They included Alascom (operating the Aurora 1 satellite), AT&T (the Telstar series), Comsat (the Comstar series), GE American Communications (the GE Americom and Satcom series including those which GE purchased from RCA), GTE (the Spacenet and G Star or GeoStar series), Contel ASC (formerly American Satellite Corporation), Hughes Communications (Galaxy series), MCI (SBS formerly owned by IBM), and Western Union (Westar series). GTE merged with Contel in 1991. Numerous other companies leased transponder capacity in bulk or own one or more transponders. Competition is expected to reduce the number of satellite operators in the United States to four big companies. They most likely survivors are AT&T, GE, GTE, and Hughes Communications.

Other countries have followed the lead of the Soviet Union, Canada, and the United States in launching domestic communications satellites. The Soviet Union operates the GORIZONT satellites and France the Telecom series satellites. India, China, Mexico, Brazil, Japan, and Australia operate domestic satellite systems to serve their national, social, and economic development needs. The Aussat (Australia), Brazilsat (Brazil), and Morelos (Mexico) satellites were launched in 1985. India's satellite communications system (InSat) was built to provide an inexpensive means of improving the educational standards for the millions of citizens living in underserved areas. Japan is served by two JCSat satellites launched in 1989. A domestic satellite communications system, called Kopernicus, has been deployed by Germany. It is designed to deliver voice, data, and video services in the Ku-band and Ka-bands (20–30 GHz).

Many communications satellites are operated by regional groups which use them on a shared basis. The European Community Satellite (ECS) system which provides satellite services to European PTTs is operated by Eutelsat. Intersputnik satellites supply satellite services to the sixteen members of Intersputnik, formed in 1971 by the former Soviet Union and Eastern European nations. Arabsat, formed in 1976, provides communications services to twenty-two member countries of Arab League through two satellites launched in 1985. The Palapa satellite system serves countries in Southeast Asia (Indonesia). PanAmSat uses its Simon Bolivar satellite to provide regional Caribbean and South American services and is expanding into international services. AsiaSat, owned by Cable & Wireless and China International Trust and Investment, serves Southeast Asia, including China, through the AsiaSat1 satellite launched in 1990. The Andean countries of South America are planning a regional satellite system called AS-ETA to serve their joint needs.

Intelsat, in particular, has played an important role in using satellite communications technology to bring the world closer together culturally, economically, and politically. According to its 1988–89 annual report, which commemorated the company's twenty-fifth anniversary, Intelsat was providing global communications from thirteen satellites stationed over the Atlantic, Pacific, and Indian oceans and servicing more than 600 sites through 800 or more antennas measuring between 3 feet and 100 feet (1 and 30 meters) in diameter. Using nine of these satellites, it provided thirty-two television channels of coverage of the 1988 Summer Olympics in Seoul, South Korea, in 1988 to fifty countries. In spite of its monopoly on international public telecommunications services, it has had to face growing competition from the rapid growth of international optical fiber communications networks that telephone companies began laying under the Atlantic, Pacific, and Indian oceans in the late eighties. It has also had to fend off competition from regional and international satellite companies, including PanAmSat, for example, which provides international services across the Atlantic to the United Kingdom and West Germany as well as Chile and Peru and AsiaSat in Southeast Asia and Orion Satellite Corp., which provides North American and European coverage. For these reasons, Intelsat has had to continually upgrade its facilities. The Intelsat VI series, which began operating in 1989, has a capacity of 24,000 voice circuits and three television channels, and each of the five Intelsat VII series satellites, which it began launching in 1992, are capable of carrying 90,000 two-way voice circuits.

DIRECT BROADCAST SATELLITES: THE PROMISE AND THE DISAPPOINTMENT

Of all the developments in telecommunications, none has been more feared by nations, national governments, and cable television and broadcasting industries around the world than direct broadcast satellites. Since the launching of the Sputnik in 1957, Canada and countries in Europe, Asia, and Africa have felt severely threatened by the fact that direct broadcast satellites (DBS) could beam signals directly into homes and destroy their culture and their cultural industries. And they fought vigorously in international fora to ensure that this did not happen.[3] It was Japan, however, that made the most progress in the development of a DBS system, at least up until 1990. Japan launched the BS-2 direct broadcast satellite in 1984 and a second, the BS-2B, in 1986 after the first failed.

By the end of 1987, it was providing two channels of television services to over half-a-million households using forty-five cm. (18 in.) dishes making it the first country in the world to provide a DBS service on a commercial basis. Japan has been using DBS satellites as a means of promoting the use of its high-definition television (HDTV) system.

European governments accelerated their plans for introducing DBS services in the late eighties. In 1986, the British Independent Broadcasting Authority (IBA) selected a consortium of Britain's big media companies, called the British Satellite Broadcasting (BSB), to operate a high-powered DBS system. The British Broadcasting Corporation was a member of the consortium. Its chief rival, Sky Channel, owned by Rupert Murdoch's News International and operating since 1982, was developing a DBS service using Europe's medium-powered Astra 1 satellite system. In 1990, after spending in excess of a billion dollars competing with one another, BSB and Sky Television agreed to merge to form BskyB. Germany launched the first of its two TV-SAT DBS satellites in 1987 and France launched its TDF-1 DBS satellite, in 1988. The European satellite consortium Société Européenne des Satellites launched the first Astra DBS satellite in 1990 and a second in 1991. Both were designed to broadcast directly to European audiences. By the fall of 1992, the Astra satellites were beaming twenty-nine channels, carrying news, entertainment, and specialty programs to European homes. They included Eurosport, Satellite Jukebox, CNN International, and TV Asia. BSkyB had become one of Europe's leading satellite pay TV companies with 1.5 million paying subscribers and an estimated 1 million others who were receiving the signals illegally. Its most popular channels were Sky Movies Plus, Sky Sports, and Sky News. A DBS system, called Tele-X, is under development by the Nordic community of Sweden, Norway, and Finland.

DBS systems are also under development in other countries, including China, for example. Satellite broadcasting has been slow to develop in Asia because most countries regard the reception of foreign broadcast signals as a form of cultural imperialism so they have erected barriers to keep them out. Malaysia, for example, has effectively banned satellite broadcasting. China passed a proclamation in October 1993 banning the possession of satellite dishes. Hong Kong restricts television viewing to Cantonese language broadcast signals. For these reasons, Star Television, the joint venture between Hong Kong's Hutchison Whampoa and Hong Kong's Mr. Li Ka-shing, which began broadcasting to Asian audiences in 1991 over the AsiaSat1 satellite system failed to develop its target market. It was successful, however, in developing a market in India, Taiwan, and Israel which were also covered by the footprint of the satellite.

DBS developments in the United States lagged those in other countries. In 1982, the FCC awarded construction permits to nine of twenty-one companies that had applied for permission to provide DBS service. In spite of this, none were operational five years or even ten years later. At least two developments changed things in the early nineties. One was advances in satellite technology which made it possible to reduce the size of receiving dish to that of a napkin and bring its price to under $1,000. The second was the development of digital video compression (DVC)[4] which makes it possible to provide as many as 150 channels or more over a single satellite (or cable television) system and it promises to usher in the 500 channel era.

GM/Hughes Electronics along with the United States Satellite Broadcasting Consortium, Paramount Pictures, and the Disney Channel deployed these new technologies to launch America's first DBS service. On May 17, 1994, DirecTV began broadcasting 150 channels of programs to a potential audience of forty million American homes equipped with 18-inch receiving dishes. Forty of these were cable channels while forty to fifty were pay-per-view movie channels. Hughes has estimated that the venture will generate $1 billion annually by the year 2000. It is DBS systems like DirecTV that Canadian broadcasters and cable television companies are most fearful of because of the effect they could have on their industry in the nineties. This is why the Canadian broadcasting and cable television industries refer to them as "death stars." One of the first broadcasters to take advantage of the opportunity to launch a service via DirecTV, however, was Canada's publicly owned broadcaster, the Canadian Broadcasting Corporation (CBC).

Competition to DBS in the United States, however, has been coming from terrestrial cable companies, which are also using DVC technology to multiply the capacity of their systems. Time Warner, now one of the biggest media conglomerates in the world, began delivering 150 channels of television content to 3,000 subscribers in the New York borough of Queens in 1992. The service, called Quantum, provided seventy-five channels of conventional programming with additional channels dedicated to delivering pay-per-view movies beginning every thirty minutes. Canadian cable television companies and Canada's domestic satellite company, Telesat Canada, are using digital video compression technology as a means to launch their own DBS service to protect themselves against U.S. death stars in 1995. This is another example of the big-stakes poker game that cable television and DBS companies along with telephone and radio communications companies have become engaged in to determine who will win the right to provide the hundreds of channels that home owners around the world could want in the future. Although it is still too soon to predict, a widely held view exists in the industry that DBS services will develop but serve a highly specialized niche market for delivering perhaps many tens or perhaps hundreds of pay-per-view programming services to rural and urban households by the late nineties.

SPAWNING THE VSAT REVOLUTION

One of the big breakthroughs in satellite communications in the eighties was a service developed for the commercial business market called VSAT, the acronym for very small aperture terminals that measure approximately 1.2 meters (four feet) in diameter. These earth stations are much smaller, less bulky, and, therefore, more portable, mobile, and less expensive to purchase and operate than their predecessors. They are capable of carrying a wide variety of video, data, and voice traffic in an integrated and economically efficient fashion. IBM was one of the early developers of VSAT technology which it used as the backbone of its interactive satellite education network for providing a variety of two-way interactive audio and full-color video communications services in the early eighties over the SBS satellites. Hughes along with AT&T, GTE, and Contel Communications now dominates the commercial VSAT industry in the United States. Businesses began using these services in the eighties to conduct live presentations and hold meetings by teleconferencing via satellite.

Retailers have been in the forefront in using VSAT networks and services. Wal-Mart, for example, was one of the first retailers to begin using a VSAT network in 1985 to connect more than 750 of its stores nationwide. Today, its national VSAT network provides the foundation of a logistical support system that no other retailer can match.[5] Sears, Roebuck had also built a nationwide VSAT network by 1988 which it used to allow regional offices of its Sears Merchandising Group to hold various types of meetings and conferences with Sears Headquarters in Chicago. By 1991, it had expanded its network to forty-three two-way and 850 one-way terminals which it used to hold meetings and conferences and make product debuts. One of the biggest VSAT users in the world is Chrysler Corporation which, by 1990, had built a network of more than 6,000, two-way Ku-band earth stations for transmitting live sales messages, service updates, technical information, and press conferences to its dealerships across the United States. Apple Computer, AT&T, ComputerLand, Hewlett-Packard, General Motors, Tandem Computers, United Airlines, and Occidental Petroleum also became big users of satellite television in the late eighties. Knight-Ridder, Associated Press, Dow Jones, and the U.S. Weather Service use VSAT facilities for broadcasting news, weather, and financial, economic, and other kinds of information to their customers. The Hospital Satellite Network and the American Hospital Association use VSAT facilities to broadcast television programs to a majority of hospitals throughout the United States. And the Automotive Satellite Telecommunications Network provides automobile dealers with courses and programs for sales, marketing, and management personnel. VSATs are also being used to broadcast stereo music and audio programs including background music to retail drug and grocery stores.

International VSAT (IVSAT) services have become a booming business in more recent years with hundreds of financial institutions, hotel chains, and manufacturing and retailing companies like Holiday Inn Worldwide, Visa International, and Volkswagen AG using them to link their global operations with one another and with their headquarters. AT&T, MCI, and Unisource are major suppliers of IVSAT services. Intelsat also provides IVSAT services through IBS, its Intelsat Business Services package of services.

But satellite communications companies are having to innovate and move faster and in smarter ways to stay ahead of terrestrial competitors by developing and holding onto niche markets. Successors to VSAT, called USAT and TSAT, for example, allow them to do that.[6] USAT is the acronym for ultra-small aperture terminals which are satellite systems that use terminals with a diameter of less than .5 meters and cost as little as $450–$1,000. These can serve small businesses as well as homes for broadcast receiving dishes, and they are beginning to compete with coaxial and optical fiber cables (witness DirecTV) for delivering pay television and data communications to the home. TSAT, the acronym for T-carrier small-aperture terminals with a diameter of 2.4 meters, is designed to carry private business telecommunications traffic at 1.544 megabits per second and can be used for voice, data, and video transmission. As described below and in the next chapter, suppliers are developing other new and innovative applications of communications satellites including global mobile telephone service, electronic mail, and message communications as well as navigation and positioning services.

THE REVOLUTION IN CELLULAR COMMUNICATIONS

The forces of technological innovation, global competition, and creative destruction opened a second front in the eighties, catapulting a variety of new wireless (radio) communications services to center-stage of the ongoing telecommunications revolution. It began with the inauguration of mobile radio in the seventies and cellular telephone in the mid-eighties and has since been expanded by developments in mobile satellite, packet radio, and a variety of cordless and other personal communications services. These promise great changes later in this decade because they have the technological and economic potential to provide homes; individuals; and cars, trucks, ships, and aircraft with inexpensive, high-quality voice, facsimile, data and image, and even video communications. By making it possible for people to keep in contact with one another and with computers and databanks as well as vehicles by voice, message, and mail and to exchange information wherever they are in the world, developments in radio communications are creating a ''mobile society''—a society continually on the move and continually in contact with people, computers, organizations, and events wherever they are taking place in the world. They are making it possible to create mobile offices and a mobile workforce.

The principles of cellular radio were conceived at Bell Telephone Laboratories in 1947, but users had to wait over three decades until microelectronics and computer switching technologies became available in the seventies and eighties so that large numbers of subscribers could enjoy its superior quality and economics. AT&T was one of the first companies to become active in field trials to test the technical and economic feasibility of the new service beginning in Chicago in 1977. Responding to growing numbers of applications and user demands in the late seventies, the FCC developed operating rules for the new industry in 1981. To ensure that market forces would predominate, the FCC decided to issue licenses to two operators in each territory—one to the local telephone company and one to a competitor. Developments have taken place so rapidly since then that few players have been able to keep up with the exploding demand for services which has been fueled by, among other factors, the rapidly declining costs of hand sets. Growth was so rapid in some of the big urban centers in the late eighties and early nineties that their systems became saturated within months of making huge investments in plant and equipment to increase their capacities.

By 1989, the number of cellular subscribers in the United States had topped 3.4 million and was growing between 30–40 percent annually. By then, the major players were attempting to build nationwide networks through mergers and acquisitions. McCaw Cellular was the undisputed leader in the acquisitions game. Having built up a substantial presence in small urban areas, McCaw Cellular succeeded in purchasing Lin Broadcasting in late 1989 for $7 billion. Lin Broadcasting had franchises in five of the top ten cities of the United States, including New York, Los Angeles, and Dallas. This acquisition put McCaw on the road to becoming the largest supplier of cellular services. The cellular industry continued to chalk up record growth rates reaching revenues of $10 billion in 1992. By then, it had begun to take on strategic importance for the entire telecommunications industry, not only because of rapid growth of demand for voice service, but because it represents an easy and relatively inexpensive means of completely bypassing the networks of the local telephone companies. It also became attractive to interexchange carriers because it offered them a means to avoid paying access charges to the local telephone companies.

Both Sprint and AT&T made strategic moves in the U.S. cellular industry in 1992. In that year, Sprint paid $2.5 billion for Centel, one of the biggest companies in the industry. In November, AT&T announced the purchase of a 33 percent stake in McCaw for $3.8 billion. A year later, in August 1993, AT&T and McCaw came to an historic agreement whereby AT&T would purchase all of the shares of McCaw for $12.6 billion, thus making it the largest cellular operator in the United States. The acquisition is perceived by many to be strategic to the future of AT&T as well as McCaw and the telephone and cellular industries. For AT&T, the acquisition offers a quick and inexpensive way to get back into the local telephone business without violating the provisions of the MFJ. But McCaw will also play a key role in AT&T's strategic plan to provide any kind of communications services "anywhere and anytime." Like other players, AT&T sees a massive migration from wire to wireless communications in this decade, and it wants to play a leading role.

Cellular carriers have been switching to digital technology as quickly as possible to meet the explosive growth in demand and for other strategic reasons. Digital cellular is attractive because it promises to lower the investment cost per subscriber and decrease the cost of making a call. It also makes communications more secure and enables private and enable carriers to provide much better quality and more reliable services. Finally, digital technology enables suppliers to provide new services such as database access, facsimile, and electronic mail as well as other voice and nonvoice communications services where the growth in demand is expected to be especially rapid in the nineties. The biggest problem with digital cellular is that there are two competing standards. The first and most widely used, TDMA (time-division multiple access), increases capacities by a factor of three to seven. The competing technology, called code division multiple access (CDMA), can multiply the capacities by a factor of up to twenty. Although it is more expensive to install than TDMA, CDMA's higher capacities has been attracting more and more operators in the United States and Asia.

Regional and national cellular operators in North America are also collaborating and linking up at the international level to create a ''seamless'' nationwide and continentwide cellular network. In February 1992, McCaw and Southwestern Bell announced a partnership called Cellular One to create a ''seamless'' national cellular network. In February 1993, fifteen U.S. and Canadian wire-line carriers with cellular franchises, including six of the seven regional holding companies, announced that they were banding together to create a North American brand and service identity called MobiLink, with the objective of providing ''seamless'' cellular roaming on a nationwide and North America-wide basis. Further integration of the North American market including Mexico as well as possibly South American markets can be expected in the months and the years ahead.

CREATING A PERSONAL COMMUNICATIONS REVOLUTION

Cellular telephone has been generally perceived as a business service rather than a service for individual or personal use, primarily because of its expense. Other kinds of wireless radio communications services for home use are currently under development. These include cordless telephones and personal communications systems (PCS), which many believe are superior to cellular telephone in the long run in terms of technology and economics. PCS systems use smaller cell sizes, typically covering several blocks, operate at much higher frequencies, use lower power receivers, and are less expensive to use than the services offered by the cellular telephone companies. They also have greater traffic capacities than cellular networks and are subject to less congestion. PCS services are expected to eventually compete on a cost basis with ordinary wire-based telephone service. For these reasons, telephone, cable television as well as other companies including manufacturing concerns have been positioning themselves for what many believe will be a mass market in the late nineties. The most serious problem with PCS, however, has been the availability of sufficient spectrum but this has not prohibited developments from taking place at a breath-taking pace around the world. But national and international bodies are taking steps to resolve the spectrum problem.

In 1992, members of the ITU's World Administrative Radio Conference (WARC) voted to allocate frequencies in the 1.7 to 1.9 gigahertz band for the provision of PCS services. The FCC has given PCS a very high priority on its national industrial competitive agenda. In January 1993, it allocated the 2-GHz band for "emerging" wireless technologies, including PCS. In September 1993, it announced it would set aside 160 MHz of spectrum specifically for PCS.[7] This will make it possible to accommodate up to seven competitors in each region. By late 1993, over 200 companies had been granted experimental PCS licenses. Telephone companies and most of the big cable television companies, including Time Warner, Cox Cablevision, TCI, and Comcast are well represented in these field trials. The scramble is already under way to build nationwide PCS networks. In 1994, Bell Atlantic, for example, announced the formation of a consortium to build a nationwide PCS network.

THE GLOBAL CELLULAR AND PCS SCENE

The revolution in wireless communications has become a global phenomenon with industrialized, newly industrializing, and developing countries implementing or planning to implement cellular and/or PCS services. The European Commission has established its pan-European cellular radio program (GSM) as the centerpiece of its plans to harmonize the radio communications activities among its member states by developing a single digital mobile telephone network for the whole of Europe. An equally important objective is to re-establish European communications companies as world-class manufacturers. The European GSM system is one of the most technically advanced in the world in terms of its capacity, speed, efficiency, and the scope of services that it can provide. Even nonmember Scandinavian, Eastern European, and some Asian countries are adopting the GSM standard.

In Britain, the Department of Trade and Industry (DTI) has been one of the most proactive promoters of wireless communications technology, primarily as a means of building local and nationwide networks that will compete with those of Mercury and British Telecom. Like the United States, Britain issued cellular licenses to two companies in each service area—one to Cellnet, in which British Telecom has a 60 percent stake and the other to Vodafone. Vodafone now offers cellular services nationwide, and it is active in over a dozen cellular developments throughout the world. Britain's Department of Industry also issued licenses to three companies in 1990 to develop and operate personal communications networks. Mercury Personal Communications, a joint venture between Cable & Wireless and US West Communications became, in September 1993, the first to offer a commercial PCS service. In early 1993, the Department of Industry issued radio licenses to three companies including Vodafone and Ionica to operate radio-based telephone services on a national basis. Ionica expects to be in business in early 1995. All are expected to completely bypass the local wireline networks of telephone companies but interconnect with their switches. Mercury Personal Communications also plans to reach a nationwide penetration of 90 percent by the end of the decade. Other countries in Europe are also actively promoting the development of PCS services. Germany, for example, inaugurated a PCS service in late 1993 operated by BellSouth, Vodafone, Veba, and Thyssen.

Countries in Eastern Europe—in Russia, Hungary, and Poland, for example—in Southeast Asia, in Hong Kong, China, South Korea, Singapore, and in Mexico and South America are building or planning to build and operate cellular and PCS networks as a matter of high national priority. But they are going about it in a radically different manner than in the past. To gain access to the technology and promote foreign investment, most have adopted a policy of issuing licenses to foreign carriers. European and American carriers, especially regional holding companies, are among the biggest winners in this big sell-off of licenses. PacTel, the wireless subsidiary of Pacific Telesis, is in partnership with cellular operations in Germany, Portugal, Japan, Sweden, and Belgium. Bell Atlantic owns 42 percent of Isacell, Mexico's second largest cellular company. In Hungary, Westel Radiotelefon, a joint venture between US West Communications and Matav, the state-owned Hungarian PTT, is expected to have a nationwide cellular network in operation by the end of 1994. Some of the most rapid developments are in Mexico, China, India, and other developing countries where radio technology holds the promise of launching them into the twenty-first century even before it arrives.

THE MOBILE DATA, MESSAGING, AND PAGING COMMUNICATIONS REVOLUTION

The rapid development of wireless technology along with the spread of personal laptop computers with wireless communications capabilities is also spawning a mobile data communications revolution, and manufacturers and cellular telephone companies are gearing up to cater to a mobile data communications market boom which, by some estimates, could reach between $8 to 10 billion by the end of the decade. Mobile data communications services appeal to companies with large sales forces or field service technicians or other kinds of operations, such as airlines, realtors, banks, couriers, and wholesalers and retailers in addition to insurance claims adjustors and traveling executives, for example, who are always on the move but need instantaneous access to information and, therefore, databases. Personal computers with wireless communications capabilities offer a natural solution for companies and even individuals with these problems.

Federal Express was one of the first companies to exploit the potential of wireless data communications for private purposes. In 1977, it built a wireless network to tie all of its offices, planes, and couriers to its computers in Memphis so it could capture information on every package and trace it from the time it was picked up to the time of its delivery. The technology was critical to enabling the company to guarantee next-day delivery around the world. It was only a matter of time before other suppliers began offering a mobile data communications service on a commercial basis. Ram Mobile, a joint venture between Ram Broadcasting Inc. and L. M. Ericsson, was one of the first companies to do so in 1989. In January 1990, IBM and Motorola announced a joint venture to provide commercial mobile data communications services nationwide. The service, called the Advanced Radio Data Information Service, or Ardis, combined IBM's private packet radio data communications system and Motorola's international shared-use radio network. The service allows users to enter orders, query databases, and transmit messages via the Ardis network through two-way, wireless, handheld data terminals. In the fall of 1992, Ram Mobile announced a national wireless commercial electronic mail service over its nationwide packet radio network. By late 1993, the service was available in over 6,000 cities and towns. Ardis became available in 8,000 cities in fifty states in 1994.

All of the major mobile radio companies have been gearing up to cater to the booming market for mobile data communications services which many expect will be created by the widespread use of personal computers and communications devices such as those produced by Apple, IBM and others in the latter part of the nineties. McCaw plans to have its packet data communications service available in 100 cities by the end of 1994. Motorola has opened up its Ardis network to cellular vendors, and IBM and eight cellular carriers are collaborating to develop a common standard for transmitting data over cellular networks. Not wanting to be left behind, BellSouth purchased 49.9 percent of Ram Mobile in 1992. Packet-switched cellular networks are also under development in Britain (Cognito), Japan (City Media), France (Telecom Mobile Data), and Germany (Telecom Datex-P). Within a few years, data communications users will be able to roam anywhere in North America and Europe and eventually around the world without having to worry about where they are.

THE MOBILE SATELLITE REVOLUTION COMPLEMENTS THE LAND MOBILE COMMUNICATIONS REVOLUTION

Developments in mobile satellite technology are adding considerable momentum to the telecommunications revolution that is under way, reflecting the fact that satellites have a basic natural advantage over terrestrial systems especially for global, mobile communications service applications. In other respects, they are both complementing and competing with the terrestrial cellular telephone and the PCS revolution. Satellite systems that provide communications services for ships at sea (so-called Maritime Mobile Satellite Services or MMSS), for aircraft (Aeronautical Mobile Satellite Services or AMSS) as well as for trucks and cars on the ground (Land Mobile Satellite Services or LMSS) have been under development for a number of years, and voice, data, message, facsimile, and even video communications can now be delivered via satellite to all three user groups. Because of their attractive economics, flexibility, and ease of use, especially in a highly dynamic mobile environment where people, vehicles, and machines are always on the move, satellite technology and satellite services are driving many of the recent developments in mobile communications.

Mobile satellite communications had its beginnings in the WARC Conference of 1971 when frequencies were allocated for mobile satellite services. In 1973, the International Maritime Organization, a special agency of the United Nations, began hosting a series of conferences to discuss the creation of an international mobile satellite system. In 1976, delegates from forty countries agreed to establish an international body to manage commercial maritime communications via satellite. In 1979, member countries signed an agreement establishing the International Maritime Satellite Organization (Inmarsat) to provide international, two-way mobile telecommunications services. Inmarsat began providing mobile communications services in 1982 to commercial and private vessels over the Atlantic, Pacific, and Indian oceans using transponders leased from Comsat General's Marisat satellites, launched in 1976. By 1989 Inmarsat was providing maritime satellite communications services using Intelsat V, ESA's Marecs and Comsat General's Marisat satellites to 9,000 mostly sea-based users such as ships and rigs at sea. By 1990, the company was providing service to any ship at sea almost everywhere in the world as long as it had a registered identification number.

Mobile satellite services began becoming available to aeronautical users in the late eighties when several consortia began field-testing satellite communications services between aircraft and ground locations using Inmarsat satellites. British Airways began a commercial trial of a satellite-based telephone service called Skyphone in February 1989 which enabled passengers to make direct-dial telephone calls to almost anywhere in the world for $9.50 per minute. In 1989, a consortium consisting of SITA, the international cooperative of 355 airlines, and Teleglobe Canada, France Telecom, and Australia's OTC, agreed to invest $60 million to develop an aeronautical mobile satellite service for commercial operation in 1990. Today, airline passengers can phone anywhere in the world from an aircraft so long as they had a credit card using the services of Skyphone, GTE Airfone, SITA, or Comsat Corporation, for example, and they can communicate via their laptop computers with terrestrial databases and electronic mail networks around the world. Pilots and air traffic controllers can communicate with one another better through mobile satellite communications, and better information can be provided, for example, on the precise positions of aircraft, thus improving the safety of air travel. And, through Hughes Communications' WorldLink, the world's first cable television system in the sky, launched in 1993, they can access a whole range of entertainment, shopping, leisure, communications, and tourist information services.

Land Mobile Satellite Services are also under rapid development to provide mobile communications services on a continentwide basis, not only for urban areas but for rural and remote areas as well. In 1985, twelve companies applied to the FCC to construct nationwide mobile satellite systems for voice services. In 1987, the FCC concluded that a single system would best serve the public interest. In 1988, a group of seven companies, including Hughes Communications, McCaw Space Technologies, Mobile Satellite Corporation, Skylink Corporation, and Transit Communications, formed the American Mobile Satellite Consortium (AMSC) to provide land mobile and aeronautical and maritime mobile communications services throughout North America and in cooperation with Telesat Mobile International (TMI) on the Canadian side. By 1996 the AMSC-TMI partners hope to provide businesses, vehicles, and individuals throughout North America with two-way mobile voice, data, and message communications services that were so popular in the Dick Tracy comic strip in the sixties.

A number of international consortia are also betting billions to design and operate a new generation of communications satellites in low earth orbit (called LEOSATs) to supply mobile telephone services for personal uses on a global basis. In June 1990, Motorola announced plans to invest up to $2.2 billion to develop a "seamless worldwide telephone system" by the end of the decade. The system, called Iridium, will involve as many as sixty-six low-orbit satellites designed to extend cellular service to remote U.S. and overseas locations. The satellites are expected to work together as a digitally switched communications system in space to relay voice, data, facsimile, and paging signals anywhere in the world. Iridium is expected to become operational in 1998. Because the proposed system could bypass the networks of the PTTs, Motorola had to make concessions to many governments to get the frequencies it wanted. It passed a major hurdle in 1992 when members of WARC voted to allocate the spectrum it asked for to transmit signals on the same frequencies worldwide. Other consortia have been formed to compete with Iridium. Loral and Qualcomm, for example, have proposed a system of forty-eight satellites called Globestar for a 1997 launch. TRW has proposed a twelve-satellite global system called Odyssey for 1997. At least seven other global systems, including Ellipso, Aries, Orbcomm, and LEOSAT, are also in the planning stages. An eighth, Teledesic, backed by both William Gates and Craig McCaw, plans to invest $9 billion in sophisticated star wars technology to create a web of 840 satellites that will provide global voice, video, and multimedia services. Almost all of systems are designed to provide communications anywhere in the world.

Inmarsat has been expanding its mobile satellite services to provide improved services for its maritime customers as well as for aeronautical and land-based users to fend off growing competition from other global and regional mobile satellite communications systems. In October 1990, it launched the first of a new generation of satellites (Inmarsat II) and a second in March 1991 which are capable of providing telephone, telex, electronic mail, facsimile, and data services for ships, aircraft, and land mobile users. One of these provides a telephony group call for simultaneous facsimile transmission to groups of ships to inform them of matters of common interest, such as weather charts and newsletters. Inmarsat has also developed a twelve-inch diameter portable terminal with the capability of providing two-way data messaging and emergency-alert services. It is also attempting to pre-empt competition from Iridium by building its own global satellite communications system. In the fall of 1992, Inmarsat announced plans to invest between $1.5 and $2.5 billion to build an international satellite system to enable consumers around the world including those in remote areas to communicate with one another through handheld terminals.

GLOBAL RADIO POSITIONING AND NAVIGATION SATELLITE SERVICES

Mobile satellite communications companies have also been developing new kinds of services for navigation, position determination, and location purposes for land, maritime, and aeronautical uses. Such services, called radio determination satellite services (RDSS) are used for tracking the movement of trucks, trains, ships, and airplanes as well as providing communications to and from their headquarters. Trucking companies, for example, can use these services to reduce repair and maintenance time, cut costs, and increase the efficiency of their fleet management operations. Companies can also use RDSS for safety and security purposes. Geostar Corporation, formed in 1982, was one of the first companies to operate a mobile satellite communications system. By 1988, it was providing services for radio location, position determination, and navigation as well as for collision avoidance, voice messaging, and database access. In November 1989, it announced RDSS capabilities aboard GTE Spacenet Corporation's GSTAR III satellite, allowing companies to automatically track and report locations of trucks, trains, ships, and airplanes anywhere in the Western Hemisphere, from the Arctic Circle to the middle of South America. Another company, Omninet, began providing RDSS services in May 1988. A third, called Qualcomm, was providing mobile satellite services in 1989 to its customers through 5,000 Ku-band antennas, about eleven inches wide and four inches high at a cost of about $4,000 each. Inmarsat began offering RDSS services over its Inmarsat satellite in 1990.

The mother of all RDSS systems, however, is the Global Positioning System (GPS) or Navstar, a system of twenty four satellites developed by the U.S. Department of Defense, which provides 24-hour, all-weather coverage.[8] Signals from the satellites are sufficient to pinpoint the position of the receiver within sixteen meters. By adding other information from a stationary receiver, accuracies to centimeters can be achieved. GPS proved itself in the Persian Gulf War in January 1991 when soldiers were able to accurately determine their position at all times. Since users do not need costly and specialized navigation systems, the benefits of GPS can be quite substantial. The number and variety of civilian user organizations is potentially unlimited. Trucking companies can use them to dispatch their fleets faster and more efficiently. Airport personnel and pilots can use the information for more accurate positioning of aircraft and for automated landings in bad weather conditions. Other important uses include precise surveying, geological studies, and synchronizing global digital communications.

The Eastern Block's Global Navigation Satellite System (GLONASS) also provides GPS services. Iridium and Loral-Qualcomm's Globalstar system are also planning to offer positioning services when their systems become operational later in the nineties. The European Space Agency (ESA) is testing a mobile data communications satellite system called Prodat on its Marecs satellite, and France's national space agency Centre National d'études spatiales (CNES) has established a company called Locstar to develop a European radiodetermination satellite system.

GPS devices began appearing as mass-market consumer items as early as 1992, the year that Sony Corporation introduced the Pyxis GPS system, priced at $1,195. Motorola introduced the Traxir at a price of $1,295 in the same year. These devices can be connected to laptop computers enabling users to watch the progress on a map which scrolls on the screen. Panasonic's handheld KX-G5500 can use the information to calculate the distance from another position as well as the necessary bearing and speed to get there. In January 1994, Sony and General Motors announced navigation systems for installation in automobiles. All of the big automobile companies plan to offer GPS systems as options on their cars in the future.

OPTICAL FIBER COMMUNICATIONS: SUPERSONIC TRANSPORT SYSTEMS OF THE TWENTY-FIRST CENTURY'S INTELLIGENT SOCIETY

Another kind of telecommunications revolution has been under way since the early eighties as a result of developments in optical fiber technology, and it is complementing and competing with the revolutions in MSAT, VSAT, DBS, and cellular telephone and PCS services. Optical fibers are the new space-age transmission systems that companies are using to wire up offices and factories everywhere and create a new optical network work environment. They are penetrating buildings and core urban areas and entire countries and continents and are well on their way to wiring up the entire world community. Over the next decade and beyond, optical fiber technology promises to completely overhaul the world's century-old telephone system as well as cable television systems. It will bring such twenty-first century services as high-definition television, interactive television, video-on-demand services, video teleconferencing, and tele-banking, teleshopping, tele-education, and teleworking services into the living rooms in homes of most nations, even though it could cost hundreds of billions of dollars.

Optical fibers first became deployed by telephone companies in their high-density long-distance national and international networks as well as by businesses in their local area networks for wiring up buildings for data, voice, and video communications. At the same time, they opened up windows of opportunity for new companies to enter the rapidly growing and highly lucrative local and long-distance telecommunications business in spite of the formidable presence of established telephone companies and long-distance and international carriers. In the United States, Japan, and Britain, dozens of companies began installing optical fiber networks in the eighties along any kind of right-of-way they could find within and between major cities—along railways and highways and along or even inside abandoned oil or gas pipelines. Railway, hydroelectric, and oil and gas pipeline companies also got into the act since they had ready access to the necessary local, regional, and national rights-of-way. A number of companies also began using optical fibers to wire up some of the biggest metropolitan areas in the world to serve the private networking needs of big corporations. Today, optical fibers have become one of several key strategic technologies for telephone and cable television companies in their race to create and dominate the broadband multimedia infrastructure of the twenty-first century.

BUILDING NATIONWIDE OPTICAL NETWORKS

AT&T successfully field-tested optical fibers at speeds of 44.7 megabits per second in Atlanta in 1976, and tests were subsequently carried out by GTE and ITT. One of the first optical fiber links was laid between New York and Washington, D.C., soon after AT&T and eight Bell operating companies received FCC approval in 1981. In November 1984, AT&T announced plans to build a 10,000-mile (1.7 billion circuit mile) nationwide optical fiber network. Sprint completed a 23,000-mile nationwide optical fiber network in 1986. By 1988, both AT&T and MCI had completed their nationwide installations. United Telecommunications also built a 23,000-mile (1.2 billion circuit mile) national network. Railway companies, taking advantage of their valuable regional and national rights-of-way, also joined in. Fibertrak, a joint venture between Norfolk Southern Corporation and Santa Fe Southern Pacific, built an 8,000-mile (2.4 billion circuit mile) network over Southern Pacific's rail rights-of-way. Other national optical fiber networks along with regional networks were also constructed. Southern New England Telephone Company and CSX Corporation formed a joint venture called Lightnet which built a national 5,000-mile network. Regional optical fiber networks were also built by Williams Telecommunications, Southernet, Litel, Microtel, and Consolidated Network which formed a national consortium called the National Telecommunications Network. By 1989, however, the industry was beset by enormous overcapacity and a price war ensued causing prices of long-distance telecommunications services to plummet. Mergers and consolidations in the industry followed.

Nationwide optical fiber networks were deployed throughout the eighties as a high national priority in Canada, Japan, France, Germany, and the United Kingdom and throughout Asian countries. In Japan, companies like Japan Telecom Company and Teleway Japan Corporation built nationwide optical fiber networks in competition with NTT. In Canada, Stentor, the organization that represents Canada's major telephone companies, completed one of the longest fiber optic installations in the world, in March 1990. The 7,000-kilometer network, which extended from the Atlantic to Pacific ocean at a cost of $750 million, crossed peat bogs in central Canada, cut through the solid rocks and swamps of the Canadian shield, winded up and down three mountain ranges between Alberta and British Columbia, and crossed rivers and streams in the Rockies over 200 times. Unitel, Stentor's competitor, completed its coast-to-coast optical fiber network in the same year. In June, 1993, Stentor completed a second 6,500-kilometer coast-to-coast optical fiber and digital microwave link.

One of the most ambitious national optical fiber programs was announced by NTT, Japan's national carrier, in 1990. In that year, it revealed plans to invest $250 billion to link all parts of the country with optical fibers to create a nationwide broadband infrastructure by the year 2015. The European Community is also investing heavily in optical fiber networks on a continental basis, and countries throughout Asia, especially Singapore, Hong Kong, Malaysia, and Thailand, are carrying out ambitious plans to build optical fibers nationwide.

T1S, T3S, OS1S, AND OS24S: SUPERSONIC TRANSPORT SYSTEMS OF THE INFORMATION AGE

Optical fibers spawned the business communications revolution in the eighties by making it possible for Fortune 500 companies to lease or own the information-age equivalent of a two-, four-, or even an eight-lane superhighway over which they can mix and transmit voice, data, and video communications. The basic unit of these digital transmission systems, called a T-Carrier T1, was introduced into the intercity network by AT&T back in 1962. These operate at a speed of 1.544 megabits per second (Mbps) and have a capacity of twenty-four, 64 kilobits per second digital voice circuits. Twenty-eight T1 channels can be multiplexed into a higher capacity T3 channel which operates at a speed of 45 Mbps and has the capacity of one full broadcast quality television channel. But these are becoming obsolete because optical fibers can carry much more traffic at much higher speeds. The new standard for optical fibers is called SONET, the acronym for synchronous optical network. SONET speeds begin at 51.84 Mbps (called OC-1) and proceed in equal increments to OC-12 (622.08 Mbps) and OC-48 (2.49 gigabits per second of Gbps), and so on. These are 3,000 times faster and have 30,000 times the capacity of their predecessors. Suppliers like AT&T and Northern Telecom advertise their fiber products as having "self-healing" capabilities, that is, they are capable of restoring themselves in milliseconds thus making them secure and invulnerable to power failures or other problems.

Optical fibers are now bringing high-speed, high-capacity digital transmission systems within the range of affordability of an increasing number of companies. General Motors, General Electric, American Express, and Citicorp, for example, and public utilities, universities, and governments at all levels often have sufficiently large volumes of information and communications traffic to justify leasing T3 and SONET facilities either locally, nationally, or internationally. And more and more Fortune companies have been, or will be, turning to systems such as these to satisfy their growing communications network requirements in the nineties.

TELEPORTS, METROPOLITAN AREA NETWORKS, AND THE WIRED CITY

Big urban centers in the United States and around the world also bore the brunt of the optical fiber revolution in the eighties as a new class of telecommunications supplier, called competitive access providers (CAPs), began installing high-capacity digital, optical fiber networks in the core areas to interconnect large companies such as banks and financial service companies with long-distance carriers or tie the local offices of long-distance carriers into their national networks.[9] These so-called metropolitan area networks (MANs) were created by laying cables under city streets or stringing them over telephone and electric utility poles or through subways, coal tunnels, and along railway and highway rights-of-way. CAP operators typically provide voice grade lines and high-speed digital T1, T3, and SONET facilities, often at a reduction over those offered by the telephone companies. Most offer little or no value-added or protocol conversion services. Long-distance companies and large financial service companies became big users of metropolitan area networks in the eighties which they used to tie their local offices together and connect to national and international carriers.

Metropolitan area networks became synonymous with the international industrial competitiveness of many big city administrations around the world in the eighties. The first MAN operator was Teleport Communications Inc., which was formed in 1983 as a joint venture between Merrill Lynch, Western Union, and the New York Port Authority. City authorities in New York, San Francisco, Los Angeles, Chicago, Amsterdam, Tokyo, and London, for example, and even those in some newly industrializing countries jumped onto the bandwagon, and they too began installing optical fiber networks at a frantic pace for their biggest telecommunications users and interconnecting and integrating these with other national and global city centers by national and international satellite, microwave, and optical fiber facilities. From them, access to the most advanced telecommunications network in the world became a way of attracting business from other centers.

In addition to New York, Merrill Lynch Teleport Technologies, the arm of Merrill Lynch which owned teleports operations, was operating teleports in Boston, Chicago (where regulators designated it a public common carrier), San Francisco, Los Angeles, and Houston by 1989. Metropolitan Fiber Systems (MFS), its main competitor, had set up operations in Chicago, Boston, Baltimore, Minneapolis, and Philadelphia and was constructing facilities in Houston, Los Angeles, and San Francisco. According to *Telecommunications Reports*, the weekly news service covering national and international telecommunications developments, a total of 2,456 buildings in 116 cities spread across forty-five states were served by twenty-one competitive access providers in 1993. Teleport Communications had operations in twelve metropolitan centers and MFS in fourteen. Others included Institutional Communications in Washington, D.C., Philadelphia Fiber Optic, Inter-Media Communications in Florida, New England Digital Distribution Inc., Eastern Telelogic in Pennsylvania, and Diginet Inc. in Chicago and Milwaukee.

Telephone companies have also become very active in building and testing SONET-based fiber rings in major cities in the United States and even cable television companies were showing increasing interest in getting into the business as well by 1993. In January 1994, MCI announced the formation of a new subsidiary, MCI Metro, with a $2 billion budget to build competitive access networks in twenty major metropolitan areas by the end of 1996. As we shall see below, CAPs, cable television operators, and telephone companies are now engaged in a fierce battle for control of the local distribution network.

GLOBAL OPTICAL FIBER HIGHWAYS

International telecommunications carriers, led by the big three—AT&T, British Telecom International (BTI), and Kokusai Denshin Denwa Corporation (KDD) of Japan—have been leading the charge to rewire the globe, or rather to "fiberize" it by deploying the technology to expand the capacities of their Atlantic and Pacific links by orders of magnitude and to interconnect these with other regional networks. The first fully optical transatlantic link, called TAT-8, was inaugurated on December 14, 1989. It had a capacity of 40,000 telephone calls. In March 1992, TAT-9 was inaugurated into service linking the United States, Canada, the United Kingdom, and France. It had a capacity of 50,000 circuits. Six months later, TAT-10 was brought into service linking the United States with Germany and the Netherlands. TAT-11 subsequently came into service in September 1993, linking the United States, United Kingdom, and France. Both systems have capacities of 80,000 simultaneous telephone calls, double that of TAT-8. These links interconnect with optical cable networks in the Mediterranean Sea and the Baltic Sea which connect with those in Italy, Greece, Turkey, Israel, and the Scandinavian and Eastern European countries.

Work is in progress way to lay TAT-12 and TAT-13 cables across the Atlantic Ocean as well. These will have significantly higher transmission capacities (five gigabits per second or 500,000 calls, ten times that of TAT-9) which is achieved by using optical rather than electronic amplifiers. Interconnecting with these will be the Columbus optical cable network, linking the United States, Spain, and Mexico, and the CANTAT-3 cable, linking Canada and the United States with Denmark, Germany, and Eastern European countries via the Baltic Sea.

Optical fiber links have also been proliferating across the Pacific. On April 24, 1989, the first transpacific optical fiber cable called TPC-3 was placed into service linking the United States and Japan. Costing $700 million and with a capacity of 40,000 telephone calls, the cable stretched 8,271 miles from California to Japan via Hawaii and Guam. No sooner was it brought into service when a consortium of thirty international carriers announced construction of a second optical fiber cable to link the United States directly to Japan. TPC-4 came into service in 1992 with a capacity of 75,000 telephone calls. Another optical fiber link, called the H-J-K Cable System, linking Hong Kong, Japan, and Korea, came on stream in 1990. It connects with the Hawaii-4/Transpacific-3 cable system. AT&T and KDD are major partners in these systems as well.

In May 1991, Pacific Telecom Cable Inc. and the Japanese consortium, International Digital Communications, began commercial service on the 5,200-mile North Pacific Cable (NPC) linking the United States to Japan. A spur cable linking Oregon to Alaska was announced a month later. The Australian Telecommunications Commission and the New Zealand Post Office completed the 30,000 kilometer (TASMAN-2) optical fiber cable system linking Australia and New Zealand to North America in 1993 and plan to complete a link with Asia by 1995. Work is also in progress to construct a new high-capacity (TPC-5) cable across the Pacific by 1995. It will use the same optical technology as TAT-12 and TAT-13.

Private transoceanic optical fiber cables were also being laid. In 1988, a consortium of companies including Britain's Cable and Wireless and Sprint began laying an optical fiber cable system across the Atlantic. In the fall of 1989, the world's first privately owned transatlantic telecommunications cable called PTAT-1 was inaugurated into commercial service. The new facility, called GLOBAL FON, has since been expanded to offer other services including integrated voice, facsimile, data, and video teleconferencing and other services.

Optical networks are also proliferating throughout Eastern Europe and Africa. In the former Soviet Union, the Ministry of Posts and Telecommunications and a consortium of international carriers (including US West, KDD, STET, British Telecom, Australia's AOTC, and Deutsches Bundespost Telekom are constructing the trans-Soviet fiber cable. The trans-European link (TEL) connecting Germany, Poland, Hungary, and Czechoslovakia was inaugurated in January 1994. Optical networks are also proliferating throughout Africa. In August 1992, the 3,280 kilometer EurAfrica fiber optic cable system went into service linking France, Portugal, Morocco, and the island of Madeira. It interconnects with SAT-2 for handling service to South America and became linked into the Columbus-2 system in 1994.

TELCO-CATV CONVERGENCE: TECHNOLOGY DEMOLISHES THE BOUNDARIES BETWEEN TELECOMMUNICATIONS AND CABLE TELEVISION

Optical fibers have the great advantage that they can carry many hundreds of high-quality video signals and voice, data, and information services in an efficient and economical manner. For these reasons, they set off a race between telephone and cable television companies in the late eighties and early nineties to create electronic superhighways that would reach into the homes of an entire nation and open up vast new economic opportunities. Visionaries and futurists saw these leading to the creation of new generations of smart home appliances, for example, that combined the functions of television, computers, facsimile machines, and telephones and of being capable of providing home banking, electronic mail, picture telephone, and customized television channels in addition to electronic information services ranging from home shopping to the delivery of entire newspapers electronically.

Many obstacles stood in the way of realizing this vision. Extremely high investment costs and the question of what kind of services households wanted and how much they were willing to pay for them were but a few of the very serious impediments to realizing these goals. One of the most serious obstacles for them was regulatory. In the United States, for example, legislation passed in 1970 banned the cross-ownership between the telephone and cable television companies, and the Cable Communications Policy Act, passed in 1984, established for the first time a national policy for cable television. The Act freed cable operators from rate regulation and from having to provide access channels for public, educational, and government use. It also prohibited local telephone companies (and broadcasting stations) from owning cable systems inside their home territory. By the end of the eighties, over 90 percent of American homes subscribed to telephone service but only about 50 percent subscribed to cable television service even though cable passed about 80 percent of American homes. By then, optical fibers had formed the backbone of the long-distance telephone network, and telephone companies became intent on installing them into their local distribution systems directly to the home. They then began pressuring the FCC and Congress to scrap the legislation and the regulations that banned them from offering cable television services. By the late eighties, all of the Bell operating companies in the United States had become engaged in fiber-to-the-home (FTTH) trials to test the economic and market potential of integrated telephone and cable television services in dozens of American communities. Among the most notable were Hunters Creek, Florida; Perryopolis, Pennsylvania; and Cerritos, California. Similar field trials were launched in Britain, Japan, Canada, and elsewhere.

The years 1991 and 1992 proved to be landmark years for the telephone, cable television, and broadcasting industries as well as the information and entertainment industries in the United States in terms of regulatory and political developments. In October 1991, a federal appeals court abolished the order prohibiting telephone companies from providing information services.[10] Congress also voted to reimpose local rate regulation on cable television companies in order to curb soaring subscription fees in the same year, and the FCC ruled that broadcasters, which were suffering from a continuing decline in viewers, could buy into cable television operations and vice versa. Finally, in July 1992, the FCC agreed to allow telephone companies to offer video-dial services to businesses, that is, to offer their networks to independent programmers on a common carrier basis and sell switching and gateway services, billing, and other enhanced functions.[11] All of these decisions heightened the drama and the seemingly inevitable clash between telephone and cable television companies.

By 1992, telephone companies had completed their field trial evaluations and became convinced that the deployment of fiber almost to the home—that is, to the curb (FTTC) or the pedestal, which served between four to eight homes—made good economic sense, based on the cost and demand considerations and the kinds of services these systems could carry as well as the fact that these systems could be upgraded to carry additional broadband services. In that year, the first large-scale deployment of FTTC systems were announced. In the fall of 1992, Ameritech awarded contracts totalling just under $1 billion for "next-generation digital loop carrier" systems for installation in areas with high application service needs such as business and dense residential areas. It is planning to provide 2.5 million customers in Indiana, Ohio, Michigan, Illinois, and Wisconsin with access to optical fibers and another 2.5 million with access on demand by 1995. Within days of Ameritech's announcement, BellSouth placed a similar order and with this the race to create the optical digital network of the future was underway. In January 1993, NYNEX announced that it would begin awarding contracts for 400,000 fiber lines, and US West unveiled plans to build a mass-market video network combining fiber, copper, and coaxial cable. Pacific Bell announced plans in April of the same year to deploy an integrated broadband network to reach half of its residential and business subscribers within ten years and serve all customers by the year 2015.

Cable television companies have been responding to the accelerating pace of competition and technological developments by deploying optical fibers as well as digital video compression which enables them to deliver as many as 150 channels over ordinary coaxial cable systems. Time Warner, the largest cable television operator in the United States, began operating the 150-channel Quantum service in Queens, New York, in late 1991 and was building a far more ambitious interactive, multimedia system in Orlando, Florida, to provide television, data, and telephone services. Its biggest rival, TCI (Tele-Communications Inc.), the largest cable operator in the United States with 20 percent of the subscribers nationwide, has also been hatching ambitious plans. On April 12, 1993, it announced that it was embarking on a $2 billion program of investments in optical fibers using DVC technology to create an "information superhighway" in 400 cities across the United States by 1996. Then, in March 1993, Time Warner announced plans to build its own "electronic superhighway" to American homes to enable them to receive videos, newspapers, and educational content within minutes of ordering them and educate and entertain themselves at home, shop for furniture and clothing from home, as well as play video games with others on the network.

All of the big cable television companies began entering into strategic alliances and joint ventures with telephone companies outside their own territory in 1993 to develop the information and entertainment supermarkets of the future. On May 17, 1993, Time Warner announced that it had sold a 25.5 percent stake in its Time Warner Entertainment division to US West Inc. for $2.5 billion. Toshiba Corporation, Time Warner Cable Group, Warner Brothers, and Home Box Office are also involved in this venture which plans to offer a full complement of broadband, interactive voice, video, and information services in about two dozen metropolitan areas by 1998. Big deals were announced between Bell Atlantic and TCI as well as Southwestern Bell, and Cox Cable Communications, but these were revoked within weeks after the FCC ordered cable companies to lower their rates. Other regional holding companies are going it alone. Pacific Bell, for example, announced plans in November 1993 to invest $16 billion to deploy a hybrid fiber and coax transmission over the next seven years to bring video-on-demand and other services to five million households in California by the end of the decade.

Cable television companies are now talking about 500 channel television as being the standard in the near future and eventually as many as 1,000 channel television in the home—all made possible by developments in digital video compression and optical fibers. Even a 5,000 channel television universe has been bandied about. Stunning developments like these have raised both hopes and fears about the future of the cable television industry. Optimists revel about the opportunities presented and the seemingly unlimited scope of choice of programming services that home owners will be able to access in the future. Pessimists point out that the proliferation of channels will frustrate and bewilder consumers, fragment the industry, drive away advertisers, and eventually destroy the industry altogether.[12]

But dramatic technological advances have also been taking place to further speed up the pace of change and expand the scope of competition and choice in the local services marketplace in the United States. By 1993, for example, advances in particular so-called asymmetrical digital subscriber line technology (ADSL) made it technologically feasible and economically attractive to deliver as many as four video channels and high-speed digital data services in addition to voice to the home over the twisted copper networks of the telephone companies. Telephone companies began deploying the new technology in field trials in the same year to test the markets for these new services. Northern Telecom and the seven regional holding companies unveiled a system in November 1992 to give home owners video-on-demand over ordinary telephone lines using a VCR-like control device by the end of 1994. AT&T is also actively testing new technology to deliver video services on demand via both the telephone and cable television networks. But the competition does not stop here. New technology now makes it feasible for cable television operators to offer telephone service over their networks at a cost of between $200 and $300 per subscriber, and operators in the United States, Britain, and Canada have begun installing the technology and offering the service.

Another alternative local broadband distribution system, developed by a company called Cellular Vision Technologies and Telecommunications in the United States, is also in the race to develop the premier local broadband distribution system of the future. Dubbed by some as a form of wireless cable television, it operates much like cellular telephone but in the 28 GHz frequency band and is capable of delivering dozens of television channels to homes and businesses. Because it does not employ wires, it promises to involve less capital investment and operating expense, and it can be deployed much more rapidly. Bell Atlantic is deploying the new technology to provide cable television services in the New York area by 1995.

Institutional and regulatory developments have been taking place in parallel with technological developments as the competition heats up. In August 1993, a U.S. Appeals Court issued a landmark ruling that the statutory prohibition barring telephone companies from providing video programming directly to subscribers in their service area was unconstitutional. And weeks later, in September 1993, the FCC ruled that local exchange carriers could provide wireless cable television services within their operating territories. These decisions could pave the way for head-to-head competition between the telephone and cable television operators. On the other hand, they could lead to phone companies acquiring cable television systems or joint ventures between the two industries.

THE BATTLE FOR CONTROL OF THE LOCAL DISTRIBUTION SYSTEM OF THE FUTURE IS UNDERWAY

Both cable television operators and telephone companies in the United States and other countries are looking at other ways to strengthen their position for what is rapidly becoming a battleground for control over the local distribution network of the nineties and beyond. This network, many believe, will consist of interconnected networks comprising not only cable television and telephone networks but cellular, personal communications, and microwave and satellite networks, as well. Cable companies like Time Warner, Cox Cable Communications, Comcast Corp., and TCI, for example, have been positioning themselves for what many consider will be highly lucrative markets for personal communications services where they will compete directly with the telephone companies. Cox Enterprises, which is heavily into broadcasting, cable television and newspapers, was successful in gaining experimental PCS licenses in San Diego and New York in 1991 where it is using its cable networks to relay signals between cells. Comcast is into PCS, cellular, optical fiber networks, and fleet dispatch services. AT&T is now a full participant and competitor in this battle for control of the local distribution networks through McCaw Cellular. MCI is another. In July 1993, MCI announced the formation of a consortium of 150 cable television, telephone, and publishing companies to build an $8 billion network to cover 75 percent of the nation. Meanwhile, the RBOCs have been mounting a vigorous campaign for permission to enter the long-distance market.

Cable television companies are also attempting to take advantage of the opportunities in the corporate market by teaming up with competitive access providers such as Teleport Communications Inc. and Metropolitan Fiber Systems which have the technical and managerial know-how to build and operate sophisticated T1, T3, and SONET-based telecommunications networks which more and more big businesses are demanding. CAP suppliers got a big boost in their competitive battle with the telephone companies in 1989 when the New York Public Service Commission gave New York Telephone ninety days to unbundle its services and give business customers separate prices for links and ports allowing them to buy from any carrier. In 1992, Cox Enterprises and TCI made a joint bid to purchase all of Teleport Communications. The fortunes of CAP suppliers and cable television companies further improved as a result of two decisions of the FCC in September 1992 and August 1993 which effectively removed all barriers to CAPs offering switching as well as transmission functions. These decisions are expected to open the door to a "robust network of networks" in which the switched networks of LECs (local exchange carriers) and others interconnect with the LEC's switched access services as well as compete with them.

Developments have been accelerating in Europe, especially in Britain, which has completely eliminated all of the legal barriers prohibiting cable television companies from offering telephone services and provides long-term incentives for cable television operators to supply telephone services. Britain has also relaxed its rules on foreign ownership, and companies like NYNEX Corp., Southwestern Bell Corp., TCI, and Vidéotron of Canada are active in the U.K. market. By 1992, U.K. cable companies had invested over 1 billion sterling in Britain's cable television networks, giving 1,750,000 homes access to broadband services. Plans are in place to invest 5 billion sterling in these networks before 1998. By June 1993, the United Kingdom had more than 170,000 cable telephone lines, according to the U.K. Cable Television Association. That is, they offered both telephone and cable television services. East London Telecommunications, now controlled by Bell Canada Enterprises, began offering combined television and telephone services in the London borough of Redbridge in 1993. And Vidéotron, another Canadian cable television operator in Britain, obtained a license to offer telephone service over its coaxial distribution system in 1994. British Telcom is preparing to offer video-on-demand over its telephone lines after receiving permission from the Independent Television Commission in September 1993.

Developments are accelerating on the Continent. Belgium is the most cabled nation in Europe with 88 percent of all households plugged into cable television networks in 1993. In West Germany, where cable subscribership reached 33 percent in 1992, the Deutsche Telekom has committed itself to optical fiber. In 1993, it commissioned four contractors to install FITL (fiber-in-the-loop) systems to serve 230,000 businesses and households in thirty seven urban sites in the former East Germany. It expects to serve approximately 1.2 million households by 1995.

THE EXPLOSION AND CONVERGENCE OF COMPETING AND COMPLEMENTARY DELIVERY SYSTEMS AND THE EVOLUTION OF THE NETWORK ECONOMY

The great clash between the cable television and telephone and radio and satellite communication companies which many have been predicting for decades has finally arrived. This battle, which will be fought throughout the remainder of this decade and into the next century, could have an enormous impact not only on the telecommunications and cable television industries, but on almost every other industry as well. Technology is running rampant over the entire information and communications landscape, changing the technological and economic underpinnings of the industry as well as the nature and quality of services delivered, while creating new and different ways to deliver information, communications, and entertainment and retail and financial services to homes and businesses. Competition and technological innovation are accelerating the convergence not only of computers, telecommunications, cable television, and broadcasting but of publishing, banking and financial services as well as retailing and providing new sources of competition for all of them.

At the same time, all networks are becoming increasingly interconnected and integrated with one another, and competition and cooperation are growing on an intramodal and intermodal basis. Optical fibers are competing with the copper distribution systems of the telephone companies and the coaxial cable systems of the cable television companies for bringing broadband services to homes and forcing telephone and cable television companies to compete for the delivery of voice, data, and video to the home. Satellites are competing with each of these for the delivery of television, telephone, and data services. On the other hand, satellites complement these by serving as backup for all terrestrial delivery systems. Wireless cable television and direct broadcast satellites are competing with coaxial cable and optical fibers for delivering broadband services to the home. Satellites are also competing with cellular radio for mobile voice, data, message, and paging services as well as complementing them in underserved areas. Cellular radio systems are competing with wireline systems of telephone companies while complementing them in other respects. Cellular is also competing with and complementing radio-paging services and radio-determination satellite services. What is emerging is a network of heterogeneous networks that compete and complement one another to supply all of the information and communications needs of individuals, homes, and businesses.

This is the nightmare facing governments and regulatory commissions and the growing number of companies in this rapidly growing and changing business in the nineties. The outcome will have a profound effect on the evolution of postindustrial society in the twenty-first century. Convergence and creative destruction are accelerating across all segments of the rapidly expanding information and communications economy, affecting not only the computer, telecommunications, cable television, and broadcasting industries but the information, publishing, banking, securities, and retail, insurance, real estate, and entertainment industries as well. These are all key pieces of a gigantic technological and economic and political jigsaw puzzle that is getting more complicated every year. Everyone will be affected by the outcome.

NOTES

1. First-generation communications satellites operated in the 8/6 gigahertz (GHz) or C-band.

2. David Rees, *Satellite Communications: The First Quarter Century of Service* (New York: John Wiley, 1990).

3. Canada is familiar with the spill-over effects of international communications satellites and their implications for national sovereignty better than any other nation. For an overview of the experience of Canada and European countries, see Heather Hudson, *Communications Satellites: Their Development and Impact* (New York: Free Press, 1990).

4. Digital video compression is an information-processing technique implemented in software that makes it possible to compress television signals by a factor of anywhere from three to eight or ten or more, depending on the content, before the signal is transmitted to the satellite and to decompress it with a special device once it is received in the home.

5. "Wal-Mart: What Makes It So Successful," *Globe and Mail*, 18 January 1994, p. B6.

6. George A. Codding, *The Future of Satellite Communications* (San Francisco: Westview Press, 1990).

7. Under the FCC's new rules, cellular companies are able to apply for licenses outside their existing service areas where they serve less than 10 percent of the population.

8. Work on the Navstar system began in 1978 when ten nations signed a memorandum of understanding pledging cooperation to develop the system for international use. The system became fully operational in 1993 when the last of the twenty-four satellites was put into orbit. Each satellite contains four atomic clocks that broadcast time data and other information identifying itself and describing its path. Receivers on the ground use the information to calculate their location. For more information, refer to "Who Knows Where You Are? The Satellite Knows," *Business Week*, 10 February 1992, pp. 120–121. For a history of Navstar/GPS, see "The Global Positioning System," *IEEE Spectrum*, December 1993, pp. 36–46.

9. For more information on telecommunications and urban development, see William Dutton et al., *Wired Cities: Shaping the Future of Communications* (New York: G. K. Hall, 1987), and "Reinventing New York: Competing in the Next Century's Global Economy" by Hugh O'Neill and Mitchell L. Moss, Urban Research Center, Robert Wagner Graduate School of Public Services, New York University, 1991.

10. Under pressure from the U.S. Court of Appeals, Judge Greene agreed to lift the MFJ restrictions on RBOC entry into information services under certain conditions on July 25, 1991. A federal appeals court subsequently abolished the prohibition altogether in October. See "Court Lets Baby Bells Branch Out," *New York Times*, 8 October 1991, p. D1.

11. But it limited the ownership of video programmers of local exchange carriers to 5 percent and reasserted the prohibition of telephone company ownership of cable television companies in their serving areas.

12. Mark Starowicz, one of the more insightful executives at the Canadian Broadcasting Corporation in Toronto, stated in a speech given in New York in April 1993 that the coming 1,000 channel universe will result in the ''complete reordering of the consumer marketplace, the transformation of retailing and distribution as we know it . . . [and the creation of] a sort of televisual mall . . . [that will] reorder the political world . . . [and make] the political landscape . . . more vulnerable to demagogic and charismatic leaders, . . . [and fiercely challenge] the nation state's capacity to define its agenda.''

Chapter 6 ──────────────────────────────

The Intelligent Infrastructure

The optical fiber and satellite and radio communication networks that carriers and nations around the world are building represent one of several key technoeconomic developments that are contributing to a radical restructuring and transformation of industrial society. Complementing these are the ongoing microchip and computer revolutions and the marriage of computers and telecommunications, in particular, which are having equally dramatic impacts on all sectors of the economy. This marriage or fusion involves the incorporation of information-processing, storage and retrieval and intelligence features into everything from telephone and television sets to office and factory equipment and their integration and interworking with personal computers, engineering workstations, and personal, mobile, communications devices through advanced telephone, cable television, satellite, cellular telephone, and personal communications networks. These are being integrated in varying degrees with on-line data banks and banking, securities trading, and reservations systems. The fusion of all of these hardware devices, systems, and networks together with appropriate operating systems and applications software into an intelligent information and communications infrastructure could be one of the most important developments in the history of civilization.[1]

Most of the leading-edge developments taking place in the telecommunications as well as the computer industries today in fact involve the incorporation of intelligence in one form or another into networks. All of the new custom service offerings that telephone companies now provide are made possible through the intelligence features of the new generations of digital switches which telephone companies began installing in the eighties.[2] Intelligent technology is also critical to such developments as digital video compression, high-definition television, interactive television, video-on-demand, video teleconferencing, and broadband multimedia networks. This incorporation of intelligence into all equipment and all networks in turn is driving the convergence of the computer, telecommunications, cable television, broadcasting, entertainment, banking, and education and entertainment industries. The implication is that intelligent networks have become strategic to all services and all industries now and in the future.

However, the question of whether this intelligence should reside in the networks of the telephone, cable television, or other telecommunications companies or in the networks of third-party suppliers, like information and computer service companies or banking and financial services companies, for example, or in the computer systems, terminal equipment, and networks of private companies has always been, and continues to be, an extremely important and controversial public policy and corporate policy issue. The issue is important to banking and financial and retail services companies as well as those in the publishing, databank, advertising, and broadcasting industries, since they will increasingly rely on intelligent networks in the future to provide services to the public. In fact, the operation and organization of the evolving intelligent economy will depend on where this intelligence resides, what functions and functionalities it performs, and how much access and control users, telephone companies, and third parties exercise over it.

Since all organizations will be incorporating intelligence in their own networks in the future and since these must interwork with one another and with public networks, it is becoming difficult if not impossible to make a clear and consistent distinction between the networks and network functionalities and operations of corporate users, telephone companies, telecommunications carriers, as well as those of information, banking, financial, retail and others, including postal service suppliers.

The distinctions and boundary lines among all these industries have been eroding and evaporating for a decade or more, and they can be expected to further erode and eventually disappear in the next decade and beyond. By then, an entirely new industrial organization and a new institutional structure will have evolved as the result of the interaction of intelligent technology, corporate strategy, and competitive market forces. For all of these reasons, the marriage or convergence of computers and telecommunications is taking on increasing importance to every company and every sector of the economy. But it is particularly important to regulatory and antitrust authorities and, therefore, to governments because of the enormous monopoly power that this control over information, communications, and banking and financial networks and content will allow some companies to gain and wield in the future.

THE INTERNET AS FORERUNNER OF THE ADVANCED INTELLIGENT INFORMATION-COMMUNICATIONS INFRASTRUCTURE OF THE FUTURE

Perhaps the best example of an intelligent network infrastructure and one that could serve as a portent of things to come is the Internet, the name given to the supernet of computer networks which had grown to comprise more than 9,000 interlocking networks, 750,000 host computers, and as many as 20 million users in over 102 countries by the end of 1993.[3] The Internet is already by far the biggest computer network in the world, but the number of users and its traffic volumes are continuing to grow exponentially. In fact, at the 1994 rate of growth of accounts (20 percent per month), the number of users could reach well over one billion by the year 2000 according to forecasters.

The Internet is many things to many people, which probably explains its explosive growth in recent years in terms of the number of networks and users that are accessible through it as well as the growth in the amount and variety of content accessible through it. One of its most popular applications is electronic mail because it permits users in every part of the world to communicate instantaneously with one another. Users can also distribute documents and engage in conferences and meetings. The Internet also allows users to access scientific databases maintained by the U.S. Geological Survey, Department of Energy, and the National Oceanic and Atmospheric Administration. Users can access software databases, interactive entertainment content, and obtain weather information, including digital photographs of weather patterns taken from satellites. They can also access commercial database publishers like DIALOG and Mead Data Central and exchange electronic mail with users on the networks of MCI, AT&T, CompuServe, America Online, and Prodigy. Internet users began adding audio and video content to their networks in 1993 so that millions of users access and retrieve lectures and video clips on demand via their PCs.

The rise of FreeNets represents another example of the potential of intelligent networks or information networks to transform the world. FreeNets are community-based computer networks that are provided free of charge to the residents of the community, hence the use of the word "free." Carriers, computer service suppliers, equipment manufacturers, school boards, and federal, provincial and/ or state, and municipal governments typically provide the funding for these to operate. By 1994, FreeNets were in operation in several dozen locations around the world, mostly in the United States, but in other cities such as Ottawa and Victoria in Canada as well as cities in Finland and Russia. Like the Internet, the FreeNets give residents of a community access to electronic mail and databank information on community events, entertainment, weather, and education content, and engage in discussions, and participate in conferences and provide access to the Internet. It is the likes of the Internet and the FreeNets that could evolve into a new socioeconomic institution in the future.

THE STRATEGIC IMPORTANCE OF INTELLIGENCE IN PUBLIC AND PRIVATE NETWORKS

As described in chapter 4, intelligent technology has played a strategic role in particular in the convergence battle between the telecommunications and computer industries in the past three decades or more. Local telephone companies, long-distance carriers, and equipment manufacturers have been incorporating as much intelligence as possible into their public networks as a matter of strategy to enable them to extend their control over transmission and switching into the evolving markets for network management and enhanced communications services. The computer and office equipment industries, on the other hand, led by IBM, have designed as much intelligence and network functionality as possible into all of their equipment and systems since the early seventies to enable them to protect their markets and supply these same new services.

Each industry has enjoyed certain strategic advantages and each has had a disadvantage in areas where the other has been strong. IBM, for example, has the biggest installed base of computer systems worldwide and dominated the computer business, at least until recently. It also used its proprietary systems network architecture (SNA) and its systems applications architecture (SAA) and other standards to protect this captive market and maximize the flows of revenues from its new products. The telephone companies, on the other hand, have owned and operated by far the biggest captive base of communications equipment in the world. Nothing can match the public telephone network in terms of its sheer size, universal accessibility, complexity, dependability, reliability, simplicity-of-use, and guaranteed profitability. Telephone companies worldwide have also been the most active participants in international standards-making bodies such as the ITU and the International Standards Organization, for example, in establishing an international open system interconnect (OSI) standard that all equipment manufacturers and carriers can adhere to so they can market their products worldwide.

Regulatory and policy-making authorities in most countries have been making every effort to ensure that the telephone network evolves to meet the needs of all users by ensuring that all suppliers of services have unrestricted access to the network. The FCC, for example, has adopted an open network architecture (ONA) philosophy so that all suppliers can interconnect their equipment and supply their services over the public network in the future. It has ordered regional holding companies (RHCs) to unbundle network access elements and offer these to everyone at market prices, thus, all of the RHCs now supply these unbundled features at a price. Governments in Europe and Asia have adopted similar safeguards.

TELEPHONE COMPANIES CREATE THE "INTELLIGENT TELEPHONE INFRASTRUCTURE"

As explained above, telephone companies, have been busy incorporating as much intelligence as possible in their switching and transmission networks so they can provide just about any kind of voice, information, and video service on demand. The fundamental building block of the new telephone network is an expensive piece of equipment called the central office switch, or CO. Its purpose is to perform the all-important function of switching and interconnecting subscriber lines for completing telephone calls. The latest generation of CO systems such as AT&T's AESS and Northern Telecom's Digital multiplex switches (DMS) are essentially digital computers (hence, the concept of digital CO). This means that they are capable of providing all of the functionality of computers, including the capability to process information in the form of digital data and of voice, images, messages, and even video as well, and to store and retrieve and manipulate them according to programmed instructions. CO systems also serve an all-important network control function. Besides switching lines, they assign and dedicate circuits among users, control access to the network and perform functions that ensure network security and reliability and facilitate network monitoring and repair. They are thus capable of achieving much higher levels of network efficiency and performance than their nonintelligent predecessors.

Central office switches are also capable of providing a wide variety of other services including call accounting, billing, and related management information services as well as directory information services that telephone companies can market to their customers. And they can be used to provide automatic call distribution services and automatic answering service for companies in the business of providing travel, credit card, reservations, retail, and telemarketing services. CO systems can also be programmed to automatically forward incoming calls to specific individuals or groups of individuals and eliminate the need for human operators. Other services include electronic voice mail, message, and image communications. Digital switches also provide access to public or private databases, including directory and yellow pages information services, and they can provide access to specialized processors, such as speech recognition and synthesis and voice response systems, for example. AT&T's CONVERSANT Voice Information System, for example, introduced in 1992, recognizes and responds to the human voice. AT&T uses its system to handle long-distance calls, even those collected and billed to third parties, as well as in those involving credit card transactions, checking bank balances, and placing catalogue orders. Other carriers, including Sprint, MCI, British Telecom, and Bell Canada, also make extensive use of speech synthesis and recognition systems.

The real brains and the central nervous system of the new generation of telephone system is a sophisticated control and intelligence system called Signaling System Number 7 (SS7). This is a superfast, super-reliable, high-performance computer processing and communications system superimposed upon, but integrated into, the traditional telephone network for the purpose of efficiently and optimally controlling and managing the entire network and giving it the capability to provide all manner and variety of services in the future. The system is connected to all of the central offices and switching systems in the telephone network by a fast packet-switched network that serves to control and coordinate their operations in an integrated fashion like a giant computer system. This computerized, software-based system is critical to the new telephone and telecommunications systems operating today and in the future. Implementation has not been without its problems, however. A single software glitch in AT&T's SS7 system on January 15, 1990, caused the collapse of the company's nationwide network. It led to a nine-hour service disruption and deprived millions of Americans of telephone service.

The SS7 system functions from a computer database containing relevant information about all of the resources available on the network and all network subscribers, including the services which each has contracted for, together with a log of activities of each and the demands each is making on the network. Its chief purpose is to provide subscribers with the network resources they need to communicate. The information is used to exercise control over the entire telephone network in such a way that each user is supplied with the resources that he or she needs when he or she needs them, with the highest possible level of efficiency, service quality, and timeliness. This new system makes it feasible and attractive to supply many other kinds of services that were previously impossible or too expensive to provide. Telecommunications companies, for example, are using intelligent technology to bring nationwide 800 (toll-free) and 900 (billed on a per-call basis) services to the public along with on-line information and database services including directory services, and they would like to see this network infrastructure evolve in the future to become the universal medium for providing retail transactions and banking and securities services. These and many other kinds of services are made possible through the services of the database query facility and the capability of the system to share intelligence among switches, databases, and intelligent peripherals on the network.

The new telephone systems effectively operate like a gigantic distributed, time-shared, information-processing, and communications system to provide a whole class of custom local access services (CLASS) which can be tailored to meet the needs of the most discriminating telephone subscriber. These services include call forwarding in which an individual can have his or her calls forwarded to another location such as another office or to one's home. Call-back features instruct the telephone system to automatically set up a call at a later time when the line is free. Subscribers are also able to park a call temporarily, redial a number automatically, or set up a conference call by himself or herself. Other functions and capabilities include incoming call identification so that subscribers can see the number of the calling party displayed on a small screen in the telephone set. Call screening and call blocking give subscribers the ability to better control, select, and manage incoming calls. Priority calling and distinctive ringing along with electronic directory services, electronic mail and message services, and voice mail are other features. These are only a few of the new custom local access services being engineered into the new telephone system that are accessed, managed, and serviced automatically by the intelligent technology being incorporated into the telephone system.

Telephone companies have accelerated their efforts to bring these and other services to market because they see this as important to their growth and profit. But they have other more ambitious and strategic reasons for deploying the new intelligent telephone technology as we shall see below. One of these is the provision of integrated services digital networks. Another is software-defined or virtual telecommunications networks services. Intelligence technology is also critical to bringing on-stream the new broadband, multimedia services that will dominate the new telecommunications environment in the late nineties. It also provides the foundation for providing universal, personal, portable numbering so that every person can be accessible anywhere in the world through a unique telephone number.

THE INTEGRATED SERVICE DIGITAL NETWORKS

Telephone companies around the world have also been deploying intelligent technology for the past decade or more to create a new technology platform, called ISDN, the acronym for integrated services digital network. As the name implies, it was conceived by telephone companies as a means of building a universally accessible transport facility capable of supplying the entire range of services from voice and data communications to message, image, and ultimately video services, including teleconferencing, for all businesses and residential subscribers. It thus constitutes a single-vendor strategy. That is, it has been designed as an all-in-one solution to satisfy all the communications needs of most business customers and household subscribers in the future. But ISDN has been slow to catch on due in large part to the fact that it has been primarily technology-driven rather than market-driven by the telephone companies. The momentum to adopt ISDN nevertheless has been developing.

Many governments outside North America view investments in ISDN as an essential element in their future economic growth. In some countries, ISDN is being deployed as a public service offering and an investment in infrastructure. NTT, for example, began providing public ISDN service nationwide in Japan in 1992. Germany is also deploying ISDN as a national infrastructure. In France, ISDN, or Numeris, is the result of a long-term national program that began in the early seventies to modernize the nation's telephone and telecommunications system. France Telecom achieved nationwide ISDN coverage in 1990 together with international linkages with the United States, Belgium, Japan, and Germany. Other countries are accelerating the roll-out of ISDN as a matter of national industrial policy. The republics of Korea and Singapore, which have made telecommunications the centerpiece of their development plans, are pushing ISDN as a means of playing a bigger role in the world economy. Singapore, for example, wants to position itself as a major global telecommunications hub in the Pacific.

ISDN has been slow to develop in the United States where it is being deployed as a corporate network service. It was not until July 15, 1991, for example, that Southwestern Bell, BellSouth, Sprint, and Bell Communications Research succeeded in completing the "nation's first cross-country, all-public network, integrated services digital network call." Some headway is being made in making ISDN available nationally. AT&T, for example, achieved ISDN accessibility nationwide by the end of 1994. Some public utility authorities in the United States are taking a more constructive approach to ISDN. In the winter of 1992, for example, the Massachusetts Department of Public Utilities determined that New England Telephone's ISDN basic service is a "basic, monopoly service." Some are optimistic that ISDN will be deployed as a matter of national priority under the Clinton administration, which has put heavy emphasis on investments in economic infrastructure to propel America's economy into the next century.

PRIVATE NETWORKS CHALLENGE THE PUBLIC NETWORK SERVICES OFFERINGS OF THE COMMON CARRIERS

Some of the stiffest competition to the deployment of intelligent technology by telephone companies and telecommunications carriers began coming from their biggest corporate customers in the late eighties. This was a time when a new generation of PBXs, LANs, and digital multiplexers came onto the market that enabled businesses to create, operate, and manage their own private networks. Many large businesses began relying on this equipment together with leased T1 and T3 facilities for accessing the growing volume of information stored in centralized mainframe computers and for networking personal computers and powerful workstations in applications involving computer-aided design and high-resolution graphics and image communications. Video teleconferencing was also becoming attractive to businesses because it promised to cut the costs of travel. This too demands high-speed digital transmission facilities.

Many large banks, brokerage companies as well as manufacturers and retailers began using PBXs in the eighties as the hub or control center to provide connectivity between in-house voice and data communications networks as well as access to public network facilities and services. Such companies typically leased T1 and T3 facilities from the local telephone company, long-distance carriers like AT&T, Sprint, MCI, or competitive access providers like Teleport Communications to interconnect their PBXs in multiple locations to create companywide networks that they could operate on their own. Some, like General Motors, General Electric, American Express, Boeing Corporation, and Citicorp,

for example, and public utilities, universities, and governments often have sufficiently large volumes of communications traffic that they can even justify
installing one or more central office systems on their premises.[4] Until recently,
these were reserved for telephone companies because they had the traffic volumes to justify them on an economic basis.

The globalization of business was also well under way in the eighties, and
more and more companies, feeling the growing heat of global competition, were
looking for ways of using their growing investments in systems and networks
to cut costs and realize strategic competitive advantages. Private networking
provided them with a means to tie together and integrate their far-flung offices
and their workers, computer systems, and other resources and integrate their
disparate voice, data, video, and image and graphics applications onto a single
facility. It also enabled them to bypass the strict regulations and high tariffs of
many PTT administrations. Private networking become attractive for many businesses for these and other reasons.

For telephone companies and public carriers, however, private networking
meant the loss of some of their biggest revenue and profit-producing customers.
This threat prompted leading telecommunications manufacturers and carriers to
use intelligent technology in yet another strategic fashion to retain and regain
these business customers. One way was with a strategy of incorporating into
their CO systems an almost endless variety of intelligence features and functionality for end users which are called "centrex services." Telephone companies, for example, can provide all of the services to a company that PBXs
provide, and they can also emulate LAN services via the intelligent capabilities
located in the CO switch. They can also provide LAN services, for example,
through a service offering called centrex-LAN, as well as ISDN services,
through centrex-ISDN. Centrex services can, therefore, be used by companies
to design, create, and manage their private networks using public network facilities in such a way that they emulate or simulate all of the functionality of
PBXs and private networks.

VIRTUAL (INTELLIGENT) TELECOMMUNICATIONS NETWORKS

Telecommunications carriers used intelligent technology in yet another strategic manner to create a new special class of telecommunications facilities and
service offerings called software-defined telecommunications networks (SDTNs
or STNs) also known as virtual private telecommunications networks (VPNs or
VTNs). These make strategic use of the capabilities of intelligent central office
systems, tandem switches, SS7 systems, and T1 and T3 digital transmission
systems together with high-speed digital multiplexers to tailor and customize
the carrier's network to meet the distinctive needs of individual corporations.

Generic virtual telecommunications networks derive their strategic advantages
from the information-processing and control features of intelligent network tech-

nology, specifically its ability to emulate and simulate a private network in much the same way as virtual memory is achieved in the computer. These software control features are designed in such a way that it appears as if each organization has a network with unlimited voice, data, and video switching and transmission capabilities dedicated to its own use. Virtual networking capabilities are based on the fact that customer locations, traffic patterns, and routing restrictions and screening functions are all defined in software and can, therefore, be changed dynamically by an operator from a command post on the company's premises or the premises of a carrier or whatever party is providing the service. This enables the telecommunications carrier to separate the way it actually manages and routes traffic over the network from the way their customers perceive and use the network. Intelligent networks give carriers the capability to create a large number of virtual private networks as part of the same shared telecommunications facility so that each of them has all the features of the most advanced, dedicated private network but at a fraction of the cost, since all of the customers share the common costs of building and operating the network.

Carriers have also designed their virtual private network offerings in such a way that user companies can gain access to the control features of the basic switching and transmission facilities so they can design and configure a national or international private-line network as if they owned it. Corporate control can, for example, be exercised either from a corporate premises through the PBX or through the central office. A company can, for example, dynamically reconfigure its virtual private network from its PBX, monitor its operation, and manage and control its own accounting and billing operations. Special software features also enable individual companies to create their own unique numbering plan. VTNs are conducive to very flexible arrangements so they benefit both carriers and their customers. Customers can have the option of using their own equipment and operating staff or those of their supplier. VTNs thus keep large customers on the public network while enabling them to gain the advantages of a private network which they can manage, configure, and control as they like.

All three big interexchange carriers in the United States announced virtual networks services in 1988, and the race was on to sell the new service nationally and internationally. AT&T announced with great fanfare that it had signed up Ford Motor Company, E. I. du Pont, and General Electric to its software-defined network (VTN) service. Ford converted twenty-eight internal data networks and one voice network into a single nationwide integrated digital network with T1 access in all of its locations. General Electric signed a five-year, $300 million contract for an all-digital, intelligent network to integrate all of its voice and data traffic for its 100,000 or more employees at more than 1,000 locations onto AT&T's T1 backbone network. MCI announced that it signed up customers for its Vnet virtual network service offering and U.S. Sprint for its Virtual Private Networking Service.

All three carriers took their virtual telecommunications offerings into the international marketplace and signed up multinational companies like General

Electric, Citicorp, and Merrill Lynch, for example. General Electric announced contracts in the spring of 1989 with AT&T, British Telecom, and France Telecom to build a worldwide private network to provide integrated voice, data, and video communications services to its employees in its offices in the United States, France, the Netherlands, Belgium, West Germany, Switzerland, Italy, Ireland, and Spain. The network was expanded in 1990 to connect to the Far East, Australia, the Middle East, and South America. GE claimed the network enabled it to become more competitive by allowing it to exchange information faster, to make quicker decisions, and reduce the need for overseas travel. Merrill Lynch awarded a five-year, $150 million contract in June 1989 to MCI to link its computers and voice systems with 730 brokerage houses in thirty-three nations. Citicorp announced a $46.5 million contract to AT&T for its Virtual Telecommunications Network Service and a similar $80 million contract with MCI to provide "global voice and data telecommunications services" for its 3,000 locations in ninety-two countries.

Virtual private network technology has been deployed in many other countries, including Canada, France, Germany, Japan, and Singapore, for example. Cable & Wireless completed its "global highway" of cables linking Europe, North America, and the Pacific Rim in May 1991. It advertises that its global virtual private network (GVPN) offers end-to-end voice, data, and image communications services at every region of the world. One of its customers, Esso, began using GVPN to link 139 sites in the United States and the United Kingdom in 1993. Virtual network facilities now constitute a rapidly growing segment of the national and global telecommunications industry. By 1993, over twenty countries were being served. They now provide an essential facility for many large corporations to operate and compete globally.

It is in the corporate environment, however, where much of the demand for high-speed facilities is being generated and where the convergence of computers and communications and the development of intelligent networks are having some of their greatest and most profound impacts. It is here too where many of the really big innovations and some of the most important decisions are being made about how best to design, build, and manage intelligent networks and maximize their economic, organizational, and other competitive advantages. The development of enterprisewide networks in particular represents one of the most important forces that is driving the creation of an intelligent corporate network infrastructure at the present time, and this is complementing the development of public intelligent networks infrastructures.

THE EVOLUTION OF ENTERPRISEWIDE NETWORKS

The corporate computer environment underwent dramatic changes in the late eighties and early nineties as a result of the introduction of new generations of personal computers and office and factory systems based on Intel's 80386 and 80486 and Motorola's 68030 and 68040 microchips. This meant that computer power could be economically distributed wherever it was needed so a need arose to tie personal computers and workstations together with one another and with minicomputers and mainframes so they could communicate and interwork and share resources. It also led to something called "client-server" computing, which involves dedicating computers to specialized functions on the network as well as the development of enterprisewide networks to interconnect all of the computers within a corporation together wherever they were located geographically. The end result is the creation of an intelligent corporate network infrastructure that is transforming the nature of work and management and the culture and structure of corporations everywhere.

A generic local area network (LAN) for a large company is illustrated in Figure 6.1. Its purpose is to connect IBM PCs, Apple Macs, and Sun workstations, for example, with one another so they can communicate and share resources. So one of their most important purposes is to overcome incompatibility between all of these devices. LANs also interconnect these with specialized resources such as high-volume, high-speed, laser printers, mass storage systems, database systems, and document management systems as well as minicomputers and mainframe computers dedicated to computation-intensive modeling and simulation applications such as those used by scientists and engineers. The best known and most widely used LAN is the Ethernet LAN, designed and developed in 1980 by a consortium of vendors including Xerox, DEC, Datapoint, and Intel. IBM's Token Ring LAN and Datapoint's ARCnet are the major competitors of Ethernet. Macintosh computers communicate through Apple's AppleTalk LAN. AT&T's LAN product is called Starlan. LANs now make use of all of the traditional copper and coaxial cable transmission media as well as optical fiber and wireless radio media. Early generations of LANs transmit data in the low megabit ranges. Ethernet LANs, for example, which are based on coaxial cable, communicate at speeds of up to ten Mbps while Token Ring LANs transmit at speeds of between four and sixteen Mbps. But the new LAN products coming onto the market in the mid-nineties are capable of very high megabit speeds.

The standard for optical fiber is called Fiber Distributed Data Interface (FDDI) which operates at a speed of 100 Mbps. Being fiber-based, FDDI-based LANs have all of the special features of optical fiber, including broadband capabilities, noise immunity, low signal degradation, ease of upgrading, light weight, and small size. These features are gaining importance for a growing variety of broadband applications especially communications with or between mainframes or serving as the backbone transmission systems for interconnecting multiple low-speed LANs, for computer-aided design, manufacturing, and engineering (CAD/CAM/CAE) applications in the factory and for radiology and other advanced medical applications in hospitals, medical labs, and doctors' offices, for example. Broadband LANs are also gaining in popularity for applications involving voice and video teleconferencing and multimedia. Both the Token Ring and Ethernet LANs are being upgraded to handle new broadband applications such as these. For example, the new Ethernet standard, called fast-Ethernet, has a speed of 100

Figure 6.1
A LAN/WAN/Enterprisewide Network Environment

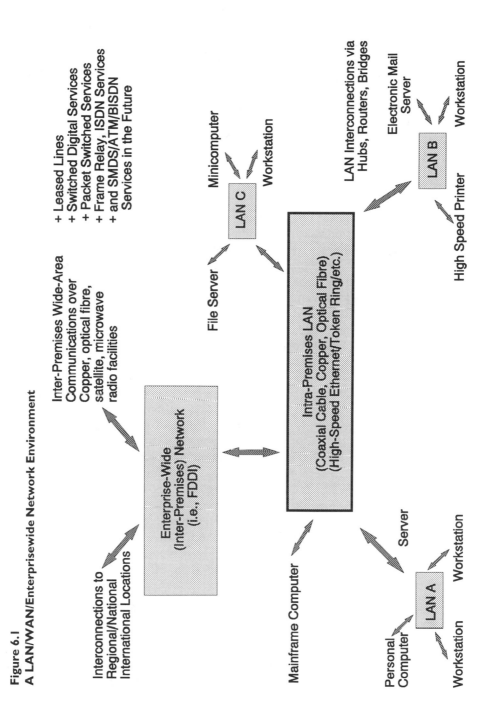

Mbps. IBM is also upgrading its Token Ring LAN to handle broadband multimedia applications. But new technology is also making it possible to deliver optical fiber speeds of 100 Mbps over shielded copper pairs. This so-called CDDI technology (copper distributed data interface) holds considerable promise over FDDI because the transmission media is very inexpensive and does not involve special optoelectronic equipment to convert between electronic and optical signals. Wireless LANs are also gaining in popularity.[5]

LANs can be interconnected with one another in a variety of ways to form wide area networks and enterprisewide networks that enable many hundreds or thousands of users located in a single building or several buildings in the same area or spread throughout a metropolitan area or across the country or across the world to communicate with one another and share information resources. Organizations interconnect LANs on their own premises by hubs, routers, and bridges. Suppliers are building more intelligence and higher performance into these devices to provide them with greater processing, communications, and switching capabilities. LANs communicate with one another over long distances by facilities and services offered by local telephone companies, interexchange carriers, competitive access providers such as Teleport Communications and Metropolitan Fiber Systems, for example, and by value-added network suppliers, such as Telenet. Corporations can interconnect their LANs, for example, by private lines or switched digital services, by packet-switched services, or by integrated service digital network (ISDN) services.

The spread of personal computers and LANs has in effect transformed the corporate computing environment into a distributed information processing, communications, and intelligence system. Intelligence of one kind or another is being built into all devices attached to the network so they can perform specialized tasks and communicate with one another. The network operating system is the central resource for controlling and managing the entire network, all of the resources attached to it and accessible through it and for ensuring that the appropriate processing and communications hardware devices, software and information resources are made available to each and every user on the network when they are required. It thus serves to ensure that the network and all of the resources attached to it are used most efficiently and that users are given the best possible quality of service. The leading network operating system is Novell's NetWare product. Runners-up include Banyan Corporation's Virtual Networking System (VINES), IBM's LAN Server, and Microsoft's LAN Manager.

THE "CLIENT/SERVER" MODEL OF CORPORATE COMPUTING IN THE NINETIES

To an increasing degree, the predominant architecture for computer networking in the nineties incorporates what is called in the technical jargon a ''client-server'' philosophy, as shown in Figure 6.2. This involves delegating responsibilities for specialized tasks such as number crunching, database, and communications, in-

Figure 6.2
A Client-Server Architecture

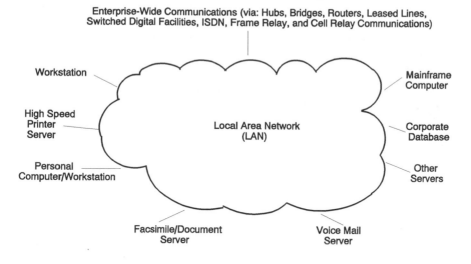

Enterprise-Wide Communications (via: Hubs, Bridges, Routers, Leased Lines, Switched Digital Facilities, ISDN, Frame Relay, and Cell Relay Communications)

Workstation

High Speed
Printer
Server

Personal
Computer/Workstation

Local Area Network
(LAN)

Mainframe
Computer

Corporate
Database

Other
Servers

Facsimile/Document
Server

Voice Mail
Server

cluding electronic mail, for example, to specialized computing devices, called servers, the purpose of which is to service individual PCs and workstations, or "clients." "A client-server environment," according to *Datamation*, "provides standardized services such as data and file management, print services or communications interfaces . . . [over a network] and also runs local applications programs . . . [assigning] to each computing element the tasks for which it is best suited. It also allows users to access programs and data transparently, without having to know where the network resources reside, either physically or logically."[6] When a user, for example, initiates a request for information on a specific topic, a request is automatically sent out over the network and the information returned can be from many databanks. Because of the way they are designed and the way they distribute processing loads, client-server systems significantly cut down on communications traffic, thus contributing overall to a more efficient operational system. Because clients and servers can be added or deleted from the network without disrupting others on the network, modifications are much simpler and easier to make. They are also much less vulnerable to problems arising in any part of the network.

Client-server systems also significantly enhance user productivity by making extensive use of applications program interfaces (APIs). These are software interfaces which allow users to write individual programs to access and use information resources on the network, such as printers, databases, and electronic mail facilities, without having to worry about technical details or program instructions. Appropriate instructions are built into APIs so they are executed when users invoke them in their programs or access them with a click of the mouse.

IBM, Microsoft, Novell, Apple, and almost every other supplier are designing APIs into their operating systems and software programs for this reason.

Client-server systems are important because they offer a much more economical and operationally efficient alternative to the highly centralized mainframe computer environment of the past, and they enable corporations to reduce their extreme dependency on highly centralized mainframe computers and minicomputers. The new LAN-client-server environment of the nineties has extremely powerful resources on the network dedicated to such activities as number crunching, records management, and database intensive applications which, until recently, could only be economically handled by mainframe computers or large minicomputers. According to a growing number of industry observers, these resources will become available on client-server systems in the nineties at a fraction of the price of those achieved from mainframes. Meanwhile, mainframe computer and minicomputer manufacturers have made sure that they are not frozen out of this new information processing environment.

IBM and DEC, for example, have designed all of their new computer product lines to serve the new client-server market of the nineties. IBM's strategic vision is to make its mainframe computers function as mammoth corporate servers or central libraries or repositories for storing and accessing all kinds of information in the form of text, numbers, digitized voice and images, and even video content. Local area networks and client-server systems are thus shaping up to play a strategic role in the evolution of a fully integrated and fully functional corporate resource-sharing information and intelligence infrastructure in the nineties and beyond.

THE SYNERGIES OF NETWORKING AND WORKGROUP TECHNOLOGIES

The networking of computers together with client-server systems is critical for the future because it will allow organizations to realize the economics of resource-sharing and ultimately the strategic and operational synergies that can only be derived from sharing all of the information and intellectual resources of the entire organization. Since enterprisewide networks provide the connectivity necessary to make all corporate units interact, interwork, and share resources, they have the potential of enabling all individuals in the organization to cooperate and collaborate as never before and to operate as a single enterprise unit, unencumbered by distance, time zones or hierarchies, people or politics, and, as importantly, by problems relating to inaccessible information. By enabling everyone in the organization to access and use information and communications systems and software and information resources, by making information resources available to all workers when and where it is required and in the format required and by providing a means for all workers to interact and communicate with one another and cooperate and coordinate their activities, enterprisewide networking is making true resource-sharing possible. In all of these ways, the new LAN-client-server environment is contributing to a more efficient information-processing and decision-making organization and ultimately a more efficient economic system. Properly managed, the new infrastructures are capable of delivering enormous but practical operational synergies and economic benefits. For these reasons, they are strategic to survival, competitiveness, and profitability in the new age.

These synergies and economic benefits are nowhere more evident than in the growing variety of "workgroup" or "groupware" applications which now constitute the leading-edge of computer applications software. Groupware software, for example, permits users to interact with one another in simple but sophisticated ways over the network through electronic mail, gain access to each others' agendas and meeting schedules, set up meetings and engage in group conferences, and query one another's databases in situations involving cooperative and collaborative computing applications such as engineering design, customer services, report writing, and so on. This is resulting in major increases in productivity, and it holds the potential of creating considerable strategic competitive and operational advantages. The first successful groupware product was Lotus Notes introduced in 1991 by Lotus Development Corp. It was in response to its spectacular success that Microsoft introduced Windows for Workgroups in the fall of 1992. It offers peer-to-peer file, printer, and clipboard sharing, E-mail capabilities, group scheduling and chatting functions, and simple network-monitoring tools. Groupware is the focus of many of the new product offerings of Novell and IBM as well. More sophisticated groupware applications involve videoconferencing, collaborative computing, and cooperative document and engineering design applications, which will be discussed in the next chapter.

THE CORPORATE INFORMATION INFRASTRUCTURE OF THE FUTURE

The enterprisewide network will evolve into a more advanced and robust corporate intelligent infrastructure throughout the nineties as the state-of-the-art continually shifts to workgroup and multimedia applications involving the sharing and communications of various mixtures of voice, text, graphs, image, and video content among individuals. Multimedia will increasingly come to dominate office automation applications involving records management as well as document creation, storage, retrieval, and distribution. CD-ROMs with both read and write capabilities will become an increasingly cost-effective storage medium for applications involving the storage and retrieval of electronic business forms, documents, images, and eventually video content. Innovations in multimedia technology will propel developments in electronic records management and workgroup applications such as electronic mail, computer-aided design, video teleconferencing, and database applications. These will drive many kinds of applications in business, government, scientific research and development, and in education, training, medicine, and health care. Special voice messaging, facsimile and document, image and video servers are, therefore, likely to become common in the enterprise networking environment of the future incorporating these developments. Multimedia applications will also create demands for broadband LANs for carrying voice, image, graphics, and video communications traffic.

Some of the products that have resulted from the enormous investments in research into artificial intelligence, such as expert systems, neural networks, chaos theory, and fuzzy logic will undoubtedly become incorporated into many standard business applications, especially in the banking, brokerage, and securities industries, as well as manufacturing, medicine, and health care industries for analyzing complex problems that involve large arrays of data that are not easily processed by traditional methods. Voice and speech recognition and voice synthesis technologies can be expected to enter the mainstream by the end of the decade as well. These will become incorporated into sophisticated multimedia interfaces which will make computers and telecommunications systems more friendly and easier to use. All of these developments will filter their way into public use including the home and the telecommunications marketplace.

IBM, Apple, Microsoft, Intel and other leading suppliers have been developing the hardware and software platforms for the new generation of mass market computers to unleash the power of these applications. Intel led off on March 22, 1993, when it announced that it had begun shipping its pentium chip as successor to the 486 chip. In March 1994, both IBM and Apple introduced the first personal computers based on the new PowerPC chip, the key product of their 1991 alliance with Motorola. This is the first RISC-based chip designed for mass markets. The battle to develop a new software platform is also under way. In July 1993, Microsoft announced its new Windows NT operating system, boasting its pre-emptive multitasking and multithreading capabilities, its portability across various hardware platforms, and its built-in peer-to-peer networking capabilities.[7] IBM has been aggressively promoting its OS/2 operating system in competition with Microsoft's Chicago (Windows 4.0) operating system as the successor to Microsoft's DOS-based Windows system. Apple has also brought a new operating system, System 7.5, to market for its new PowerPC-base line of computers. NeXt Computers has entered into alliances with Sun Microsystems among others to promote its operating system which has built-in multimedia capabilities. IBM, Sun Microsystems Novell, and other leading suppliers of UNIX operating systems announced the formation of a consortium allowing them to work together to standardize on a single UNIX operating system to counter a threat of Windows NT.

This new generation of PCs has multiuser, multitasking, and electronic mail and communications capabilities built in like most workstations which use the UNIX operating system. They are also capable of handling digital signal processing applications and integrate voice, graphics, image, and video communications applications into a single system. And they will also make extensive use of object-oriented programming software which promises to significantly simplify programming and enhance the productivity of programmers.[8] Finally, they will increasingly depend on reliable speech recognition and synthesis capabilities.

Many of the most promising computer applications will require the most advanced features that this new generation of computers and operating systems have to offer. Applications involving multimedia, videoconferencing, and workgroup software together with CAD and medical imaging, for example, will require very high-speed, high-quality telecommunications services, and this, in turn, has accelerated developments in broadband switching and transmission systems. At least four technologies are vying for the multibillion dollar markets that these applications are expected to create in the nineties and beyond. These are frame relay, switched multimegabit digital services (SMDS), asynchronous transfer mode (ATM), and broadband ISDN (BISDN). Frame relay is a more advanced, efficient, high-speed version of the packet-switching technology that came out of the ARPANET in the seventies. Local telephone companies, interexchange, and international carriers have been deploying frame relay facilities for several years because it is a mature and proven technology and because it is inexpensive. SMDS and ATM are what are called in the industry cell-based transport systems. ATM is the high-speed, fiber-based networking protocol that operates by dividing multimedia transmissions into small, fixed-length cells and sending them off to their destination where they are reassembled.[9] SMDS is a competing technology which the Bell Operating Companies have developed on their own to meet the demands of broadband communications applications in the future.

Although none of these are without inherent disadvantages, it is widely believed that ATM will dominate developments in advanced, intelligent, networks in this decade and beyond because it is viewed as having the flexibility to efficiently integrate all existing and future switching and transmission facilities and services. This is of considerable importance in the heterogeneous, internetworking world that is emerging in which circuit-switched and packet-switched networks and ISDN and frame relay networks will have to co-exist with one another in public networks and within the same organization. ATM is expected to provide this internetworking connectivity while providing a smooth migration and transition path to the intelligent broadband network of the future. Developments in ATM as well as enterprisewide networks and optical fiber and copper transmission systems are expected to bring broadband services to the desks of large corporations in the large urban areas possibly by the year 2000.

CREATING THE INTELLIGENT MULTIMEDIA INFRASTRUCTURE

Meanwhile, telephone companies, software developers, cable television, broadcasting, motion picture and entertainment, and publishing companies along with manufacturers of microchip, computer and telecommunications, and consumer electronic equipment have been gearing up to create the public intelligent multimedia network infrastructure of the future. Although the playing field is intensely competitive, all of the major players have become engaged in a variety of strategic alliances and joint ventures as a means of developing the new markets. In the last chapter, we saw how cable television and telephone companies have teamed up to create the broadband network infrastructures to the home. Both cable television and telephone companies have also begun installing ATM equipment in their networks so they can provide multimedia services. A number of computer equipment manufacturers have also designed video servers and have teamed up with cable television and telephone companies to offer a variety of services to the home including home shopping and video on demand. NCube, for example, which is a leading supplier of supercomputers, has turned its expertise into building video servers. Oracle Corporation has developed an interactive media server which uses Ncube's server that is capable of providing CD quality sound and full motion picture quality video. AT&T also has a video server on the market.

Several other consortia are also developing a black box that attaches to the television set that turns it into a two-way multimedia system. AT&T and Silicon Graphics, IBM and Bell Atlantic, as well as Digital Equipment, Intel, and Microsoft are in joint ventures to develop these. Other companies like Zenith Corporation already have home computers on the market with a built-in cable television interface which allows home owners to access databases. Games manufacturers—Nintendo, Sega, Atari, and Commodore along with a company called 3DO which is partly owned by AT&T—are trying to crack the home market with 32-bit and 64-bit game machines. Sony, Toshiba, Panasonic, Philips, and other consumer electronics companies are also in the running.

Leading software developers like Microsoft, Novell, Lotus, and Apple have also forged alliances with telephone companies and equipment manufacturers to have their software products and their standards incorporated into the telephone network and every other kind of device possible in the home, the office, and the factory. This way, they hope to transform the telephone network into a true intelligent information infrastructure through which they can control heating and lighting and other kinds of equipment in the office, the factory, and the home. Microsoft, for example, has developed a suite of software products called "Microsoft-at-Work" which allows telephones, computers, and office equipment to interwork and interact in a seamless environment and access advanced features of Microsoft's products. The company completed agreements in 1993 with over sixty equipment manufacturers and telephone service suppliers to implement its software in their new products.

Novell and Lotus are moving their networking standards into the public network as well. In 1993, Novell signed an agreement with AT&T to implement its Netware standards into AT&T's switches so that computers and telephones can interwork as well. Novell has also redesigned its network operating system to deliver NetWare-based services over the "broadband information highways" that are under development. Its standards will be incorporated into factory machinery, refrigeration and cooking equipment, point-of-sale systems, facsimile machines, copiers, and other office equipment, as well as fast food chains and environment and securities systems. Lotus and AT&T also announced a deal in 1994 to deploy a national Notes Public server network. Apple Computer is also working with manufacturers and telephone companies to have its software architectures incorporated into their products. All of these alliances will result in the creation of new intelligent and interactive architectures of every kind of machine and device, possibly before the decade is out.

Services such as E-mail, voice mail, facsimile, and database access as well as access to the Internet are among the most important targets of many of these joint ventures. Another is multimedia applications including teleconferencing. AT&T became the first manufacturer to debut a personal (analogue) video telephone in January 1992. A growing number of manufacturers, however, have introduced personal video teleconferencing systems based on the Macintosh and PC computer platforms. Intel, IBM, Northern Telecom, and the Bellcore, for example, are among these. One of the first on the market was Northern Telecom's VISIT system, for example, which is capable of delivering a wide range of multimedia applications, including videoconferencing, over both Macintosh and IBM PC computers. It also allows users to share computer screens and computer files and manage voice and facsimile communications. These applications are expected to get a big boost now that the PowerPC-based computers are on the market. Advanced PC-chip designs with digital video and signal processing capabilities could become the central processor of a device that could serve as the entertainment-communications center of the home-of-the-future. Publishers, information service suppliers, and databank service organizations are working with computer service and telephone and cable television companies to provide electronic newspapers via the electronic highways in the years to come.

The product of all of these alliances will likely be the integration of computers, telephones, and television sets to the point that they will become indistinguishable from one another. This may happen by the end of the decade. The telephone and the television set will come to resemble a computer that will take on the functionality of both the telephone and the television set. All will have built-in multimedia capabilities of one kind or another. Also before this decade is out, most home computers will likely be capable of accessing both the cable television and telephone networks, displaying live television transmissions, accessing, retrieving, and playing audio and video productions on demand, as well as performing the usual telephone voice mediation. The culmination of this convergence will be the creation of an advanced, intelligent, multimedia information and communications infrastructure. Although it is not possible at this early stage to describe in detail what this infrastructure will look like, in terms of its specific hardware, software, and network architectures, it is possible to provide a conceptual view of it and what some of its capabilities might be.

CONCEPTUAL VIEW OF THE INTELLIGENT
TELECOMMUNICATIONS INFRASTRUCTURE

The intelligent multimedia telecommunications infrastructure of the future will in all likelihood represent a true convergence and integration of all of the various transmission, switching, and microchip, computer and software technologies, and systems applications and services described above. It will consist of networks of competing and cooperative networks that interconnect and interwork with one another in varying degrees. This infrastructure will comprise satellite networks, telephone networks, cellular networks, broadband wireless networks, personal communications networks, and other kinds of hybrid networks that innovators will dream up. And it will eventually interconnect and extend throughout all parts of society, connecting homes, offices, libraries, educational institutions, medical clinics, banks and financial service companies, retailers, and even government agencies. It will also connect with aircraft in flight, and cars, trucks, and ships at sea, and people on the move wherever they might be. Since all of these network infrastructures will make intensive use of digital computer technology, they will be capable of doing all of the many hundreds and thousands of things that computers can do, from integrated voice, image, and video communications to speech synthesis and voice recognition. That is, they will have true multimedia capabilities built into them.

The intelligent broadband telecommunications infrastructure of tomorrow could offer corporations, households, and individuals anywhere access to an almost unlimited variety of services, including electronic mail and document distribution, home shopping, educational, news, and news analyses services. It could make vast multimedia libraries available to the masses allowing them to access, select, and receive an expanding selection of content extending from high-definition television and full motion pictures to live entertainment programs such as broadcasts from the Metropolitan Opera on demand. Individuals and families could ultimately have the capabilities that large businesses have today to conduct videoconferencing sessions from one location in any nation to any other. The advanced intelligent communications infrastructure could eliminate many of the physical, geographical, and economic barriers for working at home, and it could make working at home productive endeavor that could in turn enhance the competitiveness of nations. These and other applications could, therefore, have dramatic implications for travel, transportation, energy, and the environment, as well as for the whole concept of work and organization and the location of economic activity.

The possibility and potential benefits derived from hundreds and millions of individuals, homes, and businesses interacting throughout the world on a one-to-one, one-to-many, or many-to-many basis opens great opportunities for learning, education, entertainment, cultural exchange, world development, and human understanding. These are just some of the potentials of broadband intelligent multimedia telecommunications technology, and this is why governments perceive investments in advanced telecommunications infrastructures to be crucial to economic growth and competitiveness. For these reasons, they are perceived by industry, futurists, and governments throughout the world to be grand economic enablers that will propel social and economic development well into the next century.

Figure 6.3 illustrates the intelligent, multimedia information and communications infrastructure of the future. This infrastructure will comprise a network of telephone, cable television, optical fiber, radio, satellite and microwave transmission network which interconnect and interwork with one another. It will provide multimedia voice, data, image, and video services, along with electronic mail, document communications and videoconferencing services via combinations of circuit-switched, packet-switched, and ISDN facilities as well as by the more advanced SMDS, ATM, and BISDN facilities. All of the heterogeneous computing, switching and transmission facilities that are being deployed today and will deploy throughout this decade will evolve to constitute the essential infrastructure for every organization and every industry and every sector of the economy.

NOTES

1. For an in-depth analysis of the political economy of intelligent networks, refer to Robin Mansell, *The New Telecommunications: A Political Economy of Network Evolution* (London: Sage Publications, 1993).

2. Bell-Northern Research, the research arm of Northern Telecom, has estimated that as much of 90 percent of its investments in research and development into telephone switches are software related. The company boasts that the software for its DMS switch has more than 19 million lines of code. By comparison, the program needed to launch, operate, and track NASA's space shuttle has 3.6 million lines of code.

3. For a history of Arpanet and Internet, see Jeffrey A. Hart, Robert R. Reed, and François Bar, ''The Building of the Internet,'' *Telecommunications Policy*, November 1992, pp. 666–689.

4. Boeing Corporation, for example, which has been a leader in building and operating its own private network, operates one of the largest private (ISDN) networks in the world. In 1993, its network comprised a backbone of five of AT&T's biggest (#5ESS) central office switches and 95,000 lines, and it linked 160,000 people in the United States, Japan, and Europe.

5. Wireless LANs also made their debut in the corporate communications environment in the early nineties. Motorola announced a wireless LAN (Altair) offering in the fall of 1990. NCR also announced a wireless LAN called WaveLAN. Like all wireless applications, these could have a promising future because they provide users with the mobility that wire-based LANs cannot provide, and they also have economic advantages since they require little or no investment in infrastructure. For these reasons, they could have a big impact on the information processing environment and on organizations in the nineties.

6. ''Where Client/Server Fits'' and ''Defining Client/Server,'' *Datamation*, 15 July 1991, pp. 36–38.

Figure 6.3
The Universal, Intelligent, Multimedia, Communications Infrastructure of the Future

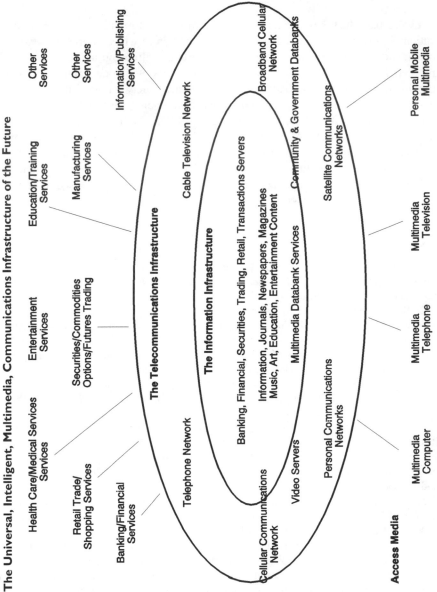

7. Pre-emptive multitasking allocates time slices to each task so that none holds up the others. Thus it is also democratic. Multithreading allows a program to execute different instructions simultaneously making tasks like database searches faster and more efficient.

8. Object-oriented programming makes use of prewritten software programs which are represented on the computer screen in the form of objects. These objects have various attributes so that programmers can simply link them together on the computer screen to accomplish a particular task instead of writing programs. For a description of the principles and pros and cons of object-oriented programming, see *ComputerWorld*, 14 June 1993, pp. 107–118.

9. ATM technology is based on cells which are fifty-three bytes in size. The fixed length makes it possible to mange network traffic so as to guarantee that a given transmission gets through in a time required for the application while the fixed length and small packet size provides flexibility for allocating bandwidth among different devices.

Chapter 7

The Intelligent Economy

Intelligent machines and intelligent infrastructures are spreading throughout all organizations and all sectors of the economy. They are initiating a transformation of industrial society on a scale of the industrial revolution that began over two centuries ago but on a time scale of several decades rather than a century or more. And every industry and every sector is being affected in one way or another. But the transformation of several key sectors, I would argue, is leading to the transformation of the economic system itself. These include the information and communications and banking and financial services sectors, which constitute what I refer to as the "central intelligence" segment or brain of the economy. These sectors are responsible for mediating the production, collection, processing, and communications of information, money, securities, and wealth, as well as the essential transactions, accounting, payment and settlement processing activities which are integral to the operation of the market economy. They thus play a critical control, coordination, and stabilization role in the organization and operation of democracy and economic system. I argue that it is through its effects on this central intelligence and control system that intelligent technology is initiating a transformation of the economic system itself as described in this and subsequent chapters. I will describe the impact of intelligent technology, sector by sector, beginning with its effects on these central control or intelligence sectors.

THE RISE OF THE NEW MEDIA

One of the most visible signs of a new postindustrial age and a portent of things to come is the emergence of the new media technologies that could initiate one of the most powerful social and economic transformations in the history of mankind in just a matter of years. The new media is synonymous with the rise of multimedia computing and communications in the workplace, the classroom, and the home, as well as in theaters and other places of entertainment. The entry of digital, interactive television, high-definition television and of digital photography, computer animation, and, of course, virtual reality into the mainstream of social and economic life is also indicative of the new media revolution. Even the Internet and the electronic superhighways and information infrastructures that companies and nations around the world are building represent integral components of this new media revolution.

The truth is that the new media is all of these. The central common element of all of the new media technologies, however, is the computer, all that it stands for, all that contains it, and all that is contained in it, connected to it, and controlled and mediated by it. The computer is the intelligent engine or brain of all of the new information and communications media devices, whether it be multimedia telephone and television sets, intelligent networks, or the intelligent superhighway itself. In fact, all of the devices and systems now and in the future, which provide the essential interface between machines and people, must qualify as components of the new media. The computer has, in point of fact, become the brain and the essential infrastructure of the new economy, and this is why it is proper to say that it is transforming the industrial and information society of the past into an intelligent, multimedia society.

THE RISE OF ELECTRONIC, MULTIMEDIA PUBLISHING

The core component of the new intelligent economy is the electronic publishing industry of which the oldest and best known segment is the on-line databank industry. The biggest members of this elite club of suppliers include the likes of Reuters, Dow Jones, McGraw-Hill, and Dun & Bradstreet. They depend on their computer-communications infrastructures to produce, collect, distribute, and market enormous volumes of business, economic, financial, demographic, and scientific and technical information electronically to their clients around the world. Companies like CompuServe, Prodigy, and America Online, for example, provide individuals and professionals at the office and at home with access to everything from news reports, weather forecasts, and stock market quotations to travel reservations, shopping, and newspapers.

Figure 7.1 illustrates how multimedia has evolved from developments in data processing, word processing, and electronic publishing and now incorporates developments in computer graphics, computer simulation, computer animation, image processing, digital photography, speech synthesis and recognition, com-

Figure 7.1
The New Multimedia Technologies

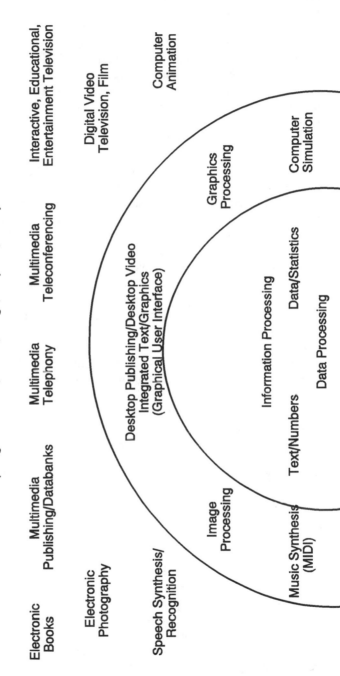

Virtual Reality
(Visualizing, Feeling and Experiencing Artificial Reality in all Dimensions)

Multimedia
(Integrated Voice/Sound/Image/Graphics/Video)

Electronic Books

Multimedia Publishing/Databanks

Multimedia Telephony

Multimedia Teleconferencing

Interactive, Educational, Entertainment Television

Electronic Photography

Speech Synthesis/Recognition

Image Processing

Desktop Publishing/Desktop Video Integrated Text/Graphics (Graphical User Interface)

Graphics Processing

Digital Video Television, Film

Computer Animation

Music Synthesis (MIDI)

Text/Numbers

Information Processing

Data/Statistics

Computer Simulation

Data Processing

puter generated music and synthesized sounds, teleconferencing, artificial intelligence, and virtual reality.

The electronic publishing industry is being expanded and transformed by the entry of the computer industry into the mass market stage of its evolution and the rise of multimedia computers which is contributing to the creation of a multimedia publishing industry. A second factor is the result of developments in technology that are catapulting CD-ROMs (or simply CDs) into becoming a universal medium for the storage and distribution of multimedia content. Electronic publishing has also been given a big boost by the growth and spread of the Internet and the communities of private and public networks attached to it. Developments such as these are creating mass markets for all kinds of personal, professional, and business electronic information, some of which already exist and some of which have yet to be produced.

The electronic publishing industry was hit by what is equivalent to a *tsunami* in 1993. That was the year in which all of these forces came together, and leading publishers took off in search of mass markets for their products and services. For the most part, their strategies involved making as wide a variety of information services as possible available electronically, in the form of text, images, and even video clippings, and using special software to enable users to personalize these services to suit their individual interests and tastes. Some companies have incorporated bulletin board and electronic mail services into their offerings. But because few publishers had the technical know-how or the delivery systems to market this information electronically, most of these involved strategic alliances between newspaper publishers, on-line databank suppliers, cable television companies, and telephone companies.

Cox Enterprises Inc. and Prodigy Services Co. were among the first to announce their intentions. Cox has extensive holdings in cable television, and it owns newspapers in seventeen cities in the United States. Prodigy is one of the biggest mass marketers of on-line services in the United States. In July 1993, the two companies announced a joint venture to market an interactive electronic newspaper service to local publishers. The service included a bulletin board, a database of print stories, expanded coverage of articles, directories, and educational services. Prodigy is also pursuing alliances with other publishers, including Times Mirror of Los Angeles, which owns extensive newspaper holdings and cable television franchises in thirteen states. The regional Bell operating companies have also entered the market in joint ventures with publishers. In June 1993, for example, BellSouth Enterprises and Cox announced plans to form a joint venture to provide electronic information services based on newspapers and classified and yellow-pages advertisements. Special software lets users customize the service for themselves. Three months later, twelve more newspaper companies joined the alliance.

Time Inc., now part of the Time Warner empire, began offering an electronic version of *Time Magazine* in September 1993 via America Online. It allows readers to provide comments and add material via an electronic bulletin board.

In the same month, Dow Jones, one of the largest suppliers of real-time electronic news in the world, introduced a digital version of *The Wall Street Journal*, called TWSJ Personal Edition. In November 1993, the *Washington Post* announced the creation of a new subsidiary, Digital Ink Co., to produce news and information products for distribution by facsimile, computer, and telephone. Its first product, an online version of the *Washington Post*, became available in July 1994. The new company uses the resources of the subsidiaries of the *Washington Post* including *Newsweek* and its broadcasting and cable television and database services. Its products combine text, graphics, photos, moving pictures, music, and sounds and makes them accessible by computers, cable television, portable computers, telephones, and wireless devices. It provides interactive communications services.

Knight-Ridder, Times Mirror, and Hearst Corporation along with IBM and MIT's Media Lab are also involved in an international consortium to develop fully electronic newspapers involving text, audio, and video for delivery directly to homes and offices via ordinary telephone lines, cable television, or cellular or personal wireless communications.[1] Knight-Ridder has designed what it calls an ''electronic newspaper tablet'' which is capable of receiving a newspaper electronically via telephone or by wireless transmission and storing it so that a person can read and browse through it sequentially or randomly like one would a newspaper. The device, which is available in black and white but eventually will be in color, will also be capable of receiving, storing, and playing back audio and video news clippings. Knight-Ridder intends to have a fully electronic multimedia newspaper by the end of 1995. It is easy to see why computers, databanks, electronic publishing systems, electronic newspapers, and telecommunications networks have now become an integral part of the world's new mass information and publishing infrastructure.

MULTIMEDIA CDs, E-BOOKS, PDAs, AND SO ON

One of the biggest promises of the new media and the strongest indication yet of its staying power is the compact disk or CD. The CD has all of the characteristics to make it a mass medium for the storage, distribution, and communications of a wide variety of information content. Its underlying digital technology and its high-capacity storage and random-access capabilities make it the preferred medium for storing and distributing not only text, statistics, and graphs, but integrated voice, images, and video content. CD technology is also interactive so it can be personalized to suit individual tastes and levels of ability, interest, and education. This is why it is on the leading edge of multimedia developments in entertainment, games, education, and training as well as book publishing and video productions.

Executives at Apple Computer felt so strongly about the potential of the CD as a universal publishing medium in 1991 that they decided to call the company's new personal laptop computer the PowerBook. Hewlett-Packard calls its laptop computer the Omnibook, and IBM calls its successful laptop the ThinkPad. Sony introduced a Walkman-like device in 1992 which came equipped with a CD for storing multimedia programs and a screen for displaying its content. According to Dataquest, a firm that monitors the industry, multimedia had become the most rapidly growing segment of the personal computer industry in 1994 with nearly 20 percent of the world's 122 million desktop personal computers being equipped with CD drives.

The CD has also facilitated the creation of a thriving market for what have become known as electronic books or E-books. These carry a wide variety of fancy multimedia content ranging from text, images, pictures, and video-to-voice, music, and natural and artificial sounds. And a growing number of publishers as well as a surprising number of other nonpublishing companies have begun producing content for them. Companies like SoftBooks Corporation of California, for example, are creating an entire line of electronic books. Both IBM and Microsoft have made big commitments to the multimedia publishing industry. One of the biggest hits in 1994 was *Microsoft Bookshelf*, which consists of seven reference works including the *Concise Columbia Encyclopedia* and *Roget's Thesaurus*. Another is *Mammals: A Multimedia Encyclopedia* produced by National Geographic and IBM. Others include *Great Literature*, which contains 1,896 illustrated literary works such as Homer's *Odyssey*, the *Oxford English Dictionary* Second Edition, and *Street Atlas USA*, which contains street maps of the United States.

Most of the big publishers of encyclopedias now produce electronic versions of their products. Compton distributes its *Interactive Encyclopedia* via CD as well as through Prodigy and America Online. Grolier has established a subsidiary called Grolier Electronic Publishing which makes its *Academic America* available via CD as well as via Compuserve and America Online. The thirty-two-volume *Encyclopedia Britannica* is also available on CD as well as via the Internet. *Encyclopedia Britannica* announced on February 8, 1994, that it was creating a new subsidiary called Britannica Online to market its encyclopedia products available electronically to universities and libraries via the Internet. The service uses a hypertext software program called Mosaic to allow users to browse through the database at random.

No discussion of the new media would be complete without reference to the new generation of personal, pen-based computers which have built-in handwriting recognition capabilities in addition to the usual information processing and communications capabilities. These represent the first of a whole new class of personal handheld computer-communications devices which Apple president, John Sculley, referred to in 1992 as personal digital assistants or (PDAs). In addition to serving as personal organizers and appointment schedulers, these also have wireless communications capabilities built in so they can communicate by facsimile, electronic mail, and voice and are capable of accessing stock market prices, airline schedules, and personal computers at home or in the office.

Many believe that these new devices will usher in a new era of "social computing."

PDAs made their debut in 1993 when Apple announced its long-awaited Newton. Since then, all of the big world computer and home electronics manufacturers have brought out their own models. EO Corporation, now a subsidiary of AT&T, introduced a much larger PDA with built-in cellular communications capabilities in the same year as Apple. Its PDA is powered by a special chip designed and produced by AT&T called the "Hobbit," which supports handwriting recognition, information-processing, and wireless communications capabilities. IBM's PDA, called "Simon," combines a cellular phone, facsimile machine, pager, and personal organizer in an eighteen-ounce unit with a retail price of $900 in 1994. It looks like a telephone but is actually a computer. It has its own icon-based, touch screen, and dial pad and is capable of operating as a pen-based note pad, an E-mail device, an appointment scheduler, and calculator. Bell Northern Research, the research arm of Northern Telecom, has designed a device, dubbed "the Orbiter," which looks like the communications device used by Captain Kirk aboard the Starship *Enterprise*. It has the features of a wireless phone, pager, voice mailbox, fax machine, caller identification system, and a post-it notes system.

Here again, most of the major players are cooperating to bring their products to market. One of these partnerships, called General Magic, was founded in 1991 by Apple, Sony, and Motorola. AT&T, Matsushita, and Philips Electronics subsequently joined in 1993. General Magic developed the Telescript programming and communications language and communications protocol that Apple has licensed to other manufacturers. General Magic has also developed an object-oriented operating system called Magic Communications Applications Platform, which it has licensed to Sony, Motorola, and Philips Electronics. Equipment manufacturers, information services suppliers, and software and entertainment companies are incorporating these new standards in their new products and services.

In 1994 IBM, Motorola, and AT&T began rolling out "intelligent" messaging systems to link wireless and wire-based networks, including cellular phones, PDAs, and E-mail networks, together. AT&T's Personal Link service employs the services of an intelligent "agent" that allows users to program it to browse electronic news services to find information. It is also capable of tracking down individuals and delivering a message. IBM's service, called In Touch, which is designed for corporate users, and Motorola's Mobile Networks Integration service have similar features.

As we shall see below, a number of software and hardware manufacturers are also working on another kind of PDA, which uses miniature computers, wireless radio, and geographical information systems as a mass information processing and communications medium for navigation purposes.

COMPUTER ANIMATION AND THE TRANSFORMATION
OF MOTION PICTURES AND TELEVISION

It is in the television, advertising, and motion picture production industries, however, where computer technology is having some of its most visible and lasting impacts. Computer technology has, in fact, created a new subculture of high-tech producers and special effects professionals who do everything on their computer screens. And a growing number of artists, animators, cartoonists, and advertisers as well as television and film producers indeed are turning to the new medium of the computer and special applications involving computer simulation and animation, 3-D computer graphics and hyper-realistic computer imagery, and information visualization together with music and sound synthesis for new sources of inspiration, creativity, and flexibility.

One has to look no further than the television set to witness their effects on commercial advertising. Artists use the latest generation of 3-D graphics software to capture through simulation and animation some of the most subtle facial expressions and movements of the body and to manipulate them in the computer and on the screen with hyper-realistic effects. Computer-generated characters animated on a television screen can move and talk and dance and sing like real people do on television. Animals can be made to have human characteristics, and humans can be made to have animal and surrealistic characteristics. Inanimate things like trees and tables and chairs can take on human-like forms and talk and interact, but in more controlled, creative and dynamic ways than the hand-drawing animation techniques of the past. Any real or unreal entity can be animated in this way using the superrealism of today's computer technology.

Industrial Light and Magic (ILM), a division of Lucas Films Incorporated, is a world leader in using computer technology as a new medium for creating motion pictures. Using one of the most sophisticated computer graphics software packages on the market, from Alias Research in Toronto, and a special graphics computer made by Silicon Graphics in California, the company created the giant water worm in the film, *The Abyss*, for which it received an Academy Award in 1989. Special computer graphics software was also used to create the liquid metal transformation of the cyborg in *Terminator II* (through a technique called "morphing") as well as scenes in the movies *Beauty and Beast, Aladdin*, and *Lawnmower Man*. Computer graphics was crucial to bringing to life the 100-million-year-old brachiosaurus nibbling leaves and the tyrannosaurus rex chasing a Jeep in the 1993 movie hit *Jurassic Park*. Companies like ILM, Alias Research, Softimage, now owned by Microsoft, and Wavefront of California are transforming the film industry and Hollywood in ways such as these. Photo-editing and tape-editing can also be done entirely in software on workstations.

Producers are now looking forward to the day when a single artist will be able to use technology to produce a feature-length film complete with sets and actors none of which really exists or use the facial images of dead actors like Humphrey Bogart to make them act out scenes they never did or could do in real life. Little wonder that special effects masters like Gene Warren, Jr., in charge of some of the most dramatic scenes in *Terminator I* and other big movie hits, believe that computer graphics represents the biggest innovation in television since its beginning.

On other fronts, various consortia of companies around the world are rushing to bring high-definition television (HDTV), digital television, interactive television, and digital audio broadcasting to market in the coming decade. Photography will become increasingly computerized in the nineties as well. Magnetic and optical disks will replace film in still cameras as computers, digital cameras, and electronic displays evolve to become the primary medium for photography. Kodak's photo CD technology, introduced in 1992, which enables print shops to transfer color photos from negatives to CDs, represents the first generation of the new technology. Fully digital still cameras and digital movie cameras are evolving in parallel developments. Computer technology in the form of synthesized music and sounds will come to dominate the music and entertainment industries in the future in the same way that it dominates film and video productions.

VIRTUAL REALITY: SIMULATING REALITY IN SOFTWARE INSIDE A COMPUTER

Of all the innovations that have been made possible by developments in intelligent technology, none is quite so bizarre as well as exciting as "virtual reality" or "artificial reality." Virtual reality or virtual technology (VR or VT), uses the most sophisticated three-dimensional graphics software, computer animation, simulation, and natural and artificial sight and sound together with real people and moving images to simulate reality, texture, action, and interaction in growing degrees of detail and realness. The new technology enables individuals to obtain a dynamic representation, visualization, or virtual facsimile of the real world on a television display screen, together with appropriate audible natural and artificial sounds including music and spoken words, and to interact with this virtual creation visually and manually with the hands through a "data glove," for example, and through sounds and spoken words in such a way that, from the point of view of our senses, it represents and approximates reality with varying degrees of precision. But the application of virtual technology goes far beyond the visual and audio dimensions.

By coupling the human body to the computer by transducers, virtual technology can enable an individual to become part of and to feel what is being simulated with multiple senses, that is, to "experience" virtual reality in multiple dimensions and to interact with the medium and control what is taking place in real or compressed time. In this way, the individual can become an observer or an active participant in the computer animation and simulation exercise.

A growing number of companies in the United States, Japan, and Europe—

many with lucrative grants from their governments—are actively developing virtual technology products and services for what could be a big market in the future. Working in conjunction with VT pioneers such as Palo Alto-based Telepresence Inc., MCA Inc., now a subsidiary of Matsushita of Japan, opened experimental theaters in 1992 in Los Angeles and Tokyo. These theaters were equipped with the most modern VT or "telepresence" technology. In February 1994, Sega Enterprises Inc., of Los Angeles, opened a VT theme park in Osaka, Japan, and plans to have a total of fifty built by 1997. In June 1994, Matsushita announced that it will open virtual reality theaters in Japan, Europe, and the United States. Telepresence along with other VT pioneers has carved out a niche as a "virtual reality integrator" to customize virtual environments for specific business, scientific, and entertainment applications. Another application being designed for Matsushita will allow consumers to browse for products in a "virtual showroom." Still another application allows users to "enter" a database to browse, select, and organize information with his or her hand or body. Complemented by advances in acoustic modeling or virtual acoustics, which is designed to simulate sounds from any direction, virtual technology is setting the stage for the development of applications in architecture, education, and entertainment.

VT also has very important manufacturing and military and aerospace applications. NASA is interested in using VT as a much less expensive, safer, and more rapid means of exploring space. The Virtual Planetary Exploration (VPE) system at NASA Ames is being designed to allow astronauts to explore and conquer the solar system without leaving the comfort of the earth. Using information collected through the eyes and ears of robots located on the surface of a planet and from orbiting satellites, NASA computers will be able to create artificial or virtual facsimiles of the planet's environment. Scientists, students, and ordinary people will be able to make simulated voyages to the planet, take a stroll on its surface, and examine the content of the surface with their hands or explore interesting rock formations and even penetrate the surface of the planet. On other fronts, scientists around the world are involved in a variety of projects aimed at developing virtual laboratories inside their computers to enable them to research and explore, through information visualization techniques, problems in meteorology, weather forecasting, astronomy, and nuclear physics. Artists are exploring its potential as a new medium for creativity and expression.

VT technology is becoming available to the millions of owners of personal computers around the world. IBM announced a virtual reality software package called VR Toolkit in the spring of 1993 that enables professional users, such as engineers, medical doctors, and sales people to develop practical virtual reality applications programs for their workstations. And Autodesk Incorporated, producer of AutoCAD, the most popular engineering drafting program for personal computers, announced the Cyberspace Development Kit in the spring of 1993. It enables engineers to add natural properties such as gravity, friction, and so on to AutoCAD objects and enable engineers to see wheels turning, beams bending and breaking, and fluids flowing over a wing, for example. Using video goggles and a data glove, engineers are now able to manipulate computer-aided designs in 3D. Virtual reality, artificial reality, and virtual technology thus represents the ultimate in man-machine interaction. It is giving new meaning to the word "experience." And it is giving rise to a radically new information and communications medium that could further transform the reality of work, entertainment, education, and learning in the twenty-first century.

THE EVOLVING BANKING AND FINANCIAL SERVICES INFRASTRUCTURE

The banking and financial services sector represents another strategic information processing and communications intensive sector that is also on the leading edge of the business and economic revolution being brought about by intelligent technology. A global intelligent banking and financial services infrastructure is under development to complement the intelligent information and communications infrastructures, and the two are contributing to the creation of a computer-based, global marketplace for the trading and exchange of all manner of wealth, capital, and financial instruments as well as goods and services. Computerization has reduced money to a series of digital electronic or photonic pulses that travel around the world at or near the speed of light over a telephone wire, a satellite channel, or a fiber optic cable.[2] It has increased the capital intensity and economies of scale and scope of banking and financial operations and reduced transactions costs by orders of magnitude. Computerization has reached the point where it is not only economically attractive to automate the entire banking and securities and commodities trading processes around the world but it has also made it an absolute necessity for competitive reasons.

Automated teller machines (ATMs) and retail point-of-sale (POS) terminals are among the most visible signs of the banking and financial services revolution but these are only a part of the enormously huge and hidden national and international electronic money and payments infrastructure that computerization has enabled institutions to create. ATMs typically operate in a network environment and serve as branches of most banks and financial institutions, and they complement and substitute for the traditional branches that are built of timber, mortar, and brick and staffed with people. The variety of services that ATMs are capable of providing is continuing to grow beyond the usual deposit, withdrawal, and bill payment features and now include a wide variety of cash and investment management services.

Computerization has also brought with it a variety of new electronic media which complement and substitute for the medium of paper money, and it is making it possible to create a completely electronic money-mediated society. The new substitutes for paper money include the magnetic strip "credit" card and its much more sophisticated descendants, the so-called "debit card" and "smart card," which are competing with one another. Debit cards permit individuals to instantly and automatically debit their bank accounts when they make a purchase at a retail store through the use of direct communications links between retail outlets and banking institutions. Banks have been aggressively promoting debit card technology to compete against nonbanks and nonfinancial institutions that have used computers and other technologies to enter the banking business and now offer a whole range of financial services through ATM and POS systems as well as credit cards, for example.

The smart card is indicative of what may eventually be in store for everyone. Typically, it resembles a credit card in size but has a microcomputer with memory and display embedded in its design which makes it capable of storing, retrieving, and processing medical, financial, and other kinds of personal information. The smart card announced by AT&T and NCR in late 1992 even has voice-recognition capabilities built in, so it can identify the user of the card by comparing his or her voice with a prerecorded voice print stored in memory. Thus, it has the capability to serve as a security and identification card in addition to a medium for purchasing theater tickets, life insurance, and so on, from a vending machine. Since it can also store and retrieve personal, financial, and medical information, it could also have important medical implications. Smart cards are gaining widespread popularity in Europe and Asia as well as North America. As the electronic mediation of money continues to grow and gain momentum in the future, the debit card and the smart card will probably make both money and checks obsolete in the years to come.

Electronic banking infrastructures have fundamentally changed the way money is managed by financial institutions, corporations, and individuals. Computer-communications networks tie thousands of ATMs together into networks and connect them with bank branches and corporate headquarters and interconnect them with other banks and financial institutions and payment settlement systems around the world. High-speed, high-capacity computer-communications networks such as SWIFT, CHIPS, and FEDWIRE also connect banking and financial institutions around the world with one another and with their central banking authorities. It is through highly secure private computer networks such as these that central banks are able to monitor, control, and stabilize the enormous volumes and flows of global funds on which the health of the global economy now depends. By effectively constituting a gigantic global computerized switching system for all of the uses of money, these sophisticated networks of computers and communications systems permit money to be accessible and used just about anywhere in the world at any time of the day or night. All of the computers and telecommunications systems that are deployed in the banking and financial services sector worldwide now constitute a global financial infrastructure in its own right.

The next logical step in this process is giving the hundreds of millions of individuals throughout the world on-line access to these infrastructures so they can do their banking, make payments, and invest their money and capital anywhere in the world from their home, their car, their office, or on the beach. This is precisely what many banking and financial services companies along with telephone companies, retailers, and on-line service providers are now trying to achieve. When this happens, the technoeconomic process that was initiated by the invention of the transistor and the computer almost five decades ago will be complete but the implications for business and society will be far-reaching.

COMPUTER-BASED GLOBAL EXCHANGE AND TRADING INFRASTRUCTURES

Computerization and the telecommunications revolution are contributing to the transformation of industrial society not only through their effects on information and communications media and money, but on the securities, commodities, and investment industries as well, and the way capital and wealth are created, invested and traded and exchanged around the world. Innovations in technology and the provision of financial services have dramatically lowered transactions costs in the securities, brokerage, investment, and commodities and futures trading economy by orders of magnitude. This includes not only the costs of producing, accessing, processing, and communicating information, but the costs of initiating, executing, and expediting the trading and exchange and payments and settlements processes. Among other things, this has made it economically attractive to invent dozens upon dozens of new "derivative" instruments to trade, such as options and futures contracts, stock index futures, and options on futures contracts, for example, and many more newer and lesser known instruments such as swaps that only highly trained specialists understand. It was instabilities in this evolving global computerized financial infrastructure that triggered the 22.6 percent drop in the New York Stock Exchange in October 26, 1987, which sent shock waves throughout all of the regions of the world and precipitated record declines in London, Tokyo, Paris, Frankfurt, Singapore, Hong Kong, and Sydney.[3] Computerization can also be linked to the phenomena of deregulation, securitization, disintermediation, and globalization which have transformed the banking and financial services sector in recent years.[4]

Computer networks have also made it possible to significantly expand the geographical operations of all exchanges thus making them more universally accessible for people and organizations everywhere. Computerization has also enabled exchanges to expand into many kinds of new services including information services which they have always had but could not economically access, process, package, and market until now.

The basic technological infrastructure is already in place to enable any company, financial institution, or government to interact and invest capital and trade and transact business anywhere in the world—automatically. Databanks of information accessible on-line by global telecommunications networks already provide traders and speculators with the essential raw and processed information from all over the world to make this possible. Sophisticated artificial intelligence software enables them to simulate complex portfolio insurance and arbitrage strategies involving options, futures, and index futures on securities, commodities, and foreign currencies. Traders can access and play computer-based securities, commodity, and currency markets throughout the world using either primary and derivative instruments or both against one another in different markets. Specialists can make trades on public or private networks at any hour of the day or night in any trading zone in the world, simply by posting a "for sale" sign on one of the growing number of electronic bulletin boards that have been set up for this purpose.

Several brokerage companies have even been experimenting with neural networks and pattern-recognition techniques as a way of improving investment strategies. Some researchers claim that these technologies could eventually enable a single company to control and even dictate the level of international currencies.[5]

The forerunner of the stock exchange of the future could be systems like Instinet, owned by Reuters PLC; Quotron, owned by Citicorp; and Globex, the fully automated electronic system, developed by Reuters for the Chicago Mercantile Exchange and the Chicago Board of Trade. Globex was created to enable Chicago to better compete and dominate the market for round-the-clock and round-the-world trading in options and futures contracts. The service came on stream in June 1992, after five years of development. By March 1993, it was giving traders in Chicago, New York, London, and Paris access to the three major world markets for trading leading options and futures contracts from a single computer screen. Reuters is expanding Globex to handle the entire range of financial instruments including bonds and equities.

Fully automated, global trading systems like Globex could eventually inflict serious damage on the traditional exchanges, like the New York Stock Exchange which has continued to maintain its physical trading floors, its floor specialists, and its open-cry trading system, in spite of the loss of trading volume to the more automated exchanges. Many in the industry now recognize that it will be only a matter of perhaps another decade until the automation and globalization of the entire securities industry will result in the demise and ultimate abandonment of the physical trading floors altogether. This has already taken place in London and Toronto.[6] Similar action on the part of other exchanges could result in the creation of a network of local, national, and global computer-based trading systems capable of trading any and every kind of financial instrument, perhaps by the year 2000. This infrastructure will further centralize and decentralize and redistribute economic activity throughout the world, and it will transform paper capitalism and the nation-state into a form of global electronic capitalism.

ELECTRONIC DATA INTERCHANGE AND ELECTRONIC COMMERCE

It is in the automation of the information and transactions processing and communications activities associated with the trading and exchange of goods and services, known as electronic data interchange (EDI) where computers and communications systems also promise to have a lasting economic benefit on the marketplace and on the transformation of the economic system as a whole. EDI refers to the use of the computer (and telecommunications networks) rather than paper as the medium for facilitating the trading and exchange of all goods and services. All of the information associated with the procurement, payment, and delivery of goods and services, including order forms and customs, insurance and transportation forms, and invoices and bills of lading, for example, when prepared on a computer, can be transmitted electronically between companies in seconds over the networks of EDI service suppliers such as IBM, AT&T, General Electric, Arthur Andersen, and Electronic Data Systems. EDI cuts down and eliminates labor-intensive and paper-intensive activities associated with the creation, storage, retrieval, processing, and transportation of paper documents. It also eliminates duplication of effort in the data input and conversion process, cuts down on errors made in keying in data, and speeds up the processing of information, thereby contributing to a much more efficient, timely, and functional order-processing, payment, inventory control, and delivery system.

By making the required information readily available and accessible in electronic form, EDI enables purchasers, suppliers, shippers, insurance companies, and customs offices to access and share a common database of information allowing each to input and manage information relating to its own function. Purchasers and suppliers and transportation companies can instantly monitor the whereabouts of their cargo and reduce the incidence of lost or stolen goods. Shippers can make more effective and efficient use of their fleet through better transport, scheduling, routing, and loading of goods. EDI also improves the efficiency of customs clearance activities, thereby facilitating trade in goods and services across international borders.

EDI is important as well because it complements a variety of other computer- and communications-based services, of which just-in-time (JIT) inventory control systems, pioneered by the Japanese and now in common practice throughout the world, along with electronic funds transfer services (EFTS) and electronic mail and message services (EMMS), are among the most important. These new services are becoming increasingly important to all companies and all industries. Since the mid-eighties, for example, EDI has become a prerequisite to doing business in the automobile industry. General Motors and the Ford Motor Company, for example, decided then that they would not deal with suppliers who do not use EDI, and its adoption has spread throughout the industry. As global competition heats up, time delays become more critical in determining success. Companies are being forced to look to new technology and services such as EDI to improve their productivity as well as provide better service to their customers.

THE NEW MANUFACTURING INFRASTRUCTURE

Manufacturers have a growing array of intelligent production and management systems resources at their disposal to speed up and improve the quality and efficiency of their production processes and even to transform the nature of

enabling them to optimize their operations to achieve maximum profitability, efficiency, timeliness, and customer satisfaction. It also allows them to concentrate most effectively all of the resources of their worldwide production facilities to serve the needs of individual customers which also have worldwide operating units.

To achieve the strategic and operational competitive advantages that EDI, JIT, MRP, and other advanced manufacturing systems have to offer, manufacturers have to design, implement, and use their electronic infrastructures accordingly. Typically, this means making electronic connections with their suppliers using satellite, optical fiber, microwave, and telephone networks so they can coordinate and schedule deliveries and control inventories. Computer and communications networks also connect them forward with their distributors, dealers, and agents enabling them to keep in contact with their customers and the marketplace by the hour and by the minute of every working day. Systems and networks such as these now interconnect hundreds and thousands of manufacturers and service suppliers throughout the world so that when a final sale is made, it triggers a series of orders, messages, and commands that cascade backward through a long chain of command into other suppliers and throughout the entire manufacturing sector. This information cascades further back throughout the resources and services sectors and ultimately back into the manufacturing sector, triggering further economic activity in all of them. In this way, advanced computer and communications infrastructures are facilitating the integration of all manufacturing and related services and resources sectors into one big interdependent world system.

The dream of futurists is to build a fully automated and computerized factory system. This may be just around the corner. Europe, Japan, and the United States have programs in place to develop manufacturing technology for the twenty-first century that will take full and complete advantage of all of the potentials of intelligent technology. In 1990, Japan proposed a ten-year, $16 billion program to pool international resources from industry, university, and government in the major industrialized countries, develop a worldwide standard for future factory automation, and integrate factory technologies from the various countries to create an "intelligent manufacturing system." The United States and Europe have developed their own advanced manufacturing technology programs. America's "twenty-first century manufacturing enterprise strategy," designed by fifteen U.S. executives in the summer of 1991, "envisions nimble car makers that will take an order, then build and deliver custom-made, defect-free cars in only three days."[9] The manufacturing systems in the next century will take maximum advantage of computer-based systems including CAD/CAM, CIM, MRP, JIT, EDI, and satellites and optical fiber networks, as well as other technologies, including virtual reality, to achieve maximum efficiency, flexibility, and customization along with high quality and upgradability in all aspects of the production process.

OVERLAYING AND AUGMENTING THE
TRANSPORTATION INFRASTRUCTURE

It was innovations in transportation technology that precipitated the development of the railway, highway, and airline infrastructures throughout this century and brought the world community closer together, integrating it physically, economically, politically, and culturally. Today, it is advances in computers and telecommunications that are transforming the transportation sector. A global intelligence network is being created to overlay the transportation systems and networks of the world, linking ships and aircraft, trains and trucks with central offices across the continents. Global positioning systems (GPS), radio determination satellite systems, and mobile satellite systems are beginning to link them together and interconnect them with terrestrial radio communications and cellular telephone networks and even telephone networks. These are being linked to computer systems that automatically monitor and control the movement of goods, machinery, equipment, and people. Electronic navigation and landing systems are improving the safety, reliability, and efficiency of the airlines industry. State-of-the-art electronic charting systems also provide ships with digitized maps showing shipping channels, water depths, obstructions, buoys and lights, for example. These maps can be overlaid with information obtained from the ship's radar so the skipper can see at a glance the position of his ship and all others in the vicinity. Alarms automatically warn when a ship enters shallow water or is on a collision course.

Trucking and taxi companies are using digital computer communications technology to enable them to keep in touch by voice, data, facsimile, and even video communications so they can better coordinate their activities and improve customer services. Companies in the courier business depend as much on advanced computer and communications systems as they do their fleet of aircraft to enable them to keep track of every piece of the millions of parcels, letters, and reports they pick up each day for next day delivery. The postal service administrations around the world are also adopting this same technology to enable them to better compete.

Leading international airline and telecommunications companies are investing tens of millions of dollars to create an advanced electronic information and communications infrastructure to enable passengers wherever they are located in the world to communicate via telephone, laptop computer, E-mail, and videoconferencing links with those on the ground. The world's airlines are already served by three computerized reservations systems. The American Airlines' Semi-Automated Research Environment (SABRE) system is used by travel agents in more than sixty-four countries and more than fifty airlines around the world. Its main rivals are Covia, now in a joint venture with several European airlines that operate the Galileo reservations system and Mozart which is operated by another consortium of world airlines. Automated reservations systems have now spread to hotel and motel chains and their capabilities have been expanded to provide a variety of other services, including theater tickets, car rentals, and insurance, for example. All of them together provide the essential information and communications infrastructure to improve the efficiency of the world's airlines, hotel, motel, and entertainment industries.

Automobile companies and federal and state governments in the United States and other countries are just beginning to tap the potential of advanced computer and communications systems to improve the efficiency, safety, and convenience of their highway systems. The Intermodal Surface Transportation Act of 1991 authorized the expenditure of $659 million in federal funds over five years to develop "intelligent vehicular highway systems" (IVHS). The IVHS program envisions a future when all cars will be equipped with computers and video screens and computerized maps of the major highway systems and other navigation aids. Road sensors and cameras along the highways will monitor traffic flow. IVHS systems promise to provide drivers with information on highway and weather conditions and traffic flow and alert them by voice or computer of traffic congestion, traffic accidents, and road pile-ups and advise them of taking alternate trouble-free routes. Automatic toll booths along major highways will enable governments to collect fees without the need for drivers to stop. Systems such as these could significantly reduce highway congestion, cut pollution, and conserve valuable energy resources, while improving the efficiency of the highways systems of major cities and improving driver safety and satisfaction. Governments in Japan, Canada, and the European Community are developing similar programs. All of the big manufacturers are involved in these programs.

THE GEOGRAPHICAL INFORMATION INFRASTRUCTURE

A wide variety of high-tech developments such as those identified above are evolving and converging to create a worldwide electronic navigation infrastructure. A rapidly growing geographical information systems (GIS) industry is already in existence. It caters to the many needs of a wide variety of companies and governments, in addition to the automobile and trucking industries, for example. The GIS industry converts maps and other information into digital form and develops and sells computer hardware and software programs to manipulate the data by users on their computers. Leading companies in the United States, including Intergraph the Environmental Systems Research Institute, McDonald Detwiller, and SHL System house in Canada are active in this new industry. By 1992, the United States had over 100 geographical databases and over 200 software packages to choose from. Industry revenues totalled $3.5 billion in that year.[10] Road Scholar Software of Houston produces a GIS software database called City Streets covering 170 cities in the United States and 80 in Europe. Another company, Wessex Corporation, introduced a package of twenty-two CDs containing digital maps of every street in the United States in 1994. Yet another company, Etak, a database developer owned by Rupert Murdoch's News

Corporation of Australia, is also computerizing the streets in America and Europe.

Manufacturers of automobiles and computer and consumer electronic equipment manufacturing companies are cooperating with software producers to bring these new generations of products to market. Siemens, Apple, and Sony, for example, have been cooperating to develop a portable CD-based MAPMAN device for mass markets. Sony Mobile Electronics, a subsidiary of Sony Corporation, and Etak Inc. announced a computerized navigation system, in February 1994, for tourists and travelling sales people. The system uses global positioning system technology and detailed road maps with street names to display location on a five-inch color computer screen. The information can be used to locate restaurants, parks, shops, nightspots, museums, and so on. General Motors and a company called Zexol introduced a similar system in 1994 and others are expected to follow.

Geographical information systems serve a wide variety of industries. Telephone and gas companies can use it to monitor and maintain their buried infrastructure and make repairs. Governments can use it to better manage urban development projects, land registration records, and emergency vehicle services, as well as water, forests, and wildlife, and other environmental protection uses including pollution control. GIS can also be of considerable benefit to police and law enforcement agencies and companies can use it for determining the best location for a new restaurant or a retail outlet, for example. Industry and governments have just begun to realize the potential of this new medium.

THE INTELLIGENT INFRASTRUCTURE EXTENDS INTO SPACE

The world's electronic intelligence infrastructure now extends into outer space where earth observation satellites (EOS), orbiting high above the earth's surface, constantly monitor the earth's resources. EOS satellites are designed to pick up radio frequencies emitted from the earth's surface. These signals are then processed and converted into geological maps which can be used to identify water, mineral, and oil and gas deposits below the surface of the earth. Or they can be used to track the movement of icebergs, identify the outbreak and spread of forest fires, spot crop disease, and monitor pollution in the oceans, the air, and on land or the health of agricultural crops. EOS satellites also have very important meteorological applications. They are used, for example, to monitor the temperature of the atmosphere, track the movement of storms and hurricanes, and provide top-side photographs of weather formations for display on television in homes around the world. A growing number of organizations now sell satellite images around the world. These include the EOSAT Corporation, now owned by General Electric and Hughes Communications (now owned by General Motors) through its Landsat satellites[11] and Satellite Pour L'Observation de la Terre

(SPOT), owned by a consortium of French, Swedish, and Belgium governments, as well as its subsidiary Spot Images Corporation (Sicorp).

There appears to no limit to the use of satellite images by businesses, governments, or even individuals. In 1991, for example, EOSAT advertised in leading business magazines including *Business Week* that its satellite images can be used to detect underground water sources and hidden geological faults and identify temperature, moisture, density, and texture patterns. "Insurance companies use our data to verify damage claims after floods and other disasters," the advertisement read. "Retailers use it to track population trends in order to locate more customers. Our data helps investors make crop yield predictions for use in market forecasts. It even enables real estate developers to complete environmental impact studies."

A growing number of countries are involved in the EOS satellites business. The Soviet Union operates the V/O Soyuzkarta and India the IRS-1 earth observation satellites. Japan operates the Marine Observation Satellite (MOS) and the JERS earth resource satellite. ESA operates the ERS-1 earth resources satellite. Canada's Radarsat, the country's first earth observation satellite, uses a new technology called synthetic aperture radar (SAR) to produce the highest resolution images of the earth's surface ever made, regardless of weather or darkness. When operational in 1995, it will support mineral exploration, environmental monitoring, and crop disease and prediction and produce what developers promise will be the first 3-D surface model of the entire globe.

Satellites such as these are now strategic to the world's information gathering and dissemination networks as well as its economic, political, and military intelligence gathering activities. The French SPOT 1 observation satellite, for example, entered service only days before the Chernobyl catastrophe took place on April 26, 1986. France's Centre national d'études spatiales (CNES) was fortunate that the satellite was in a position to enable it to obtain an image of the burning reactor within hours. The Landsat 5 satellite also picked up the pictures which were relayed to journalists. Both incidences demonstrated that "commercial 'spy' satellites" have become strategic in the new age of "space-based journalism."[12] The U.S. National Environmental Satellite, Data and Information Service (NESDIS), a branch of the National Oceanic and Atmospheric Administration (NOAA), gathers, processes and disseminates data to a wide variety of users ranging from universities to television stations. Satellite signals are processed by NESDIS's computers to produce digital images which were used by allied forces during the Persian Gulf War, for example.

A satellite communications system called SARSAT (Search and Rescue Satellite) is being integrated into the world search-and-rescue system. Still another called NAVISAT forms an important part of the new infrastructure for global marine navigation systems as well as for ship-to-shore communications. Other satellite communications systems have become vital to our military and peace-keeping operations. Hundreds of military satellite systems are now a part of a global early warning system.

THE NEW GLOBAL MILITARY DEFENSE INTELLIGENCE INFRASTRUCTURE

The world witnessed the startling impact of the new intelligent technology on military defense on television during Operation Desert Storm in the winter of 1991, demonstrating beyond any reasonable doubt how dramatically technology has transformed all aspects of the art and science of military warfare, from its weapons systems and its systems for battlefield management to its command, control, and communications systems. Indeed, in the last decade or more, we have witnessed one of the most remarkable transformations in military warfare in history. The new military defense and weapons systems are truly artificially intelligent by the standards of the past. Computers and communications systems dominate every aspect of the new battlefield management environment. They are essential components of the new tanks, bombers, cruise missiles, stealth bombers, and helicopter gun-ships. Stealth bombers, for example, are able to navigate their way into the war theater undetected by conventional radar systems and consequently do not need the support of the dozens of protective aircraft that are usually required. This translates into vastly improved efficiency and cost-effectiveness of military expenditures. Computers and telecommunications networks are also critical elements in battlefield simulation and management systems and in navigation systems. Computerized Airborne Warning and Central Systems (AWACS), for example, and global satellite positioning systems such as those used during Operation Desert Storm provide the essential means of navigation and coordinating much of the activity.

Military technologists and leading companies in the defense industry are now working to create a totally electronic and intelligent military battlefield system to monitor and manage the entire world. Air, sea, and ground surveillance, defense and combat systems will become completely integrated and coordinated with one another in the future. Supersmart military surveillance, communications, and control systems will be capable of automatically identifying likely targets for destruction, then coordinating the launching and guidance of hundreds and thousands of smart weapons from the sea, air, and ground into the battle theater all with minimum human intervention. The only role that airmen, soldiers, navy crewmen, and military officers will play in the electronic battlefield of the future will be as observers and technical experts stationed in front of their computer screens in hidden, protected bunkers in locations far removed from the real battle field and the real action.

EDUCATION, MEDICINE, AND HEALTH CARE APPLICATIONS

High-technology in the form of computers, telecommunications networks, and databanks as well as imaging and automatic diagnostic systems, multimedia applications, expert systems, artificial intelligence, and CD-ROMs are gaining importance in all aspects of the education and training systems in both formal and informal educational institutions, training centers as well as in medicine and health care. The potential benefits of information technology are so significant that the Clinton administration has made the application of information technology the central focus of its efforts to cut costs and improve the efficiency and effectiveness of America's education and health care delivery system. Educational television, tele-education, distance learning, and computer-based education, training, and instruction can provide a means of augmenting and extending the traditional classroom, and all are becoming integrated into a new technology-intensive education environment. The multimedia capabilities of computers, however, could prove to be the most attractive to educational institutions in the future since it could go a long way in assisting students and adults at home, on the job, or in the classroom, better prepare themselves for the demanding work environment in the future.

Computers have already become a very powerful educational tool and medium capable of assisting both students and teachers not only in such fields as mathematics, biology, chemistry, and physics, but in geography, history, and even art. Students can hone their mathematics and science skills on their own at home or in the classroom, gain greater insight into scientific principles, and test their knowledge of history and geography, for example. They can design experiments in hypothetical chemical, physical, biological, or sociological environments and test scientific hypotheses and principles, engage in simulated business decision-making problems, and solve problems through numerical and statistical analysis. Students and faculty can perform research from a computer, or in a computer, and communicate with one another and access, share, store and retrieve software and information content. State and federal governments in the United States, Canada, Japan, and Europe are developing computer networks to share the educational resources of the schools, libraries, and colleges and universities throughout the nation and throughout the world. In Canada, for example, over 2,500 schools are linked into a national SchoolNet.

Computers and telecommunications networks along with cybernetic control devices and expert systems and artificial intelligence, it seems, are also invading all aspects of the art and science of the practice of medicine and the delivery of health care. Over the past decade or more, a proliferation of new computer-based EEG and ECG equipment along with computer axial tomography (CAT) and magnetic resonance imaging (MRI) scanners, for example, have come into widespread use, which are capable of producing two- and three-dimensional images of the body. These can be used to identify and diagnose medical problems without the need for expensive exploratory surgery. As these technologies improve in the future, costs are expected to decline and analytical techniques more refined until eventually advanced medical devices could become available to the masses.

One of the most promising new health care applications is called the electronic patient records system (EPRS) which is either in operation or under development in some big clinics like the Mayo Clinic and the Harvard Community Health Plan. Even though the basic principles have been around for several decades, EPRS systems are just now getting the attention they deserve. An automated patient records system makes use of a communications network to link highly distributed personal computers and workstations in doctors' offices, medical clinics, hospitals, medical laboratories, and pharmacies into a local or regional database so all can share the records of each patient. According to an article in the *New York Times*, a nationwide electronic patient records system could cut between $40 and $80 billion off the health care budget of the United States while improving the quality of health care at the same time.[13] They could be used on a mass scale to monitor and evaluate the effectiveness of drug treatment, for example, eliminate unnecessary exams and surgery, cut down on paper, and improve accounting and billing. Such a network could also be used to provide physicians with information on new drugs, new diagnostic procedures as well as the results of new medical research and developments. In conjunction with advancements in expert systems, for example, computers could also be used to improve the quality and speed of diagnostic procedures and make preventive medicine more cost-effective.

Improved telecommunications infrastructures could go a long way to improving the quality of medical services in small communities and rural and remote areas which could not otherwise afford such high-cost services. Memorial University in Newfoundland, for example, now provides via telephone a variety of electronic health care, and training and diagnostic testing services to the Caribbean and East Africa. Telemedicine, telehealth and teleconferencing systems along with computer-based information systems such as these promise to improve and extend the quality of medical and health care services in every nation and throughout the world.

UNIVERSAL APPLICATIONS TO ALL ACTIVITIES AND IN ALL SECTORS

Intelligent technology also has applications in the public sector as well as agriculture and resource sectors. In addition to their applications to weather forecasting and the remote sensing of the environment, computers along with satellites have become important to the exploration of oil, gas, and mineral reserves, for forecasting earthquakes and hurricanes, and spotting crop diseases and forest fires. In the petroleum industry, geologists use powerful computers to combine the data from seismic surveys to build three-dimensional models of oil reservoirs which they then use to analyze and identify the most probable locations to drill. In the mining industry, huge underground robotic machines controlled by operators at remote locations near the site do all of the work miners used to do but through cameras and cybernetic controls. Computers are becoming increasingly common on the farm where they are used to access databases and retrieve information on subjects such as the market prices and availability of livestock, grains, feed, seeds, and fertilizer, and receive tips on the latest in crop and livestock management, the application of new chemicals and fertilizers, in addition to the all-important weather forecasts. More advanced applications involving the automated feeding and cleaning of livestock are also becoming common.

Many government agencies are fully automating their operations and do away with paper altogether. The Internal Revenue Service in the United States, for example, expects to process all tax returns electronically by the end of the decade and use handwriting-recognition technology to prevent fraud. On another front, an automated electronic filing and retrieval system, called EDGAR, the acronym for Electronic Data Gathering and Retrieval system, developed by the Securities and Exchange Commission, allows tens of thousands of corporations in America to submit their financial reports electronically and the SEC to access these reports electronically. Computers are also being used to streamline customs and immigration operations. In October 1992, the U.S. Small Business Administration (SBA) turned on a national electronic bulletin board service, called SBA On-Line, which allows small businesses to query its databases and download information about the SBA's loan programs, financial management, and government procurement services, as well as publications and training services and a calendar of events. The Business Computer Network (BCNet), established by the European Commission in 1988, now provides tens of thousands of small- and medium-size businesses in thirty-five countries with access to a business matching service.

Eager to exploit any potential means of generating additional revenues, many governments have begun taking advantage of the commercial value of their enormous databanks of economic, demographic, and land registry information, either by selling this information outright or by privatizing it. Automated land registry systems, for example, are under development in many countries. These systems contain a wide variety of sensitive and commercially valuable information on the ownership and value of private properties as well as maps of the properties and surrounding districts.

Libraries are another area where computerization and automation are taking over. Public, private, and university libraries are banding together to make their holdings accessible on-line so people in distant locations can browse in search of specific publications and make interlibrary loans. And some are looking forward to the day when they will be able to access not only the holdings of libraries around the world but all of the big databanks of information throughout the world on-line. Computers and communications systems have also become essential to the efficient operation of the criminal justice system and to organizations responsible for national security. Police and law enforcement agencies maintain enormous databanks of information on criminals and even ordinary citizens. These databanks can contain personal information on everything from medical records, photographs, and fingerprints to traffic violations and criminal convictions. Databanks of information, communications networks, sophisticated software, and artificial intelligence are among the most important means by which Interpol, the Federal Bureau of Investigation, and other national and international police, security, and law enforcement agencies, communicate and coordinate their operations, share information, and improve the efficiency and effectiveness of their operations. Countries around the world are also cooperating to create a computerized information exchange to make it easier to trace runaway or abducted children. Law enforcement agencies and customs officials at airports and border crossings are being issued portable computers so they can access this information and photographs of missing children at the press of a button.

Many governments are actively preparing for the day in the not-too-distant future when they will be able to offer many of their services electronically to their citizens. President Bill Clinton and Vice President Gore have announced their intention to use information technology to revitalize and re-engineer the public service and create a more customer-driven form of government. The federal government in Canada announced plans, in April 1994, to build an electronic information highway to provide every Canadian with access to one-stop shopping for all government information services.

This brief survey serves to demonstrate that computers, telecommunications networks, software resources, and intelligent infrastructures have already become the critical underpinnings of the evolving postindustrial economy. It provides undisputable evidence that a full-blown technological revolution and a social and economic transformation is upon us. Every industry and every sector of the economy and every kind of economic activity is undergoing the same transformation, and most of these can be linked to the revolution in intelligent technology and knowledge revolution which it has initiated. The nature of work and management and the structure and operations of corporate organizations are undergoing dramatic changes as well.

In the next chapter, I will briefly describe how leading companies are using technology to break down the operational, geographical, legal, and other barriers that separate organizations, industries, markets, and economic systems, and are contributing to the globalization of everything.

NOTES

1. For a description of the possibilities and potentials of the new multimedia technologies in the future, see Stuart Brand, *The Media Lab: Inventing the Future* (New York: Viking Penguin, 1987).

2. For a preview of the implications of this new global electronic financial system for economic policy and world stability, see Joel Kurtzman, *The Death of Money* (New York: Simon and Schuster, 1993).

3. For an analysis and description of the Great Crash of 1987, refer to *Report of the Presidential Task Force on Market Mechanisms* (Washington, D.C.: U.S. Government Printing Office, 1988).

4. For an explanation of these phenomena, see Maurice Estabrooks, *Programmed Capitalism: A Computer Mediated Global Society* (Armonk: M. E. Sharpe, Inc., 1988).

5. "Can a Computer Beat the Market," *Globe and Mail Report on Business*, 2 January 1993, p. B1.

6. London abandoned the physical trading floor in the aftermath of the "Big Bang" in 1986, when the British government deregulated its entire financial services sector on the premise that this would enable it to become the world's premier financial center. According to Pierce Bunting, President of the Toronto Stock Exchange, the TSE's new electronic trading system will reduce costs, increase productivity, "contribute to the liquidity of the exchange," and enable the exchange "to compete in the global securities industry."

7. See "Keyboard Replaces Wood and Clay," *Globe and Mail Report on Business*, 22 January 1992, p. B4.

8. "How to Bolster the Bottom Line," Special Issue entitled "Making High Tech Work for You," *Fortune*, Autumn 1993, pp. 15–17.

9. Otis Port and John Carey, "This Is What the U.S. Must Do to Stay Competitive," *Business Week*, 16 December 1991, p. 92.

10. "The Delight of Digital Maps," *Economist*, 21 November 1992, p. 69.

11. The Landsat Privatization Act of 1984 brought the satellites under private ownership and control.

12. See Peter D. Zimmerman, "Civil Remote Sensing: New Technologies and National Security Policy," in Paula R. Newberg (Ed.), *New Directions in Telecommunications Policy* (Durham: Duke University Press, 1989), p. 101.

13. "New Momentum for Electronic Patient Records," *New York Times*, 2 May 1993, p. F8.

Chapter 8

Restructuring, Transforming, and Globalizing Organizations, Markets, and Economic Systems

I argued in chapter 1 that the structure, organization, and operation of economic society is to a large extent determined by its knowledge foundations and technology underpinnings as much as it is by its culture and economic and political philosophies and institutions, and that all are interrelated with each interacting with one another directly and indirectly in a variety of complex ways. I maintain that a matrix of forces exists that links the scientific, technological, and knowledge foundations of society, the systems and infrastructures that facilitate its basic information processing, communications and production and distribution activities, the structure, organization, and operation of business enterprises, the market system and the economy itself, as well as the nature and distribution of decision making and power and control in society. All constitute integral components of a single interdependent system so that major changes in any one or combination of these can initiate a chain reaction which works its way up through the various hierarchical structures of business organizations and throughout the economy as a whole until it ultimately transforms society in its entirety. This chapter will explore the effects of the current technological revolution on organizations, markets, and economic systems.

NEW TECHNOLOGY AND CORPORATE INFRASTRUCTURES AND THE NEW BUSINESS ORGANIZATION

Some of the most immediate impacts of intelligent technology are organizational in nature. The spread of personal computers, workstations, and mainframe computers linked together by local area and enterprisewide networks and all of the various corporate databanks, databases, electronic filing systems, and specialized servers connected to them together with all of the private and public telephone and telecommunications facilities that businesses now use, has evolved to the point that these now constitute a new corporate infrastructure in its own right. But it is an intelligent, information, communications and coordination and decision-making infrastructure in contrast to the passive, paper-based, manual, and electromechanical infrastructures of the past. This makes it possible to create new kinds of organizations and a new kind of economic system that, in many respects, are defined by technology and the architectures and the functionalities that it permits. It is, therefore, important that corporations exercise strategic judgments in designing and creating their electronic infrastructure to ensure that its capabilities match the organization's operational needs, the needs of its employees and customers, as well as its strategic, long-term goals and objectives. Intelligent technology is, in effect, leading to a radical operational and organizational transformation of the corporation.

The evolving corporate information and communications infrastructure enables organizations and the people, systems, processes, and activities within them to interact, communicate, and transact their affairs in more diverse ways and with greater accuracy, efficiency, and concentration than ever before, and it permits information flows and communications to take place in more of a horizontal rather than vertical manner. It, therefore, provides managers with an effective means to distribute information, information processing and decision making, and control in different ways than in the past and to redesign and reorganize their operations in new ways to create and enhance competitive advantage. It can be used, for example, to re-engineer more efficient and flexible work flows as well as design, production, and distribution and information and communications processes and organizational forms so that activities can take place in a collaborative and parallel rather than a sequential fashion, and product designers, engineers, marketers, and blue-collar and white-collar workers from various parts of the organization can cooperate in free association with one another. Authority and responsibility can be significantly delegated downward so that levels of management and layers of control and planning can be eliminated. The organizational structure as a consequence can be significantly flattened.

Intelligent infrastructures thus enable organizations to achieve a much greater degree of coordination and control over their operations. They can provide businesses with much greater freedom and flexibility and, therefore, scope of choice in how they organize themselves and undertake their design, development, production, distribution, and marketing and sales activities and where to locate these activities throughout the nation and the world to take strategic advantage of economic opportunities wherever they might be. Intelligent technology also provides organizations with the means to gain new sources of competitive advantage through economies of scale and scope, for example, and through the strategic management of people, customers, customer services, as well as information, time, geography, and financial and other resources. Organizations can use their intelligent infrastructures and workgroup technologies, for example, to pool their knowledge, experience, talent, and other resources and tap the necessary expertise immediately when the need arises, wherever it happens to be located. Intelligent corporate infrastructures thus introduce a new dynamic that allows organizations to collaborate and cooperate and focus on problems and solutions and customers and services as required.

On the one hand, intelligent technology provides workers with greater freedom and autonomy. On the other hand, it forces them to rely on one another in different ways, in different degrees, and in different intensities than before. It provides corporations with much greater freedom and flexibility in how they organize and structure their activities and operations, but, it binds them to new structures and organizational forms that are just emerging. Intelligent technology enables corporations to design intelligent infrastructures to achieve strategic competitive advantage, but only in the short term. If they are successful, the innovations will be copied by others, in which case they cease to be a source of strategic competitive advantage. Companies must then seek new and more effective sources of strategic competitive advantage to sustain them and the cycle begins over again.

Intelligent technology can be a tremendous productivity booster in ways such as those described above and in previous chapters. It can also be used as a means of enhancing creativity and innovation, especially through the use of workgroup technologies. And, by cutting down on inventory requirements and contributing to increased flexibility and customer responsiveness, it can be a strategic ingredient to "time-based competition."[1] It can also be used to cut down on and, in some cases totally eliminate, materials, energy, and paper in certain stages of production processes. Organizations can also use the technology together with appropriate innovations in management and human resource practices to change the economics of production, for example, by reducing the marginal costs of doing business and to diminish the significance of economies of scale in the production process. But corporations can also use the technology to increase the economies of scale[2] and scope in their operations and to internalize market transactions and expand into other geographical product and service markets.

The result is the emergence of new kinds of organizations in which most of their design, development, production, distribution, marketing, and sales activities are mediated by computer-based information and communications networks, software, and intellectual content. This new postindustrial corporation has been given many names. In an earlier publication, I referred to it as a "computer-mediated corporation." Brian Quinn called the postindustrial corporation an "intelligent corporation" in his book of the same title. William Davidow and Michael Malone called it a "virtual corporation" in their book of the same name. It has also been referred to as a "network-based corporation." Whatever we choose to call it, the new corporation is a much more flexibly organized and flexibly operated, knowledge-based, learning, cooperative, and collaborative entity. It is an organization in which intelligent infrastructures form the foundation of its operational structures. These infrastructures in turn enable companies to gain synergies and strategic competitive advantages from the joint operation, management, and interaction among diverse units within the same organization and with other organizations—sometimes competitors—independently of time and global geography.

Network-based, information-processing, and communications technologies and infrastructures, for example, enable suppliers and buyers and customers to realize important synergies and competitive advantages by coordinating their activities and their actions in an on-line, interactive fashion. Banking, insurance, securities, commodities and foreign exchange, options, and futures trading companies are purely information processing and network-based entities at heart like publishing, and this means that they too will eventually become completely mediated by the intelligent infrastructures under development today. To capture the synergies and competitive advantages and other benefits that they can provide, however, organizations are having to enter into new, strategic short-term and long-term contractual and electronic network relationships of various kinds. Clusters of suppliers, buyers, and wholesale and retail service organizations are being formed in the manufacturing and services sectors, with a growing variety of electronic linkages that connect them forward and backward with one another. Similar networks are spreading through the financial services sector. Network-based organizations derive their strengths and stability from their ability to interwork with one another in an on-line, interactive fashion. Even the marketplace and the economy are becoming mediated in the same way, and a network-based marketplace and a network-based economy are evolving as a result.

Intelligent technology is thus blurring and eroding the boundaries of the corporation and radically changing the meaning and definition of the firm. It is making it difficult and sometimes impossible to distinguish where the boundaries of one firm, one industry, or one sector of the economy or one national economy, for that matter, ends and that of another begins.

In addition to the delayering of corporate hierarchies and the adoption of flatter organizational structures, intelligent technology has also facilitated the decentralization of production activity and the delegation of decision making down into the corporate hierarchy and out into the field, factory, and customer levels. The rise of intelligent corporate infrastructures has also facilitated the creation a new economics of location by enabling corporations to locate plants, warehouses, and offices in strategic national and global centers without paying the usual economic and other penalties associated with coordination over time and long distances. In some cases, strategic advantage can even be achieved by colocating a plant on the premises of a customer (or supplier) and even integrating the operations of suppliers and customers to the point that they become indistinguishable from one another from an operational point of view. The intensive use and application of intelligent, multifunctional networks is also facilitating the rationalization of organizational activity at the firm, the national, and the global levels.

The intelligent infrastructure is multiplying the information-processing, communications, decision-making, and control capabilities of corporations and markets by many magnitudes. It is affecting the relationships among business enterprises in the same sector as well as in other sectors and, through these, it is affecting the structure and operation of the entire economy. It is contributing to the creation of huge postindustrial conglomerate enterprises—in the manufacturing, banking, financial, and information and communications sectors, for example—which, in some respects, resemble the structure and the operation of the Japanese *keiretsu*, the huge industrial combines which control much of the Japanese economy.[3] Unlike their Japanese counterparts, however, many of the these are electronic network-based organizations, and many do not have a financial arm. These new Western-style *keiretsu* are also different because they are being created through innovations in the strategic management of people, organizations, and intelligent technology—all primary resources of the creative destruction and economic renewal process.[4] These new corporate enterprises derive their strategic competitive advantage from internalizing many of the key transactions and trading and exchange activities that have traditionally been delegated to markets.

In other respects, the effects of the spread of intelligent infrastructures are to make the market a more efficient mediator of economic activity and allocator of economic resources in both the national and global economies. They are thus diminishing the optimum size of corporations while expanding the scope of market activity so that many more (global) players can be accommodated.

Much of the industrial restructuring and many of the institutional changes that have been taking place in recent years in the telecommunications, broadcasting, entertainment, and banking and financial services industries, including convergence, deregulation, privatization, and globalization, can thus be attributed to the revolutions brought about by computers, microchips, and telecommunications. Before describing these further, let us look at how technology and global competition are transforming the high-tech manufacturing sector itself and how companies in this sector are reinventing themselves.

THE TRANSITION FROM HARDWARE TO SOFTWARE AND SERVICES ECONOMY

Of the many thousands of technological and economic changes taking place today, none is perhaps more significant than the transition from hardware to software, that is, from an economy specializing in the production of physical hardware products to one specializing in the production of knowledge-based products, including software, and intellectual designs and content, for it has major implications for our economic future. This transition is being driven by the continuing miniaturization of semiconductor devices and the use of intelligent machines and intelligent infrastructures for the design, production, distribution, and operation of all products and services, in effect, for the computerization and computer-mediation of everything. The microchip and computer and telecommunications revolutions are contributing to the demise of the industrial economy based on the manufacturing of dumb products and machines and equipment and the rise of a postindustrial economy based on intelligent machines, knowledge, and software—the new intellectual capital of the world— and their production and application to all aspects of economic (and social and cultural, including entertainment) activity. This transition thus has important implications for every business, every government, every economy, and the world economic system itself.

The semiconductor industry continues to be a fundamental source of the new economics as well as providing much of the dynamism of the high-technology, knowledge-based economy. The process by which bulky hardware components are shrunk in size and incorporated into microchips or eliminated altogether— either because they no longer serve a useful purpose or because they are being implemented in software—is continuing to speed ahead without encountering any effective limits or constraints. The microprocessor housed in an advanced engineering workstation today has more power than the mainframe had only a decade ago, but, instead of occupying a room, it sits on the top of a desk or fits into a briefcase, and soon it will fit into the palm of your hand. The bulky, electromechanical, analogue telephone switches of the past are being replaced by fully computerized digital telephone switches in a sequence of stages that is reducing them to ever-smaller size—to the size of a cabinet, then a single circuit board, and in some cases to a single microchip. The other difference—and it is a most significant one—is that their processing capacities and functionalities are being expanded tenfold, then another tenfold, and tenfold again.

This process of condensing more hardware components onto a single chip and building greater functionality and performance into microchip designs is expected to continue into the foreseeable future. As this process continues, as the density of semiconductor circuits continues to increase, and as greater functionality and performance is built into both hardware and software, a corresponding shift in, and transformation of, industrial activity is taking place at the microeconomic and macroeconomic levels away from bulky, energy-consuming, physical devices, equipment, and machines to energy-conserving, semiconductor devices and multifunctional, intelligent machines with no moving parts and millions upon millions of software programs and intellectual program content and services that they can mediate. This too is having dramatic impacts on the nature of production and the location of economic activity in the world as well as the nature of work and management and the distribution of economic power and wealth in the world.

At the same time, the application of a broad range of computer- and communications-based tools and techniques has dramatically diminished the time and eliminated many of the steps it used to take to design, test, and produce the new generations of microchips and computer and communications systems and equipment that use them. Pure software tools, such as silicon compilers and logic synthesizers, make it possible to design semiconductor chips completely on computer screens in the "cyberspace" inside computer chips rather than in physical buildings and plants. Microchip producers use these logic synthesizers to optimize their chip designs automatically, reduce circuit lengths, and increase chip densities.[5] This makes it possible to dramatically shorten design times and reduce the costs of producing chips while increasing their speed, functionality, and performance.

The chip design revolution has given rise to "fabless" chip design firms and "semicomputer" companies in the silicon valleys of the world. Fabless microchip companies are those that specialize in the design of chips but farm out their production to silicon "foundries" in the United States, Japan, or other Asian or European countries. Companies, like Sun Microsystems, MIPS, DEC, and Apple, turned to these new design techniques in the late eighties to keep them ahead of their competitors. Other technology-intensive applications described in chapter 7, such as paperless design techniques, concurrent engineering and robotics, MRP and JIT systems cut time, material, energy, and human effort in all stages and all phases of the production process in every industry. Robots typically dominate the production and assembly processes in most high-tech manufacturing plants today, and, more often than not, they operate in multiple shifts. Fully automated factories use the latest, up-to-date flexible manufacturing systems and techniques to produce dozens and even hundreds and thousands of differentiated products on the same assembly line through the new production process called mass-customization.[6] This enables the modern assembly line to be retooled and redesigned in hours to produce any one of a dozen or many hundreds of new products. Such speed is essential to remaining competitive in the global marketplace.

As this transformation in the high-tech manufacturing sector gains momentum—as bulky, room-size cabinets, equipment, and machinery are reduced to the size of chips, as computers come to completely dominate the design process and robots to dominate the production process and as software increasingly becomes a source of added value, another kind of transformation is taking place in the organization of production. Fewer workers are required to wire, solder, and assemble components and build or mount assemblies in cabinets or to paint, transport, and maintain components, cabinets, and end products because all of the essential functionality has been built into chips. One of the results is the continuing reduction in the labor content of the high-tech manufacturing sector. Manufacturing is becoming even more technology-intensive and capital- and knowledge-intensive as a result, and employees are being laid off in the hundreds of thousands around the world. On the other hand, employment is increasing in other areas, in the design, development, and production of new customized chips, in systems design and systems integration, and in network-based applications, for example, but particularly in software applications, including those involving the production of multimedia education and training and entertainment content where the future could be particularly bright.

The strategic application of telecommunications and computer technology in all aspects of manufacturing is also contributing to the globalization of the corporation. High-speed digital data communications networks, computer-aided design, and the growing use of workgroup technologies make it possible for companies to serve global markets as efficiently as they do national markets, but with additional strategic competitive and operational advantages. At the same time, the fixed costs of doing business globally are rapidly increasing due to the need to finance higher investments in research and development, in developing new markets and distribution channels, in advertising and product promotion, as well as in building the necessary computer and telecommunications infrastructures needed.[7] Global competition, together with the speed-up in the design and development of new products, systems, and services, also means that manufacturing companies must look for new ways to write off their enormous investments in fixed costs. One way of doing this is by going global and taking market shares away from competitors. Another is through acquisition. A third is through cooperation, that is, through joint ventures and strategic alliances. And the high-technology companies worldwide have been engaging in all three kinds of strategies. The result of all of these forces acting together is a grand restructuring of the semiconductor, telecommunications, and computer manufacturing industries worldwide.

THE GREAT SHAKEOUT IN THE WORLDWIDE HIGH-TECHNOLOGY SECTOR

The semiconductor industry worldwide has been transformed by these forces as well as the shift from electronic to optical and optoelectronic technologies, and all suppliers have been teaming up to compete.[8] IBM and Siemens, for example, are collaborating to produce 256 MB DRAM chips. Texas Instruments is in a joint venture with Hitachi to produce chips, as is Motorola with Toshiba, AT&T with NEC, and Intel with Sharp. American and Japanese companies are also collaborating on producing specialized chips for multimedia, advanced graphics, and video applications, for example. Similar dynamics are at work in the telecommunications manufacturing industry worldwide, and a shakeout has already taken a great toll. Companies like Stromberg Carlson and the manufacturing activities of GTE in the United States have been taken over by others including Siemens. Siemens and General Electric of Britain took over Plessey Telecommunications in the spring of 1989. And, in a long and complex series of transactions, the French government merged its telecommunications equipment, office automation, and consumer electronics manufacturing companies to form a new company called Alcatel N.V. Collaboration is now the key to survival in the world telecommunications manufacturing industry. AT&T, DEC, and MIT are collaborators in the Wideband All-Optical Networks Consortium which is building fully optical test beds in several U.S. sites.

The computer industry has been hit perhaps the hardest of all high-tech industries primarily as a result of the shift to personal computers, powerful workstations, and client-server systems tied together by local area and enterprisewide networks, the growing emphasis on RISC-based computers, scalable processors, and supercomputers built on parallel-processing architectures, but especially as a result of the entry of the industry into its mass market stage where retailing is most important. The "commoditization" of the microchip and computer industries is affecting everything. Every European, American, and Japanese manufacturer has been hurt as a result. Victims of this shakeout include Zenith Data Systems, Amdahl Computers, and Wang in the United States, International Computers Limited (ICL) in Britain, Groupe Bull in France, Nixdorf in Germany, and Philips in the Netherlands. Their computer manufacturing operations were taken over by other companies, primarily Japanese, but Japanese manufacturers have been suffering as well.

The shakeout in the worldwide mainframe and minicomputers manufacturing industries reached a climax in December 1992, when IBM announced the first of what has turned out to be an annual massive layoff of workers, and expenditure cut of $6 billion, and a complete restructuring of its $60 billion operations worldwide. The company in effect broke itself into thirteen smaller companies—nine manufacturing and services units feeding into four global geographical operating units. DEC, the other big casualty of the shift to microcomputers and the worldwide slump, announced in December 1992 that it would split itself up into five separate corporations to target separate markets. This restructuring of computer manufacturing companies and the computer industry is still continuing as hardware devices become smaller and smaller and pack higher value, performance and greater functionality and intelligence and as the focus of activity shifts to the new knowledge-based frontiers of the economy.

THE NEW FRONTIER: SOFTWARE AND SERVICES

It is now widely agreed that the leading edge of the information revolution in the nineties and beyond is in computer and communications applications, software, and services of all kinds, including workgroup and multimedia software and multimedia content and information- and communications-related services, as shown in Figure 8.1. This view is held by Andrew Rappaport and Shmuel Halevi who wrote in a 1991 issue of the *Harvard Business Review*:

The future belongs to the computerless computer company. Value derives from scarcity. In the computer industry, scarcity now resides in the gap between power—what com-

Figure 8.1
The New Software and Services Frontier

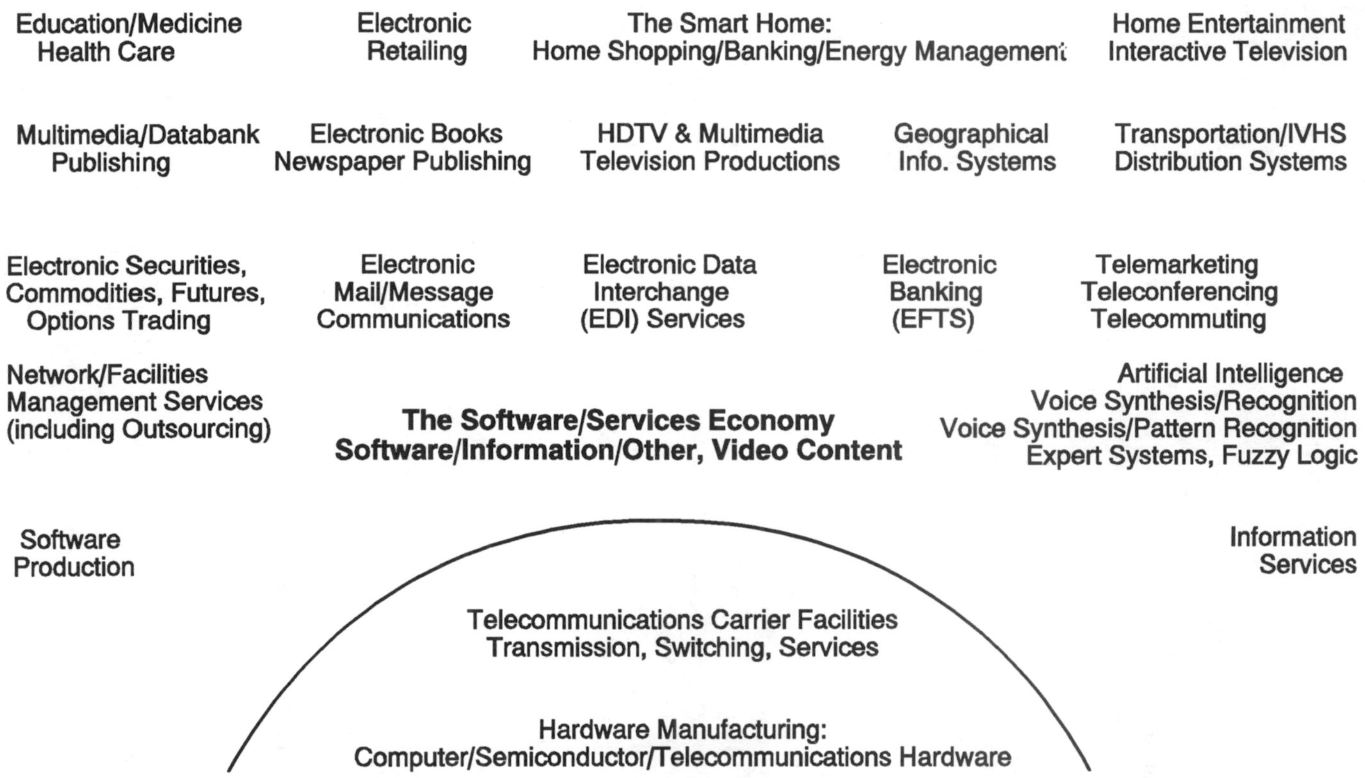

Education/Medicine
Health Care

Electronic
Retailing

The Smart Home:
Home Shopping/Banking/Energy Management

Home Entertainment
Interactive Television

Multimedia/Databank
Publishing

Electronic Books
Newspaper Publishing

HDTV & Multimedia
Television Productions

Geographical
Info. Systems

Transportation/IVHS
Distribution Systems

Electronic Securities,
Commodities, Futures,
Options Trading

Electronic
Mail/Message
Communications

Electronic Data
Interchange
(EDI) Services

Electronic
Banking
(EFTS)

Telemarketing
Teleconferencing
Telecommuting

Network/Facilities
Management Services
(including Outsourcing)

The Software/Services Economy
Software/Information/Other, Video Content

Artificial Intelligence
Voice Synthesis/Recognition
Voice Synthesis/Pattern Recognition
Expert Systems, Fuzzy Logic

Telecommunications Carrier Facilities
Transmission, Switching, Services

Software
Production

Hardware Manufacturing:
Computer/Semiconductor/Telecommunications Hardware

Information
Services

puters and their underlying semiconductor technologies are capable of doing—and utility—what human imagination and software engineering are capable of enabling
computers to do. . . . But virtually all of these [high-value added applications] . . . represent software challenges rather than hardware challenges. . . . [The consequence is that]
by the year 2000, the most successful computer companies will . . . leverage fabulously
cheap and powerful hardware to create and deliver new applications, pioneer and control
new computing paradigms, and assemble distribution and integration expertise that creates enduring influence with customers.[9]

The ascendancy of software companies like Microsoft, Lotus, Novell, Borland, Broderbund, Corel, and Computer Associates, for example, and the decline
of big hardware companies like IBM and DEC in the ranks of America's largest
industrial corporations are indicative of the growing importance of software to
the new economy.[10] Software is the focal point of all of Microsoft's new strategic corporate directions. It is aggressively promoting its Windows operating
system as the standard for everything from laptop and pen-based computers to
wallet PCs and telephone- and TV-PCs and pursuing opportunities in workgroup
software, office systems integration, as well as multimedia applications and interactive television.[11] Microsoft's new long-range vision is "Information at Your
Fingertips." It wants to make information available on demand in whatever
form, wherever individuals are. Microsoft is also a leading player in the production of multimedia CD content. Among its biggest successes have been its
Cinemania movie guide for the movie buffs and Musical Instants, Bookshelf
and its Encarte encyclopedia for the education market. Gates has created a software company called Continuum, which is aggressively buying up the electronic
rights to many of the world's art treasures for distribution on CD. Microsoft has
recently begun taking long-term strategic positions to build information superhighways in fields such as interactive television and video on demand. In late
1994, it also announced an on-line service called Microsoft Network as its first
commercial information service offering.

Even though Apple Computer is widely known as a hardware company, its
greatest strength has been in software. Indeed, the Apple Macintosh operating
system and its graphical user interface rank among the most important innovations in the history of the computer industry and are still the standard by which
all operating systems are measured. Apple has also been a world leader in electronic publishing and multimedia software, and it has slowly been shedding its
manufacturing activities so it can concentrate on new developments. Its subsidiary, Claris Corporation, is a leading supplier of software for both the Macintosh
and IBM PCs. It has struck deals with Sony, Toshiba, and Sharp to manufacture
a wide range of PDAs to leverage on its software and systems expertise, and it
is strengthening its position in multimedia through its Taligent and Kaleida joint
ventures with IBM. Apple has been strategically positioning itself in key emerging markets, including consumer electronics, telecommunications, media, and
publishing. It reorganized itself in 1992 into four new functional groupings to

better target these markets. Apple also has initiatives underway across the entire range of advanced application areas, from handheld, computing and communications devices and multimedia applications to electronic information services, telecommunications, and interactive television. In January 1994, Apple announced its entry into the on-line services market with a new service called eWorld. It provides a variety of interactive information, communications, and entertainment services in competition with Prodigy and America Online.

IBM has had to make the most drastic changes in its strategic corporate directions in its history to cope with the transition from mainframe to PC-based and network-based computing and the tide of other technological changes that have overtaken the computer industry. It has downsized, reorganized, and given more autonomy to its individual operating units, and it has put systems integration, software, and services at the focal point of its new strategic directions. It has also forged joint ventures and strategic alliances and partnerships with former rivals including Lotus, Apple Computer, Motorola, Borland, and Novell. Its biggest joint ventures, of course, are with Motorola and Apple and other companies which resulted in the development of new line of PowerPC computers which it is depending on to prime the new generation of broadband, video, multimedia, and teleconferencing applications in business and the home. IBM is also staking out a leadership position as a developer of education and training and entertainment content. It is financing an ambitious project to develop a multimedia version of the history of the world, for example, and it has an agreement with the Vatican to put its collection of rare books and manuscripts on CD so the world can access them.

IBM is also re-focusing its efforts in such areas as information services, electronic message services, electronic data interchange services, and electronic funds transfer services. It is active in data and voice networking and value-added services as well as international outsourcing through Advantis, its joint venture with Sears, Roebuck. To some, IBM is one of America's leading *keiretsu* organizations.

Software has become the strategic focus of every player in the computer industry. Wang Computers, for example, has been forced to abandon manufacturing altogether and become a software and systems company. Steve Jobs, founder of NeXt Computers Inc., announced in the winter of 1992, that he too was abandoning hardware manufacturing to concentrate on supplying software. Software is also proving to be a source of strategic competitive advantage to other computer manufacturers, including Hewlett-Packard, for example. Sun Microsystems' domination of the workstation market has also been due in large part to its software expertise. Software is a strategic source of much of the added value in hardware products and systems, and its importance is growing in information, communications, and banking and other services.

Software is an economic commodity quite like any other in terms of its intellectual labor intensity and because, once produced, its cost of electronic distribution is almost zero. Software can also be continuously upgraded in sophistication, functionality, and efficiency, semi-independently of the hardware. Software is both a factor of production and an end-product in itself. It represents the new form of capital of the computer-based, intelligent economy of the nineties and beyond.

This shift from hardware to software could have an equally dramatic effect on other manufacturing companies in the future. Indeed, the entire manufacturing sector could go the way of the American semiconductor industry in spite of the fact that, according to conventional wisdom, manufacturing is one of the least software-intensive industries in the economy. "Fabless" automobile companies, for example, could become common perhaps before this decade is out. These companies could perform much of the high-value, knowledge-based design activities while manufacturers throughout the world would transform these into final products. Like publishing, architecture, and film production, industrial product design is a knowledge-intensive, intellectual activity, which is what the evolving postindustrial economy appears to thrive on.

MOBILIZING TO TAKE ADVANTAGE OF OPPORTUNITIES IN THE NEW HIGH TECHNOLOGY, SOFTWARE, AND SERVICES ECONOMY

Some of the biggest manufacturing companies in the United States and around the world have been redesigning their corporate strategies to take advantage of the opportunities in the new knowledge-intensive and technology-intensive sectors of the economy of the nineties, in such fields as information and communications services, software development, systems integration, and facilities management as well as financial, educational, and health care services and entertainment. They include not only AT&T and IBM, but many others like General Motors, General Electric, and consumer electronics manufacturing giants like Sony and Matsushita. These companies and many others like them have been lured into the new high-technology services economy by the promise to make big profits.

General Motors has become one of the most aggressive manufacturing companies in the world in positioning itself for the new age in which mastery over high technology and leadership in systems and services are strategic to competitiveness. In 1985, it paid $5.2 billion for the giant Hughes Aircraft empire, one of America's premier high-technology companies with global strengths in the manufacturing of defense, radar, weapons control systems, and tactical guidance missiles and communications systems. In the same year it purchased Electronic Data Systems (EDS) from Ross Perot for $2.5 billion. EDS was one of the largest computer services companies in the world. GM was so impressed with EDS's expertise in systems integration that it put EDS in charge of automating its automotive production, inventory control, and retail distribution operations around the world.

Through Hughes Electronics and EDS and its other subsidiaries, GM has a growing presence in telecommunications and value-added networks services, including EDI services, and it is in the cellular phone and facilities management businesses worldwide. Hughes is also one of the world's leading manufacturers of satellite systems and equipment. Hughes Communications dominates the VSAT market in the United States with a 60 percent market share, and it is a joint owner with GE in the EOSAT venture to market earth resources information services around the world. Hughes Electronics also has great ambitions in the entertainment industry where it has invested more than $600 million in the development and launching of its DirecTV DBS satellites which began broadcasting 150 channels of news, sports, and special programming to homes throughout North America in 1994. GM is even a partner in General Magic which is developing the market for wireless, pen-based computers. Through EDS, it is a joint owner of Hitachi Data Systems which produces components and clones for IBM compatible mainframe computers. And through its General Motors Acceptance Corporation subsidiary, it has become a full-fledged financial services company.

General Electric, a $60 billion (1992) conglomerate with roots going back to Thomas Edison's invention of the electric light bulb, is another example of a manufacturing company that has shed much of its old line manufacturing businesses to concentrate on high value-added opportunities in the new high-technology, knowledge-based economy. GE has built a strong world leadership position in satellite communications, broadcasting, and information and financial services. It paid $6.4 billion in June 1986 for RCA's aerospace and satellite communications and broadcasting units, including NBC, in what was billed as the biggest non-oil merger in history. This also strengthened its global leadership position in aerospace and telecommunications technologies. GE America Corporation is also major player in satellite communications. GE combined several of its own information services units with those of RCA to create its $2 billion information and communications services subsidiary, GEISCO, which supplies communications equipment, installation, and maintenance as well as information and communications services to government, business, and industry.

Through its various subsidiaries, GE also provides a whole range of network-based information and communications services, including EDI, banking, health care, and network management and systems integration services. Genie, GE's network for information exchange, allows personal computer users to access a wide variety of information and communications services, including travel, reservations, shopping, and entertainment services. Through Kidder, Peabody, GE is also heavily into investment banking and brokerage services and through GE Capital Corporation, it is into equipment and industrial financing, insurance, consumer finance, real estate, asset management, and reinsurance. All of these are part of the General Electric Financial Services organization (GEFS). GEFS is so big that if it were classified as a bank, it would rank the eighth largest in the United States in terms of assets, and it has been one of General Electric's most profitable subsidiaries.

Other world manufacturers like GTE, Westinghouse, Digital Equipment, Control Data, Unisys, as well as AT&T have been expanding their portfolio of services in key growth areas like systems integration, outsourcing, and value-added services like database information services.

Some of the biggest consumer electronics companies in the world are also diversifying into the new software and information and communications services economy. Sony paid $2 billion for CBS Records in 1988 and $3.4 billion for Columbia Pictures in 1989. Sony has rolled these along with its electronic publishing, digital audio, and video distribution subsidiaries into a new subsidiary called Sony Software Corporation. Matsushita paid $6.6 billion for MCA, owner of Universal Studios, in 1990. Both companies have been trying to use these acquisitions to take advantage of the synergies between their consumer electronic manufacturing activities and music and entertainment content. Philips owns PolyGram, one of the world's top three producers of recorded music. Other manufacturers are following their lead. Toshiba Corporation has entered into a joint venture with Time Warner to develop the home market for interactive multimedia cable television products and services. Motorola, a world leader in the manufacture of semiconductors and mobile radio communications equipment and systems, has become active in supplying cellular and mobile communications services in Japan, Europe, and North America, and it is developing the Iridium global mobile satellite system. British Telecom has also abandoned manufacturing to concentrate on the high-growth national and global markets for telecommunications, outsourcing, and multimedia services. These are but a few of the companies strategically positioning themselves in the new economy.

TECHNOLOGY, CORPORATE STRATEGY, AND THE CREATION OF INFORMATION, COMMUNICATIONS, AND FINANCIAL SUPERMARKETS

The role played by corporate strategy, technology, and organization in restructuring economic activity is nowhere better illustrated than in the manner in which corporations are using information and information-processing power, telecommunications networks, and software to take advantage of synergies and economies of scale and scope of one kind or another and create much bigger "megacorporations" which combine a variety of activities in various sectors of the economy into something as close as possible to a "one-stop shopping" organization. These very large, highly diversified, conglomerates or "supermarkets" are especially common in what I have called the central intelligence and control and, hence regulated, sectors of the economy, that is, in information and communications and banking and financial services sectors, which are purely information processing-, communications-, and transactions-intensive. But they could become common in other sectors as well in the future. Although the strategies have not always been successful, they are indicative of the way corporations have been using technology to restructure and transform the economy. The following is a capsule summary of the strategies and successes of some of the major players.

Citicorp, American Express, and Merrill Lynch have been leaders in the strategic application of computer and telecommunications technology since the sixties. Citibank was the first bank to build a nationwide network of automated teller machines in the seventies and eighties, in spite of strict laws prohibiting banks from setting up operations across state lines. And it has been busy developing new lines of business across the entire gamut of financial and information-processing services mainly through acquisitions. It is in the credit card and credit card processing business. It has also used advanced technology to create a place for itself in the information, securities brokerage and underwriting as well as the currency trading and funds transfer services businesses throughout the world. Citicorp owns Quotron in the electronic trading business, for example, and it has targeted information services as one of its strategic goals for expansion in the nineties.

Computers and telecommunications technologies have played a strategic role in enabling American Express to build a global travelers checks and credit card services organization. Leveraging on this strength, the company successfully diversified through a series of strategic acquisitions in the eighties into the insurance, banking, brokerage, and underwriting businesses and other key industries that make intensive use of computers and telecommunications networks. Through American Express Information Services (AEIS), it provides high-volume information processing and communications services worldwide. Merrill Lynch has also evolved into a global financial supermarket over the years. It is involved in everything from investment banking and underwriting, securities brokerage, and banking and financial services to asset management, insurance, and real estate services, and it has embarked on an ambitious plan to use high-technology to create a global financial services organization.

Reuters PLC, Knight-Ridder, Dun & Bradstreet, Dow Jones, and McGraw-Hill are other leading companies that have also used computer and telecommunications technologies to take advantage of the growing opportunities in the electronic information services business. Reuters, PLC successfully diversified out of the international newswire services business in the sixties and seventies through the innovative use of technology and has gone on to develop a complete portfolio of electronic services for the global marketplace. These include international stock market quotations, international business and economic information, and currency, commodity, and securities trading services. Leveraging on its strength in the publishing industry, particularly its ownership of *The Wall Street Journal* and *Barron's*, Dow Jones has diversified into the electronic publishing, computer processing, and electronic trading services industries. It owns the Dow Jones Retrieval Service, an on-line business and financial news service, an electronic foreign exchange service, called The Trading Service, as well as Telerate, which is a major supplier of stock market information and of stock trading services. Knight-Ridder, which owns twenty-nine newspapers, has become a leading player in the electronic information service business. In 1988, it purchased Lockheed's DIALOG Information Service, the biggest on-line full text information retrieval system in the world with 96,000 subscribers in eighty-six countries. Knight-Ridder is also a leading player in the development of a fully electronic multimedia newspaper service involving not only text but motion pictures and sound.

Dun & Bradstreet (D&B) has expanded into the whole information services marketplace from its initial base in the credit information business. It acquired National CSS, a leading time-sharing services company in 1979, and it went on a buying binge in the mid-to-late eighties with the acquisition of A.C. Nielsen (1984), the largest media research company in the United States, and Interactive Data Corporation (1988), which supplies securities information and corporate performance information. Dun & Bradstreet also owns the Moody's Investor Service and supplies yellow pages and telephone directories. McGraw-Hill has also transformed itself into an internationally diversified electronic information services company to complement its book and magazine publishing and broadcasting activities. Through its various subsidiaries, including Standard and Poor's and Data Resources (DRI), it is a leading international supplier of business and economic information and econometric forecasting services which it provides in printed form as well as on-line via telephone, satellite, and CD-ROM. The company consolidated its information-related holdings into the new McGraw-Hill Financial Information Services Group in October 1993. McGraw-Hill is also becoming a major player in the multimedia publishing business. Its *Encyclopedia of Mammalian Biology,* for example, which is on CD-ROM, contains text, still images, sound, and full-motion video. It also produces computerized college text books in a partnership with Kodak.

Some of the biggest retail services companies in the United States, including J.C. Penney, K-Mart, Wal-Mart, and Sears, Roebuck, have been striving to create high-tech, information or financial services supermarkets of their own. Sears, Roebuck has also been pursuing opportunities in information processing, database, information, and telecommunications services. Sears Communications and Sears Technology Services have been providing voice and data communications and network design services since the mid-eighties. Through Prodigy, its joint venture with IBM, Sears, Roebuck has penetrated the market for home information retrieval services. In August 1992, it announced another agreement to combine Sears Technology Services and Sears Communications Corporation with IBM's Networking Systems and Services Division and IBM Information Network business into a new joint venture called Advantis. The new company offers a wide variety of services, including voice and data outsourcing, value-added network services, as well as those relating to the design, development, and integration of custom networks. Advantis competes with GE and AT&T in the international VANs marketplace. Wal-Mart has used information and communications technology to become the largest retailer in America, and it has embarked on a strategy to dominate the world in retailing.

AT&T as well as the regional holding companies have been slowly moving into the new information, communications, and financial services marketplace. AT&T has also established a considerable presence in the computer and financial services industries through its acquisition of NCR. Its Universal Card has become one of the most popular credit cards in the United States since it was introduced in March 1990. AT&T has also acquired several financial service companies including the asset leasing and financing services division of Pacific Credit Corporation. In 1991, it consolidated all of its financial holdings into a subsidiary called, naturally, AT&T Commercial Financial Corporation. Another new subsidiary, AT&T Smart Cards produces a smart card with voice-recognition capabilities that enables individuals to make airlines reservations, purchase airline tickets, theater tickets or life insurance, and pay highway tolls or it could be used as a security, identification or medical card. The smart card could give AT&T much greater clout than the credit card has given American Express, Visa, or Mastercard in the future. AT&T has also embarked on a bold strategy to create its own electronic superhighway, which it refers to as a "knowledge network." This network would tie together video servers, multimedia databanks, and other sources throughout the country. The network will provide every business and household with access to any kind of information and communications services imaginable anywhere, on demand.

It is in the media sector as described in previous chapters where technology and corporate strategy are playing a particularly crucial role in restructuring the economy, especially in the United States but in other countries as well. Here the focus of strategy has been on trying to gain as much control over the electronic superhighways as well as the content that they will carry. Telephone and cable television companies, broadcasters, motion picture producers, video producers, publishers, and databank and information suppliers have become involved in this mad scramble. The leaders include the regional holding companies as well as Time Warner, Viacom, TCI, QVC, and Cox Enterprises. In 1993, US West Communications bought a 25 percent interest in Time Warner, the second biggest cable television distributor in the United States and a major producer of television and motion picture content. Cox Enterprises, a big player in the cable television and newspapers business in the United States and hoping to become one in the United Kingdom, purchased the cable television operations of Times Mirror in June 1994 for $2.3 billion. Viacom won the takeover battle to purchase Paramount Communications in 1994. Paramount is into movie production and distribution through Paramount Pictures as well as television programming, distribution, and home video. It also owns Simon & Schuster and several other publishing companies as well as six broadcasting stations. Viacom is into broadcasting and cable television systems. This makes the merged organization one of the world's leading producers and distributors of filmed entertainment, cable programming, and published information.

CONVERGING INDUSTRIES, EVAPORATING INDUSTRIAL BOUNDARIES, AND OBSOLETE INSTITUTIONS

The effects of the strategies of companies in industries as diverse as manufacturing, retailing, and banking and financial services, as well as publishing, computer services and telecommunications, cable television, and broadcasting have been nothing less than to restructure and transform industrial economies organizationally and institutionally in recent years. In the United States, for example, it has resulted in giant nonbank financial services companies like Merrill Lynch and American Express and retailers such as Sears, Roebuck entering the banking business and big banks entering the securities brokerage, trading, and insurance businesses. Manufacturing giants like General Electric, AT&T, General Motors, Ford Motor Company, Chrysler, Xerox, and Primerica are now major players in the financial services sector. The regional Bell operating companies and AT&T have targeted information and publishing services, home banking, cable television, and video-on-demand, and multimedia entertainment services as areas of expansion. Cable television companies are positioning themselves in the telecommunications and information and entertainment services business in a big way. And traditional publishing companies are moving into software and electronic publishing and multimedia productions of personal, educational, and entertainment content.

It has been developments like these that have been driving deregulation and structural change and eroding the industrial, institutional, and legal boundaries between just about every industry and every sector of the economy. The legal, regulatory, and geographical boundaries between banking, securities brokerage, and insurance, retailing and even securities and options and futures trading are already in shambles in the United States and the institutional boundaries between computers, telecommunications, broadcasting, and cable television, as well as publishing, entertainment, and information services are also rapidly disappearing. The consequence is that the laws and legislation and the institutions that were designed to control, regulate, and administer these key sectors of the economy are now obsolete. This new technoindustrial revolution clearly has important implications for regulatory and antitrust policies in the telecommunications, broadcasting, and banking and securities industries and therefore for government.

GLOBALIZATION OF THE MEDIA

Technology and corporate strategy are playing a crucial role in the transformation of industrial economies in yet another critical way—through the globalization of the communications media. Information and communications technologies extending from CD-ROMs and VCRs to global optical fiber and satellite communications networks have made it feasible and economical to transplant every kind of content—from newspaper, magazine, and book publishing to audio, video, and motion picture content—across all media and across all national borders and to create global markets for all of them. Technology has made it possible for media giants to treat the markets of other countries simply as an extension of their own national markets from a production and delivery point of view. For the past decade or more, book, magazine and newspaper publishing industries, and music production and recording industries, and film and television production industries have become caught up in a global takeover frenzy which has concentrated and restructured these industries nationally and globally.

Robert Maxwell became prominent in the eighties as a result of his having created a global publishing and broadcasting empire that encompassed Britain, Europe, and the United States. At its height, the Maxwell empire included Pergamon Press and Macmillan, both leading international book publishers as well as the British Printing and Publishing Corporation and the Mirror Group of newspapers, Britain's best-selling newspaper chain and the Official Airlines Guide. In 1990, he launched *The European* weekly newspaper and purchased the *New York Daily News* in 1991. Since his death, the empire Maxwell created is now being dismantled. Pearson PLC, another British-based media giant, owns the *Financial Times* and publishers Longman, Addison-Wesley, Penguin, and Viking Books, and it has entered the electronic publishing business as well.

The Bertelsmann Group of West Germany is one of the largest media conglomerates in the world. It is involved in everything from printing and publishing to television broadcasting, records, CDs, and music videos on the three major continents of the world. Publishing companies like Doubleday, Bantam, and Dell and the Literary Guild along with record companies like RCA Records, Arista, and Zoo Records and Entertainment in the United States and BMG-Victor in Japan are all members of the Bertelsmann Group. In the newspaper and magazine industry, it owns *Parents* in the United States, *Der Stern* in Germany, and *Prima* in Europe. In the printing industry, the Bertelsmann Company owns Brown Publishing in the United States, and, in broadcasting, it owns RTL Plus and Premiere Pay TVF in Germany.

Time Warner Inc. is the second largest media conglomerate in the world. The merger of the two corporations in 1989 was seen as a defensive one in the face of the globalization of the media sector and the takeover of the American media industry by foreign conglomerates, including Sony and Matsushita, and it created a world-scale entertainment and media conglomerate with combined assets of $18 billion in 1989. Time Warner is a world leader in book publishing, music recordings and publishing, film making, and cable television. It publishes such well-known magazines as *Fortune*, *Time*, *Life*, *Money* and *People*. In the film-entertainment industry, it owns Warner Brothers, Lorimer Telepictures, Home Box Office, and Cinemax. In music and music recording, it owns Atlantic Records and Warner/Chappel Music. It also owns Warner Cable Communications and 82 percent of American Television and Communications.

Perhaps no other media company has been as forward looking and as aggressive in going global as News Corporation of Australia, the holding company owned of Australian media magnate, Rupert Murdoch. Since the seventies, Murdoch has been steadily building a global media empire encompassing newspapers, magazines, satellites, television stations, and production houses in Australia, United States, Britain, Europe, Asia, and South America, and he is aggressively expanding his empire by using advanced technology to create a global electronic multimedia giant of a company. The flagship of News Corporation's holdings is the 205-year-old newspaper *The Times* in Britain and it also owns *The Sun*, *The News of the World*, and *The Sunday Times* in Britain as well as the *New York Post* in the United States. News Corporation of Australia also owns publishers Harper & Row and Triangle Publications in the United States which publishes *TV Guide* and *Seventeen* magazine. In the television and film production industries, it owns 20th Century Fox and Fox TV, and, through Fox TV, it operates a network of television stations in the United States. News Corporation of Australia also controls MGM/UA Communications. In Europe, it owns 50 percent of BSkyB, Britain's biggest satellite broadcasting company, which supplies a twenty-four-hour satellite news network. Murdoch has made it clear that he plans to make BSkyB a key to the creation of a "superhighway of the air." He has an agreement to build an international digital satellite system spanning Asia, North and South America, and Europe. Murdoch's latest target for development has been Asia. In July 1993, he negotiated the purchase of a 63.3 percent share in Hong-Kong-based HutchVision Limited, parent and supplier of programs to Star TV, one of Asia's fastest growing satellite television companies, thus giving News Corporation a presence on all three continents.

Murdoch foresees the breakdown of traditional barriers separating five of the world's largest industries—computing, communications, consumer electronics, publishing, and entertainment—and their transformation into a dynamic whole, and he wants to play a role in making it happen. In 1993, he announced the purchase of Delphi Information Systems Inc. (now Delphi Internet Services), the fifth largest on-line service supplier in the United States. Murdoch's plans are to use Delphi to give subscribers instant access to news, educational material, and other information worldwide. He also wants to create an electronic newspaper, which distributes an electronic version of *TV Guide*, for example. Murdoch is also into reservations systems, travel, and tourism.

TRANSFORMING THE WORLD'S SOCIAL, ECONOMIC, AND INTELLIGENCE INFRASTRUCTURES

Corporate titans around the world have been transforming national economies and the world economy in at least one other significant way, that is, through telecommunications.

Through their massive investments in transoceanic optical fiber cables and satellite communications systems, companies like AT&T, British Telecom, Nippon Telegraph and Telephone, and France Telecom, along with Sprint, MCI, Teleglobe Canada, and Cable and Wireless, and PTTs in other countries, as well as special carriers like Intelsat and Inmarsat and many new ones like General Electric, Motorola, and GM/Hughes Electronics are building the global electronic and optical digital information, communications, and financial highways that will predominate later in this decade and the next. But they are also taking advantage of all of the many other opportunities that are opening up throughout the global economy. They are rushing in to buy up or buy into national telephone and cellular radio and personal communications operations and cable television franchises in Western Europe, Eastern Europe, South America, and Asia. In addition to providing transmission and switching services, many of them are eager to enter new and potentially high-growth markets such as international value-added network services (IVANS), to supply a wide variety of E-mail, EDI, EFTS, and other financial services as well as information, database, and trading and transactions services. Some are busy positioning themselves in the really big growth markets for software, systems integration, and network management services and outsourcing that are expected to be worth billions in the late nineties.

Here too, the world's leading telecommunications carriers are attempting to create a one-stop shopping, global services organization that supplies all of the networking facilities and services needs that their international customers need, as well as the software engineers and management personnel and the expertise to deal with dozens of foreign telecommunications administrations and different international standards. Although each would like to go it alone, none has the necessary strengths in all of the product and service markets and all regions of the world to be successful. One strategy is to buy into other companies with expertise and strengths in systems integration and value-added services to complement their own strengths. The second strategy is to forge strategic alliances and joint ventures with one another. In the process, they are creating what *The Economist* has called a new "superleague" of international suppliers.

AT&T has been aggressively building a global services organization to complement its strength as a dominant national and international carrier and service supplier and manufacturer of telecommunications equipment. Through GlobeCom, it provides a whole range of telecommunications and value-added services to international businesses including E-mail, facsimile, EDI, and advanced image and voice services. AT&T also supplies a family of videoconferencing-related services, called Global Business Video Services, which targets the needs of businesses for training, meetings, marketing, and sales. In May 1993, it announced its "WorldSource" alliance (with KDD, Japan's international carrier, and Singapore Telecom) which offers international "one-stop shopping" for voice and data services and end-to-end private line, virtual network, and frame relay data services. Another AT&T alliance, called "World-Partner," offers end-to-end global services with other carriers. A third, called

"WorldWorx," is a multimedia service provided in collaboration with Apple, Novell, and IBM. AT&T is a company that should be watched because it is the only company in the world that is strategically positioned in all of the major segments of the world's information and telecommunications marketplace, in research and development, telecommunications, and computer equipment manufacturing, and local, national, and global facilities, and services markets, and it is aggressively advancing on all fronts. AT&T is so strong, according to *Business Week*, that it could end up a decade from now ruling the world.

British Telecom has also been forging a strategy to become a dominant force in the global information and communications services economy. The company provides a whole family of end-to-end network management and data communications services to its customers from more than 1,000 locations worldwide through its Global Network Services (GNS) organization. Tymnet, a world leading supplier of packet-switching services, is now an integral part of GNS. Tymnet owns 25 percent of Network Information Services Company, one of Japan's leading computer network services companies. BT is using Tymnet to go head-to-head with General Electric Information Services, AT&T, and IBM. In October 1991, BT announced the launching of its "supercarrier" Syncordia subsidiary to provide end-to-end global network services to large corporate users. One of its most ambitious projects is called Cyclone. This is a worldwide network to which BT has committed $1 billion in investment throughout this decade to provide a comprehensive range of virtual private network services for institutional customers. The company took its first step in this direction in May 1993 when it announced it would take a 20 percent stake in MCI for $4.3 billion. The two companies have agreed to invest $1 billion to create a new company called Concert to build global networks for offering voice, data, and video services to their international clients.

Other international carriers are creating their own global services organization through strategic alliances and joint ventures. Several of Europe's biggest PTTs, including Swedish Telecom, France Telecom, Deutsches Bundespost Telekom, and KDD of Japan, are joint owners of Infonet, which supplies international value-added services on the three major continental markets of the world. Twelve of the world's largest carriers responded to the moves by AT&T and BT in 1992 by forming the Financial Network Association (FNA) to provide all of the telecommunications needs of the world's financial community. Other members include AOTC of Australia, Stentor of Canada, France Telecom, Deutsches Bundespost Telekom, Hong Kong Telecom, Italcable, Japan's KDD, Singapore Telecom, and Telefonica in Spain. The financial community is one of the most prized client groups because it is in the forefront of global networking.

Another rival of Syncordia is Unisource, a joint venture between the Dutch and Swedish PTTs, announced in June 1992. It offers international outsourcing and managed network services. A third rival, Eunetcom, is the joint venture company formed in the same year by Deutsches Bundespost Telekom and

France Telecom. On December 7, 1993, the two carriers unveiled a joint venture to provide "one-stop shopping" services to multinational companies.

Mergers and acquisitions and joint ventures and strategic alliances like these have become the norm throughout Europe and across the Atlantic and Pacific oceans. But some international carriers like Cable and Wireless (C&W) are already well represented globally. By mid-1993, the company had an ownership stake in more than forty carriers around the world, including all of the countries that are major hubs for international private-line networks. Cable and Wireless also owns Mercury Communications and Hong Kong Telecom and has a 10 percent stake in International Digital Communications in Japan. It is also part owner of Tele2, an alternative services supplier in Sweden, and a member of the Global Virtual Private Network (GVPN) group formed in 1991. Other members of the group include Hong Kong Telecom, Sprint, Teleglobe Canada and Unitel Communications in Canada, Swedish Telecom, Telstra of Australia, and International Digital Communications of Japan.

TRANSFORMING NATIONAL TELECOMMUNICATIONS INFRASTRUCTURES

Domestic and international telecommunications companies in the industrialized countries are also contributing to a new social and economic world order by buying into national carriers and investing heavily in the development of national infrastructures in North America, Western and Eastern Europe, Asia, South America, and Africa. C&W is a member of the Mannesmann Mobilfunk cellular consortium in Germany. It is building a local telephone network in the Gdansk Region of Poland. Bell Canada International purchased a 20 percent interest in Mercury Communications, Britain's second competitive carrier in the fall of 1992 to give it a foothold in the British market where it competes with British Telecom. Stentor, the consortium of major telephone companies in Canada, announced a partnership in October 1992 with MCI to create an integrated Canada-U.S. intelligent network. A few months later, in January 1993, AT&T announced that it had negotiated a 20 percent interest, the maximum amount permitted under Canadian law, in Canada's second interexchange carrier, Unitel, giving AT&T virtually unlimited access to the Canadian business market. Then, in June 1994, Deutsches Bundespost Telekom and France Telecom announced the purchase of a 20 percent stake in Sprint for $4.2 billion.

The regional holding companies (RHC) in the United States have been transformed by deregulation, competition, and divestiture into diversification and acquisition-hungry tigers, and they too are playing a key role in the transformation of the world's telecommunications infrastructure. By 1994, RHCs had become involved in more than twenty-five industrial activities in more than thirty-six countries, primarily in areas like telephone, cellular and cable television, and radio and paging networks but in international fiber optic cables, packet switching, voice messaging, and directory publishing services as well.

They have also become involved in many other areas, including computer, banking and electronic funds transfer services, network design, facilities management, systems integration, computer software, consulting and professional services in Asia, Western Europe, South America, and Eastern Europe.[12] Bell Atlantic and Ameritech were successful in purchasing 49 percent of Telecom Corp. of New Zealand for $2.46 billion in 1990. Southwestern Bell, in partnership with France Telecom and a Mexican manufacturing and mining concern, won controlling interest in Mexico's state-run telephone company, TelMex, in March 1991, for $1.76 billion. BellSouth is part owner of Optus Communications in Australia. The cable industry in the United Kingdom has become besieged by regional holding companies. In 1994, US West had twenty-three franchises passing 3.4 million homes. Southwestern Bell had seven passing one million homes, and NYNEX had sixteen passing 2.5 million homes. RHCs are heavily involved in investments on the Continent as well as Eastern Europe including Russia and Asia. US West holds franchises with partners in Hong Kong, Britain, and France to build cable television systems reaching up to six million homes. NYNEX has a 50 percent interest in a new company to own, operate, and modernize the phone system in Gibraltar. In November 1993, it acquired a 23 percent stake in Hong Kong–based Orient Telecommunications and Technology holding (OT&T) for $177 million. OT&T has a 25 percent interest in Telecommunications Asia Corporation which owns a twenty-five-year franchise to build and operate a two million line telephone system in Bangkok.

RHCs are also heavily invested in cellular and paging services ventures in such countries as Norway, Poland, France, Germany, Belgium, Greece, Japan, Argentina, Mexico, and Venezuela. Pacific Telesis has a 26 percent stake in a consortium that is developing a second West German cellular system, and it has a 20 percent stake in the Microtel Communications consortium which is building a nationwide personal communications network in Britain. US West has a 30 percent stake in the Unitel Consortium which is building a personal communications network in Britain. It also has a 49 percent stake in a Hungarian cellular telephone project. And it is a member of several joint ventures with Russian companies which began supplying cellular services in St. Petersburg in September and in Moscow in December 1991. In January 1993, US West also won the right to build a GSM mobile communication system in over a half-dozen Russian cities, sharing licenses with VART, a Russian company based in Moscow. Bellsouth has cellular investments in Argentina, Uruguay, France, Britain, Switzerland, and Mexico and paging ventures in Australia, Britain, and Switzerland. Both US West and Bell Atlantic are involved in a consortium to build cellular network and a public switched packet data network for the Czech Republic.

These are just a sample of the mergers and acquisitions and joint ventures and strategic alliances that are restructuring the telecommunications industry worldwide. Other industries and sectors are being affected in similar ways. Cross-border and cross-country mergers and acquisitions and joint ventures like these will increase in the nineties and beyond as the networks of all countries become increasingly integrated to form a seamless North American and Western European telecommunications infrastructure. European and Asian and South American countries will experience the same fate as carriers and noncarriers complete the building of a seamless infrastructure to interconnect and integrate all of the economies in the world.

GLOBAL INFORMATION AND TELECOMMUNICATIONS INFRASTRUCTURES ARE CONTRIBUTING TO THE GLOBALIZATION OF EVERYTHING

The optical fiber and satellite and radio communications infrastructures that carriers are putting into place around the world may be invisible to the naked eye but they are capable of carrying literally all of the essential information and communications and other traffic necessary to sustain the operation of global businesses. These infrastructures already carry everything from voice, data, message, image, and video traffic to money, securities, and other financial assets. They also carry the latest news and published information along with engineering, manufacturing, and architectural designs and medical, educational, and entertainment content. Indeed, they are capable of mediating all of the essential information processing, communications, and trading and transactions activities required for the global economy and the global marketplace to operate efficiently and effectively. This global infrastructure in turn is contributing to nothing less than the globalization of everything—of broadcasting, publishing, banking, securities trading, insurance, advertising, retailing, consulting, travel, tourism, manufacturing, and transportation.

In the next chapter, I will look at the implications of globalization, computerization and the rise of the high-tech, knowledge economy for governments and nation-states in the nineties and beyond.

NOTES

1. George Stalk and Thomas Hout, *Competing in Time: How Time-Based Competition Is Reshaping Global Markets* (New York: Free Press, 1990).

2. Michael E. McGrath and Richard W. Hoole, "Manufacturing's New Economies of Scale," *Harvard Business Review,* May-June 1992, pp. 102–105. Also *Technology and the Economy: The Key Relationships* (Paris: Organization for Economic Cooperation and Development, 1992).

3. Japan's *keiretsu* takes two forms: a bank-centered and supply-centered combine. The bank-centered *keiretsu* consists of 20-45 core companies centered around a bank and provides a mechanism for allocating investment to strategic industries. Supply *keiretsu* are groups of companies integrated along a supplier chain and dominated by a major manufacturer. More than half of Japan's largest 100 companies are members of six groups, and by the late eighties, according to Marie Anchordoguy, "earned some 18 percent of the total net profits of all Japanese business, had nearly 17 percent of total

sales, held over 14 percent of total paid-up capital, and employed almost 5 percent of Japan's labor force.'' For more, see Marie Anchordoguy, ''A Brief History of Japan's Keiretsu,'' *Harvard Business Review*, July-August 1990, pp. 58–59.

4. For more information on these Western-style *keiretsu*, I recommend Charles Ferguson, ''Computers and the Coming of the U.S. Keiretsu,'' *Harvard Business Review*, July-August 1990, pp. 55–70; and ''Learning from Japan: How a Few U.S. Giants Are Trying to Create Homegrown Keiretsu,'' *Business Week*, 27 January 1992, pp. 52–60.

5. ''Silicon Valley's Design Renaissance,'' *New York Times*, 6 August 1991, Section 3.

6. Motorola is well known for its success in using fully automated production technologies in producing thousands of different kinds of pagers in its plants in the United States. Flexible manufacturing technologies can provide companies with sufficient economies of scope to offset the disadvantages of small production runs. Intelligent technology can also lead to economies of coordination—of research and development, production, marketing and sales—at the national and global levels by taking advantage of networking synergies. See Michael E. McGrath and Richard Hoole, ''Manufacturing's New Economies of Scale,'' *Harvard Business Review*, May-June 1992, pp. 102–105. Also B. J. Pine, *Mass Customization* (Cambridge: Harvard University School Press, 1993).

7. Kenichi Ohmae, ''The Global Logic of Strategic Alliances,'' *Harvard Business Review*, March-April 1989, pp. 143–147.

8. In the early nineties, the cost for producing 256 Mb DRAMs, for example, has been estimated at $1 billion in research and development and another $1 billion for building a factory. In the case of telecommunications, the investment costs are of the order of $2 billion. See ''The Costly Race Chipmakers Can't Afford to Lose,'' *Business Week*, 10 December 1990, p. 186; also ''Talk About Your Dream Team,'' *Business Week*, 27 July 1992, pp. 59–60; and Carl Edgar Law, ''Merger Mania Hits Europe with a Vengeance,'' *Business Communications Review*, February 1989, p. 68.

9. ''The Computerless Computer Company,'' *Harvard Business Review*, July-August 1991, pp. 69–78.

10. In *Business Week*'s 1992 ranking of the top 1,000 U.S. companies by stock market value, Microsoft jumped from 45th in 1991 to 24th place ahead of Ford Motor Company. Novell jumped from 185th to 83rd place, ahead of Apple Computer (90th position) and Xerox (100th position). IBM, on the other hand, slipped from first place to 7th place, and DEC from 54th to 94th place. In 1992 when Microsoft's stock was trading at a high of $95, it had a market valuation of $28.4 billion. At its low in 1992, IBM was worth just below $30 billion. Statistics like these illustrate the dramatic changes sweeping through the computer industry worldwide, that is, the shift away from hardware to software and services.

11. ''Bill Gates' Next Challenge,'' *Fortune*, 28 December 1992, pp. 31–41.

12. Leslie A. Taylor, ''The World Is Becoming the RHCs' Oyster,'' *Telephony*, 27 August 1990, pp. 44–49; also ''The Baby Bells Take Their Show on the Road,'' *Business Week*, 25 June 1990, pp. 104–106.

Chapter 9

War of the Worlds

The globalization of economic activity is without doubt one of the greatest challenges that every corporation, every government, and every individual must face and cope with now and in the future. At a minimum, globalization means a growing openness in the affairs of all countries with global trade playing an increasingly important role in determining economic growth, employment creation, and the prosperity of every nation. But it also means growing economic integration and interdependence among all national markets and national economies to the point that global economic and political issues supersede and dominate national ones in importance. At a maximum, globalization entails the elimination of all physical, spatial, geographical, and temporal barriers to social and economic activity. The intelligent infrastructures that nations and corporations are building throughout the world are synchronizing and rationalizing all social and economic activity on a global scale and giving rise to the convergence of economic and political systems everywhere.

The entire world is, in effect, being transformed into one gigantic integrated common market. All economic activity and all information, knowledge, science and technology, and money, securities, and educational and entertainment content and, indeed, all of the wealth and intellectual capital of the world are becoming mediated by electrons and photons processed by computers and distributed over optical fiber and radio and satellite communications networks.

National economies are being interconnected and integrated in space and time, thus making worker and managerial skills, educational systems, and innovation and productivity strategic variables in the equation of economic success of every nation.[1]

Globalization also means that the socioeconomic and political affairs of every country are now inextricably interdependent and interlinked with one another. The monetary and fiscal policies of individual nation-states have become interdependent along with domestic regulatory policies in telecommunications, banking, and financial services. The daily turmoil in international currency markets is evidence of this. Science and technology and research and development policies are now linked with industrial and trade policies. Trade policies, industrial policies, and even cultural policies have become dependent on telecommunications, standards for equipment manufacturing, and network interconnection as well as the allocation of radio frequencies and on computer systems and operating systems architectures. All of these, in turn, influence national and international banking and financial services regulatory policies. National security and defense policies now constitute other elements in this new matrix of political interdependencies among nations. Social policy, taxation policy, and regional development and transportation and energy policies are also interdependent.

For businesses, globalization ultimately means treating all of the economies in the world as one enormous market where all resources are allocated and goods and services produced and distributed according to strict global standards of performance. For nation-states and governments, it means that it is no longer possible to protect domestic industries from foreign competition or fund all of the costly social and economic programs as in the past. It means that nations and national economies and unions and workers in the national economies of the world must compete with one another to an increasing degree for jobs, investment, and economic growth. For governments and nation-states as a whole, it signifies a profound loss of cultural, economic, and political sovereignty. For everyone, it means a loss of security, protection, and even identity.

Since every nation and every national economy must now operate in this new global context, globalization means a fundamental rethinking of national policies and priorities toward economic growth and development and trade and competitiveness. It means that nations must abandon many of the industrial, regulatory, and trade and protectionist policies they have depended on in the past to serve their economic development objectives and adopt policies that promote investment in human capital and education. In some cases, it can even require nations to completely reverse their national economic policies of the past. Industrial policies that actually promote foreign investment, for example, are superior to those which have restricted it in the past. Strategies that promote innovation and change are superior to restrictive regulatory and antitrust policies that have confined them in earlier times because they enhance competitiveness. Cooperative industrial and trade and technology strategies are preferable to the go-it-alone nationalistic approaches of the past. And, policies that promote trade are preferable to protectionist policies. Free trade and free trade agreements, after all, are far superior to no trade at all, at least from an economic perspective.

The globalization of economic activity therefore calls for a new role for government as coach of the national team of economic players—of industries and interest groups—and as the principal agent and architect responsible for managing the human, financial, and economic resources of the nation. It is governments that have the responsibility for ensuring that they, along with the production and distribution systems of the nation, its infrastructures and institutions, are operating at global standards of performance and in harmony with the global community of players.

THE SUPREMACY OF KNOWLEDGE, SCIENCE, AND TECHNOLOGY IN GLOBAL ECONOMIC AND POLITICAL AFFAIRS

The rise of global transportation, electronic information, communications, and financial infrastructures linking all parts of the world along with the integration of world economies has opened up many new and unexplored potentials for economic growth and wealth creation. But it has also exposed every company, every industry, and every government to the realities of global competition. And it has precipitated a race among the nations of the world to use almost any means at their disposal to gain strategic competitive advantage. The stakes in this international race have become so great that it now supersedes the arms race in importance.

The scientific and engineering laboratories of the world where knowledge is produced and products are designed represent the new battlefields where these economic wars are waged. The scientists, engineers, software designers, computer programmers, and content producers constitute their armies of foot soldiers and their entrepreneurs represent their commanding officers. The new weapons and factors of production are the brains and minds and creative skills of scientists, engineers, and other knowledge workers and the imagination and creativity of product designers, inventors, managers, and content producers. The new global warfare model is now based on the world control and domination over invention, ideas and information and the discovery and application of knowledge and science, technology, engineering, and managerial skills. These also constitute the new sources of global power and wealth of nations and the world.

National industrial development policies are still one of the most popular and, indeed, one of the most effective means for nations and governments to cope with the challenges they face in an increasingly globalized economy. In some respects every nation must have a strategy, be it to gain or maintain a lead in this global race, to catch up to the leaders or to simply avoid falling further behind. The strategic factors that will decide the winners include a highly educated, highly skilled and highly motivated workforce, superior management, vast amounts of capital for investment purposes, access to global markets, a superior economic infrastructure, and the capability to rapidly and efficiently innovate and develop and commercialize new scientific and technological inventions and discoveries on an ever-decreasing time scale. And nations are doing everything they can to excel in all of these areas.

The front-runners in this global race are the United States, Japan, and the European Community, which represent the foci of what Kenichi Ohmae has called the "triad" of global power. It is from this triad that economic power and control are now exercised over the global economy. Its members are battling it out for domination over all aspects of control of the development and application of knowledge and technology in the world today.[2] Japan has closed the gap that the United States built up in the early postwar years and taken the leadership in a growing number of high-technology products, including memory chips, and it now controls many segments of the intelligent hardware economy worldwide. Britain, France, and West Germany and other European countries are endeavoring to catch up or avoid falling further behind the United States and Japan. Other nations, such as South Korea, Taiwan, Hong Kong, and Singapore, are doing their best to close the technological and economic gaps with Japan, Europe, and the United States in key industrial sectors.

Each of the major players has its own institutions and chosen instruments for promoting its industrial development goals and objectives. In Japan, it continues to be the famous Ministry of International Trade and Industry (MITI), which has been credited with nothing less than creating the postwar economic miracle in Japan. In the United States, institutions such as the Pentagon, the Defense Department's Advanced Research Projects Agency (DARPA), and the National Aeronautics and Space Administration (NASA), along with a variety of public and private scientific research institutions, such as MIT and Bell Telephone Laboratories, which in large part have been responsible for America's preeminence in science and technology. The European Commission now spearheads Europe's high-technology strategy with individual states playing a strong, cooperative roles.

The national industrial policies of leading nations typically target critical enabling technologies that are perceived to have strategic competitive significance to the nation.[3] These include biotechnology, pharmacology, nanotechnology, advanced materials science, ceramics, low-temperature "superconductor" physics, medical electronics, and opto-electronic, and photonic, semiconductor technologies. Next generation computer and communications technologies as well as software and artificial intelligence and knowledge-based systems are also the targets. Critical enabling technologies such as these are viewed as being of strategic economic importance because they represent major bottlenecks which, once overcome, could lead to global leadership. Complementing these is a variety of public policies targeting the application of these technologies. National strategies also focus on the soft side of the spectrum of industrial development policies, emphasizing organizational and human resource dimensions and education and training policies, for example. The public policy mix also includes antitrust and regulatory and privatization policies, as well as government sponsorship of cooperative ventures and strategic alliances among firms, industries, and universities.

European, American, and Asian nations have been engaged in this global high-technology race for more than a decade. Their governments have been channeling hundreds of millions and even billions of investment dollars in some cases into pure and applied research and development programs involving universities, industries, and government in an effort to gain strategic competitive advantages over the others. Spearheading this new form of scientific and technological and economic warfare has become an important role and responsibility for governments in the postindustrial era. The outcome of this war could decide whether global industrial, economic, and political power will be shared and distributed among nations more or less equally, or whether it will be concentrated and controlled by one nation or by a few. This technoeconomic war could exacerbate the economic divide between the rich and poor nations of the world, or it could go a long way towards lessening or eradicating it altogether.

THE JAPANESE CHALLENGE

If we accept the fact that the United States has not had an "explicit" national industrial policy, then Japan, more than any other country, has benefited from having an explicit one. Japan's industrial policies, spearheaded by MITI, its unique industrial and technology-oriented culture and its organization of production under the *keiretsu* system are among the most critical factors that have contributed to Japan's success. But its public policies towards the production and access and distribution of knowledge and the manner in which it has applied science and technology to all industrial activities have also contributed to its rise as an economic superpower. Japan has demonstrated that knowledge, technology, and organization and human resources (in conjunction with appropriate export-oriented and protectionist trade policies) are more critical to economic growth and competitiveness than huge reserves of energy or raw materials.

Since its 1972 "Plan for Information Society," which targeted computers and information technology as the key component and focus of its industrial strategy, the Japanese government has followed on with program after program aimed at developing leading-edge technologies and scientific, technological and knowledge resources.[4] MITI also initiated a series of advanced technology projects in the eighties, ranging from fifth-generation computers, artificial intelligence, and robots to databases and satellites. Japan's fifth-generation computer project, launched in 1981, was designed to produce a new generation of knowledge-based or knowledge-processing computer systems. Its 1983 Technopolis Plan developed a blueprint for building a network of nineteen high-tech communities in lesser developed areas based on the silicon valley model.[5] These are expected to become the engines of economic growth in the twenty-first century. Its Real-time Operating System Nucleus (TRON) program was launched in the mid-eighties to develop a common set of hardware and software architectures for an integrated all-electronic society.[6] Research has been carried out to develop real-time operating systems in three strategic areas—business, home, and industrial and communications systems applications—together with an overall architecture designed to achieve full transparency across all platforms. This is one of a series of programs that Japan launched to gain world supremacy in software in the nineties when it hoped to challenge the United States' leadership in yet another high-technology field.

Since 1987, over 200 Japanese companies have been involved in the "Manufacturing 21" program, one of the most advanced and ambitious manufacturing-technology programs in the world. Japan also has an extensive program to develop and apply neural technology in many of its products for export, and it is also a leader in the application of fuzzy logic. Fuzzy logic is a mathematical method based on approximations, such as many, close to, low or high rather than explicit numbers. Japanese companies are installing fuzzy logic devices in many consumer product lines as well as automobiles, for example, to make decisions based on the behavioral patterns of their owners and users. Japanese companies are positioning themselves in these technologies to extend their domination of the worldwide consumer electronics industry into the nineties and beyond.

Many of MITI's ambitious programs have been highly successful. Companies have benefited from the knowledge, insight, and experience, especially shared experience, they have gained from participating in these programs as well as being able to share the huge costs of such developments and reduce their risk. One of the results is that Japanese companies have caught up and surpassed the United States in a growing number of high-technology areas, and they now dominate certain product lines, for example the production of some lines of high-capacity computer memories. Japanese companies completely dominate the world market for flat panel displays.

But some of MITI's most promising and most expensive projects have also been dismal failures by its own admission. In 1992, for example, Japan acknowledged the failure of its fifth-generation computer project and promised to give away all of its developments to industry free of charge. And, in February 1994, top officials of the Ministry of Posts and Telecommunications announced that the country was considering abandoning its high-definition television program in which it had ploughed billions of dollars in investments for over thirty years. Nippon Hoso Kyobai Broadcasting Corporation (NHK), Japan's state-owned broadcaster, admitted that the program was made obsolete by America's all-digital television designs. Japan has also failed to develop an internationally competitive software industry. But these failures have not deterred MITI. Soon after abandoning its fifth-generation computer project in 1992, MITI announced its so-called Real-World Computing Project (or sixth-generation computer project) which is designed to develop "flexible information processing" or "soft logic'' systems to enable computers to see and recognize objects and human facial expressions and gestures and understand human speech.

The success of Japan's national industrial strategy has brought it into increasing conflict with its major trading partners, especially the United States and the European Community, and, under this pressure, Japan has begun opening up its programs to participation by foreign companies. One of these is an international ten-year, $1 billion program, proposed in 1990, to develop an ''Intelligent Manufacturing System.'' The program would integrate factory technologies from major industrialized countries, develop a worldwide standard for future factory technologies, and pool international resources to create a twenty-first-century high-technology system. Companies, universities, and governments in the United States and Europe have been invited to participate in the project, and MITI has offered to pick up 60 percent of the cost. Japan has also invited American companies to participate for the first time in its sixth-generation computer project. IBM is a participant in this program.

The Japanese government is continuing to target other enabling technologies including new ceramic materials and satellites, as well as biotechnology and others in defense and aerospace to improve its industrial strengths. Japan is also building a commercial rocket-launching and satellite communications industries to compete with that of the United States and Europe. Another strategic target of its ambitious industrial plans is the development of a national optical fiber infrastructure leading into every home of the nation. Officials at MITI view this as a means of developing a new information-based social infrastructure. Among these is a $250 billion plan to build an advanced intelligent network (AIN) infrastructure by the year 2015. Nippon Telephone and Telegraph is also developing what it calls its Visual, Intelligent, and Personal Communications Service (VI&P), and it has plans on the drawing board to invest as much as $4 trillion in telecommunications infrastructures before year 2015. In ways such as these, Japan has clearly set its sights on becoming one of the leading knowledge developers and appliers of technology and one of the leading knowledge exporters in the world as a means of securing and ensuring its success throughout the remainder of the decade and beyond. Newly industrializing countries, particularly in Asia, look at Japan as a model for their own development, and they are challenging Japan's growing hegemony in Asia.

EUROPEAN HIGH-TECHNOLOGY STRATEGIES

National industrial strategies have played an important role in the economic development of Western Europe in the postwar period. As described in chapter 4, Britain, France, and West Germany, for example, set up national industrial projects throughout the seventies and eighties to develop their semiconductor, computer, and software industries while targeting key industrial and educational applications. These had limited success, however. By the late eighties, legislation creating a single European market was beginning to take effect, and pan-

European initiatives were overtaking national programs. Among the most ambitious European high-technology projects are ESPRIT (European Strategic Program for Research into Information Technology), a $9.8 billion program with the objective of strengthening European microelectronics technology in areas like integrated circuit design and computer-aided manufacturing and EUREKA (European Research Coordination Agency), a $15 billion, nineteen-nation program, involving 297 joint government-industry cooperative projects designed to gain strength in such fields as high-definition television and automobile guidance systems. The European Community is also spearheading a number of infrastructure projects including the $2.8 billion RACE (Research on Advanced Communications Technologies in Europe) program, which focuses on the development of broadband networks and telematic programs and the building of a number of trans-European networks for cooperating in education and training, libraries, linguistics, administration, transport, health care, and rural services.

Europe also has its STAR (Strategic Telecommunications Applications for Regional Development) Program to foster the adoption and diffusion of telecommunications technology and services especially throughout underdeveloped regions. Still another is the Joint European Submicron Silicon Initiative (JESSI), an eight-year, $4 U.S. billion venture similar to the U.S. Sematech Program. Europe has also targeted $3.2 billion for advanced materials and manufacturing technology. The European Union's Advanced Computer Research Institute in Lyons in France has developed a supercomputer which it is marketing worldwide. Most European countries now have their own home-grown silicon valleys. England has Milton Keynes and Cambridge. France has high-technology centers in Grenoble and near Paris. Germany has its technoparks in Berlin, Stuttgart, and Munich. Even Scotland has its own, called naturally, "Silicon Glen," which comprises a hundred-kilometer corridor stretching across Scotland north of Glasgow. Four hundred fifty of the largest high-tech companies in the world are located here.

European initiatives are also designed to foster the development of advanced telecommunications infrastructures, including fully digital networks and optical fibers, satellites, and digital cellular radio telephone, systems in addition to high-definition television. The European Union has its own intelligent manufacturing technology program like the Japanese and the United States and European countries, and it is broadening its efforts to gain a growing piece of the action in the global high-technology game. The European Laboratory for Particle Physics is a fourteen-nation research project that has built the world's largest atom smasher, a seventeen-mile long large electron positron collider or LEP. Europeans also have projects underway to conduct research and development in such strategic areas as new fighter aircraft, antitank, and antiaircraft missiles and plans to build a prototype nuclear fusion reactor. The Airbus consortium of companies from France, Britain, Spain, and West Germany has also become the world's number two manufacturer of passenger aircraft, Boeing Corporation being number one. The European Consortium Arianespace now controls as much as 65 percent of the world's commercial rocket-launching market and is optimistic that it can increase its share. Much of this share has been at the expense of the United States which controlled 100 percent in the seventies. The European Space Agency has built more than thirty satellites for telecommunications and meteorological and scientific research purposes, and it is building the $4.8 billion space shuttle as part of the planned international space station. The European Commission is also laying plans for the creation of what it refers to as an "European Nervous System" modeled after the Internet.

The European Union's industrial strategy has had a down side, however. In fact, European nations have fallen behind Japan and the United States in semiconductors and computer technology, and have abandoned their all-digital television program. The most unique feature of Europe's industrial strategy, however, may be its cooperative, cost-sharing approach to funding high-science and technology projects. This approach may eventually be adopted by other countries and even on an international scale, for even the United States and Japan are finding it increasingly difficult to come up with the billions of dollars needed to fund science and technology programs, especially since the end of the cold war.

REINVENTING THE AMERICAN INDUSTRIAL REVOLUTION

The United States has been slow to respond to the new global economic and political realities that have emerged in recent years but this is changing. The rise of Japan as an industrial superpower and the relative decline of American industrial power coupled with the end of the cold war and the rapid decline in the strategic importance of military power are challenges with which the United States has found difficult coping. The nation can clearly no longer depend on its vast expenditures on military weapons and space systems to stimulate its high-technology industries. The positive linkages between military expenditure, research and development, technological innovation, and economic growth are no longer as effective as they used to be. In fact, military expenditures are now widely recognized as a burden, rather than a stimulus, to economic performance and competitiveness. The economic prosperity of the United States is also threatened by its low savings rate, low investments in social and economic infrastructure, and declining educational standards. Investments in research and development are now lower in the United States than in Japan. The upside, however, is that the government, business leaders, and the public at large, according to *Business Week*, now recognize that these must be overcome if the nation is to grow and prosper.[7]

The United States began overhauling the way it manages its industrial and technology policies in the eighties, and this process has been accelerating since then. One of the ways in which the United States has done so is to adopt and adapt some of the industrial and institutional innovations pioneered by Japan. These include a more activist role for government in supporting and even leading a number of industry-specific, high-technology research and development initiatives in civilian technologies, much like MITI has traditionally done.[8] The U.S. government is also encouraging more cooperation among companies and industries, even to the point of creating its own American-style *keire.su*. Under the Reagan administration, for example, it began relaxing its antitrust laws to make it possible for American companies to cooperate and engage in "precompetitive" research and development activities. Congress eventually passed the National Cooperative Research Act which explicitly encourages corporations to undertake joint research into long-term, risky projects that are too expensive for one company to finance by itself.

The new policy thrust has had immediate and, some would say, impressive results. In 1982, twelve major corporations formed the Microelectronics and Computer Technology Corporation (MCC) with the objective of collaborating on high-risk, precompetitive research and development initiatives. Membership in the MCC includes DEC, Motorola, Control Data, and Honeywell. In the same year, IBM, Intel, RCA, and thirty-two other companies formed the Semiconductor Research Corporation (SRC) to fund basic research into microelectronics. In response to a 1987, $1 billion program aimed at restoring American leadership in semiconductor-making equipment, fourteen semiconductor manufacturers formed Sematech (Semiconductor Manufacturing Technology Corporation) to make very high-capacity, dynamic, random-access memories. In the same year, the Semiconductor Industry Association announced the formation of U.S. Memories to produce the next generation of D RAM. Members of the consortium included IBM, DEC, HP, Intel, National Semiconductor, Advanced Micro Devices, and LSI Logic. U.S. Memories has been working with Sematech to develop advanced chip-making technology using special semiconductor technology developed by and licensed from IBM.

Some of these initiatives have already produced promising results. In the summer of 1992, for example, Silicon Valley Group Limited, a product of America's Sematech initiative, announced a breakthrough in optical lithography technology that many believe will make it possible to produce chips with circuit widths of .25 microns and smaller. This could enable American companies to leapfrog Japanese technology in the production of very high capacity memory chips.

In 1988, Congress passed The Omnibus Trade and Competition Act which resulted in the creation of the Advanced Technology Program to provide seed funding for consortia of government agencies, industry, and universities to engage in areas of generic research, such as ceramics, superconductivity, and robotics, and to transfer research from government to industry. And it followed up these initiatives with the $2 billion High Performance Computing Act which was passed by Congress in December 1991. This program targets four areas of strategic importance to the future of the American microelectronics and computer and telecommunications industries and its telecommunications infrastructure, and links these to the future economic development and competitiveness of the nation. One of these, the "teraflop" initiative, is designed to support research into computer architectures, microelectronics, and software for developing high-performance computers operating in the trillions of floating point operations per second. A second initiative targets advanced software technologies and algorithms for specific applications. A third targets a national research and educational network (NREN), and a fourth targets investments into upgrading university computer science departments and increasing the number of Ph.D.s by 1995. Several of these also target the development of America's "information superhighway."

Concerned that the American electronics industry will be decimated by the Japanese domination of the high-definition television business, the U.S. government has allocated funds to finance joint ventures among leading American high-technology companies to develop an all-digital television system. AT&T's Bell Labs teamed up with Zenith Electronics. American Television Alliance became involved separately in alliances with MIT and General Instruments. The David Sarnoff Labs, NBC, and Compression Labs are also involved in a consortium with Philips Electronics and Thompson Electronics. In May 1993, the four consortia announced an agreement to pool their designs and expertise to create a single world standard for all-digital television set design. Other consortia are targeting promising high-tech developments that require huge amounts of capital investment. One of these is the Optoelectronic Technology Consortium, formed in 1992 by AT&T, IBM, Honeywell, and General Electric with $8 million in funding from DARPA. Its mission is to develop advanced switching technologies that can be used by computers and high-speed telecommunications switches. The project aims to develop equipment which, operating in parallel, will be capable of transmission speeds of 64 Gbps.

The United States has also developed its own "twenty-first century manufacturing enterprise strategy," to develop factories "that could enable U.S. industry to match and surpass the ambitious programs underway in Japan and Europe."[9] The intelligent vehicular highway systems (IVHS) program is another multimillion dollar industrial program which the U.S. government is sponsoring. Through such programs as these, America has been attempting to renew its technological and industrial leadership and develop new strengths. It is betting hundreds of billions of dollars that these industrial programs will pay off.

The United States has also put the development of a nationwide information and telecommunications infrastructure at the top of its industrial, economic, and political agenda. Besides the High Performance Computing Act of 1991, Congress also approved the Communications Competitiveness and Infrastructure Modernization Act of 1991 to "advance the national interest by promoting and encouraging the more rapid development and deployment of a nationwide, advanced, interactive, interoperable, broadband telecommunications infrastructure on or before 2015." This is the same year that Japan has set to achieve a similar goal. The Information Infrastructure and Technology Act introduced in August 1992, is intended to complement the high-performance computing initiative by supporting applications in education, health care, and manufacturing. But the number and variety and scope of infrastructure policy initiatives increased dramatically under Clinton administration, which has put the development of the nation's information superhighways at the top of its political agenda.

The changing nature of America's industrial policy is also demonstrated by the increasing leadership role that the FCC is playing as a facilitator in the development of America's telecommunications and information industries and advancing the development of its information and communications infrastructure. The FCC orchestrated the formation of the "grand alliance" of companies to establish the new world standard for high-definition television. It has also become more aggressive in recent years in the strategic management of the radio frequency spectrum as a means of achieving national industrial objectives. It has allocated generous radio frequencies for emerging radio communications technologies to stimulate the development of new wireless personal computer-communications devices and new services such as interactive newspapers and video-on-demand.

The United States has also been creating what it hopes will be more effective alternatives to special federal agencies such as the Pentagon, Department of Defense, and NASA to spearhead its industrial-technology strategy. It has redirected the efforts of many of these agencies and provided funding for its big defense contractors to enable them to pursue more commercially relevant research and development objectives that could have a direct effect on the nation's industrial competitiveness and its trade deficit. Discussions have taken place to create a civilian technology agency, similar to the National Science Foundation, which would focus on applied research and the creation of a civilian technology corporation to fund companies commercializing new technologies.

Some have argued that the main thrusts of America's current industrial policy is the creation of an new enterprise model similar to that of Japan's *keiretsu*. Many large American businesses have, indeed, taken advantage of the liberal industrial and antitrust environment by creating their own highly diversified coalitions and cooperative ventures among manufacturers, suppliers, and finance companies. Between 1986 and 1992, according to *Business Week*, "hundreds of companies . . . in industries as diverse as computers, semiconductors, autos, farm implements and motorcycles [revamped] their corporate cultures and [recast] their investment practices to form cooperative links both vertically, down their supply lines, and horizontally, with universities, research labs, and their peers."[10] These links serve to share development costs, spread risks, take advantage of synergies, and provide access to management and marketing and other kinds of expertise.

Charles Ferguson, a research associate at IBM's Center for Technology, Policy, and Industrial Development, believes that the only way the United States can reassert its leadership in the global economy is by adopting an explicit policy of encouraging the creation of more of these industrial *keiretsu*. In an article in the *Harvard Business Review*, in 1990, he wrote,

Only by building appropriate corporate complexes will U.S. and European companies be able to secure their supply base against the strategic pressures exerted by integrated Japanese competitors and obtain sufficient financial return from the commercialization of innovative designs. Only by co-operating as they compete will U.S. companies be able to rationalize major component sectors, maintain a technically competitive, non-Japanese capital-equipment and components supply base, and create long-term, reciprocal partnerships between innovative designers, standards developers, large-scale manufacturers, suppliers, and distribution channels.[11]

THE EVOLUTION OF A NEW GLOBAL ECONOMIC ORDER

The globalization of economic activity and the growing intensity of global competition together with the growing knowledge and technology intensity of economic activity are creating a new world economic and political order that affects every individual, every company, and every nation. And governments everywhere are revising and refocusing their industrial policies and their economic and political institutions, upgrading and modernizing their socioeconomic infrastructures, and mobilizing their human resources as best they can to position themselves so they can prosper in this evolving new order. The new order comprises what I will refer to as the "first-tier" bloc of countries whose economies have entered the postindustrial, knowledge-based, "intellectual capital" age. The "second-tier" comprises what have been referred to as the newly industrializing countries that have been making progress up the ladder of economic success by pursuing appropriate foreign investment, trade, technology, and other industrial policies. These countries have specialized in labor-intensive production activities in traditional manufacturing and assembly operations where their labor costs, proximity to global markets, or access to natural or other resources have given them a strategic competitive advantage. "Third-tier" countries are those that are entering the industrial stage of economic development.

First-tier countries consist of those in the global triad of economic power, that is, the European Community, led by Germany, France, Italy, and Great Britain; North America, led by the United States; and Asia, led by Japan. Second-tier countries include the so-called Asian dragons of South Korea, Taiwan, Hong Kong, and Singapore. Following closely are countries such as the Philippines, Malaysia, Thailand, and Indonesia, Mexico, and Brazil, for example. Third-tier countries consist of the majority of African, South American, Eastern European, and Asian countries including India, China, Vietnam, and North Korea.

Countries in each of these tiers are interacting with and competing with one another and increasingly with those in other tiers. Second-tier countries have been coming under growing competitive pressures from within their own group as well as from those in the third tier. They are being forced to specialize in higher-value, knowledge-intensive, technology-intensive, and skills-intensive manufacturing activities. The leaders are abandoning their previous positions to third-tier countries and putting increasing competitive pressure on the postindustrial, first-tier countries, in those areas of economic activity where they have traditionally enjoyed strategic competitive advantages and strengths.

Third-tier countries are advancing on those in the second tier by taking advantage of their indigenous economic strengths, whether they be of a human resource nature or their geographic location or their supplies of natural resources. South Korea, Hong Kong, and Singapore, for example, and even Thailand and Malaysia now view microelectronics, computer, and telecommunications technologies along with software, information, and telecommunications infrastructures as strategic to their success. These industries typically constitute core elements in the industrial strategies of almost every second-tier nation.[12] All of the leading Asian countries have even built their own silicon valleys and science cities based on Western models. Taiwan's science city is called Hsinchu, near Taipei. South Korea's is called Taeduck. Typically, these cities have their own universities, industrial parks, and accommodation for tens of thousands of research scientists and engineers. Asia's second-tier nations also put great emphasis on telecommunications infrastructure. Several, such as Singapore, now have more advanced computer and communications infrastructures than those of any member of the first tier. And they have used this to strategic advantage, particularly in their battle with Tokyo to become Asia's financial and trading center. Between 1992 and 1994, Singapore and Hong Kong outperformed Tokyo in terms of new listings and capital turnover, according to *The Economist*. In other words, there may be some scope and possibility for certain second-tier countries to leapfrog first-tier countries in the hierarchy of economic development and evolution in the decades ahead. That is what countries like South Korea, Singapore, and China would like to think.

South Korea has become a model of industrial and economic success for many developing countries and it is even threatening Japan's hegemony in the Pacific in certain areas. It has become a major exporter of very high quality, technology-intensive products like personal computers, automobiles, and high-quality stereo, microwave, and VCR equipment. Korean manufacturers are also challenging the lead of Japan and the United States in the production of memory chips. Between 1988 and 1992, South Korean companies quintupled their share of the world DRAM market to 20 percent, primarily at the expense of the Japanese. South Korea has also developed its own *keiretsu* industrial groupings that have been responsible for much of the economic success of the nation. Lucky Gold Star and Dawoo have become household names that are now associated with high-quality consumer manufacturing, like Sony, Hitachi, Panasonic, and Toshiba. South Koreans also put a great deal of value on education. About 33 percent of

South Koreans leaving school go on for a university education, more than any other nation in the world. The South Korean government has identified strategic developments in key industries which it believes will be essential for the future competitiveness of its economy. These include 256 MB chips, high-definition television sets, and transmission equipment, flat panel displays, and multimedia computers which, until recently, only highly developed economies such as Japan and the United States could produce.

Led by its government ministries, South Korea has also built five national information networks including those for education, finance, and public administration as part of its national computerization project launched in 1989. And it is also diversifying its trading relationships and focusing on emerging world markets like China and Eastern and Western Europe while negotiating a union with North Korea.

Few, if any, countries have prospered more than Singapore in the strategic application of intelligent technology in its economic development plans, in spite of the fact that it is one of the smallest nations in the world and has no natural resources whatsoever. The source of Singapore's success, according to Rajendra Sisodia, writing in the *Harvard Business Review*, has been the development of a strategy which leverages on "its single natural advantage of strategic location by establishing worldclass transportation and materials handling facilities; [extending] such 'hubbing' into the financial and other service domains by establishing a sophisticated communications and information technology infrastructure; . . . [establishing] highly sophisticated, automated, and flexible manufacturing centers; . . . [while] continuously [upgrading] the skills of its work force to keep up with the more challenging demands placed upon it; and closely [monitoring] relevant global technological developments, absorbing them as quickly as possible."[13] With the encouragement of the government, many of the world's premier high-technology companies have located manufacturing operations in Singapore, and a growing number are locating their research and development facilities there as well. They include AT&T, Motorola, Mitsubishi, IBM, Apple Computer, Philips, and Hewlett-Packard.

It is in the application of information technology and telecommunications infrastructure that Singapore stands out, however. Convinced that information technology was strategic to the country's economic future, the government of Singapore established the National Computer Board back in 1980 to oversee all of the nation's computer-related activities and to develop an industrial strategy. This resulted in the creation of a comprehensive "National Information Technology Plan" in 1986, which the government has pursued ever since. The Singapore Network Services Corporation, which was subsequently set up, has developed networks for almost every conceivable activity. These include AutoNet, which targets manufacturing automation; RealNet which serves real estate applications; and others like LawNet, PortNet, MediNet, and BizNet, which provide services to South Korea's legal, medical, and business communities. Singapore became the first country in the world to achieve 100 percent

ISDN availability in 1989, and it now calls itself the world's most networked nation for these reasons. The government has now embarked on a follow-on "IT2000" plan to create what it calls an "intelligent island." Wisely, the government of Singapore has realized that political progress must go hand in hand with economic prosperity, and it is initiating changes to make the country more democratic.

Other Asian countries are attempting to jump into the same world-class, high-technology league as the United States, the Japanese, and the Europeans. Taiwan, for example, which is noted for its manufacturing base is facing stiffer competition from Thailand, Malaysia, and China where labor rates are as much as a quarter of its own. It is attempting to move into engineering design and software development, and it is promoting its research and development capabilities. Its silicon valley is called Hsinchu, which is near Taipei.

Even India has begun reversing its highly nationalistic industrial policy approach to economic development. Under the leadership of Prime Minister Narasimha Rao, the country decided to throw its doors open to the world in 1991, and the economy has begun to prosper. India now boasts its own silicon valley in the southern city of Bangalore where HP, 3M, TI, DEC, and IBM are now located to serve the growing Asian market and export to neighboring countries.[14] Its highly educated workforce now poses a serious competitive threat to the Western countries, including the United States and Japan, especially in software development and systems design. A 1992 study by the World Bank rated India as the most attractive nation in the world for Western companies seeking offshore software development partners. The Indian government is financing investments in telecommunications networks with global linkages to enable foreign and home-grown companies to develop software products and distribute them throughout the world. Companies are being attracted not only by the potential growth of the market and skills of Indian programmers but by their wages which are typically below the minimum wage in the United States. The Indian government is playing a leading role in globalizing and modernizing the Indian economy and transforming it into a modern high-tech state.

China has been quietly but rapidly switching over to a market-based economy, and it too is putting industrial development in general and the development of its high-technology industries in particular high on its list of economic priorities. In spite of the 1989 crackdown in Tiananmen Square, China has made tremendous strides in modernizing its production and distribution sectors, attracting foreign investment, and exporting its products all over the world. These and other policies propelled the Chinese economy to grow an average of 10 percent per annum throughout the eighties, and the Chinese government has taken steps to ensure that this success continues. The southern province of Guangdong, formerly Canton which is the closest province to Hong Kong, is the geographical center of China's new capitalism. Throughout the eighties, it succeeded in achieving an average annual growth rate of about 15 percent, a rate that exceeds that of the four Asian tigers when they were at the same stage of development.

Guangdong has attracted many big high-technology companies, like Lockheed and GEC of France, and it boasts of having created a new class of millionaires.

Other centers in China such as the northern port city of Tianjin are also flourishing. Here, Motorola is targeting a total investment of $400 million by 1996 in plants to produce pagers, integrated circuits, and cellular phones as well as automotive electronics, advanced microprocessors, and silicon wafers.[15] Other high-tech companies, like AT&T, Alcatel N.V., Siemens, Philips, Samsung, and NEC are also moving into China. AT&T reached a $1 billion agreement with the Chinese government in 1993 to manufacture telephone switches, wireless phones, and integrated circuits. General Electric has targeted China as well as India and South America for its vast expansion plans in the late nineties and beyond. It plans to source as much as 25 percent of its revenues from both of these countries by the year 2000. Its plans include everything from power plants and jet engines to appliances, plastics, and medical systems.

China is also a world-leading high-tech country in other areas as well. It is one of the few countries with space-launching facilities which puts it in the superleague with the United States, Europe, and Russia, and it is marketing its launching facilities worldwide. It also has a well-developed nuclear capability, and it is one of the leading suppliers of sophisticated military weapons. One of these, the Silk Worm missile, won considerable notoriety in a number of international military engagements in the eighties, including the Middle East. Like other countries in Southeast Asia, China is promoting market-oriented and export-oriented industrial policies as well as foreign investment policies along with advanced education, high skills, and human resource policies in its efforts to become a global economic superpower. But it is also committed to creating its own unique kind of capitalism.

National and international telecommunications networks and services have also become a focal point of the economic development plans of many third-tier countries. This is because international telecommunications networks provide a means for them to take advantage of their low-wage worker population to develop thriving export market niches for information capture, conversion, and processing services for airline tickets, insurance claims, mailing lists, and coupons for credit card companies, banks and other financial institutions, as well as electronic publishing, hotel and airline reservations, and credit card authorization.[16] Ireland and Singapore were the first to develop these markets in the eighties. But countries like the Philippines and Jamaica, the Dominican Republic, Barbados, and St. Lucia in the Caribbean have also developed thriving export markets in these services. These countries are now making efforts to expand into other higher-value services involving software and custom programming services, as well as CAD/CAM applications, mapping, and geological services. This explains why the governments of these countries have put a high priority on the development of advanced telecommunications infrastructures that offer high-speed digital communications and audio and video teleconferencing and voice mail services, for example.

More and more countries are pioneering many other bold new policy directions and initiatives to achieve their national economic development goals in the nineties. The reality is that most countries—not only industrializing and developing countries, but industrialized ones as well—do not have a great deal of choice in the policies they pursue to achieve their industrial and economic development goals as rapidly as they might like. Few countries have all of the technological and engineering skills and the manufacturing base within their borders to supply all of necessary equipment and systems to build and manage the new telecommunications infrastructures, and few have the huge amounts of capital to invest into developing these infrastructures that are so fundamental to their future economic well-being. The reality is that the only way many countries can make the great leap forward is by importing the expertise, the technology, the equipment and systems, and the investment capital. And that is what many governments have been doing. They are providing incentives for foreign carriers to do the job for them.

Satisfied with the success of the privatization efforts in Britain and Japan, governments on other continents—from Poland, Russia, Czechoslovakia, and Hungary in Eastern Europe; Mexico in North American; Venezuela and Brazil and others in South America; and others throughout Asia and across the Pacific Rim as well as in Africa—have become engaged in a colossal privatization of state-owned companies to advance their telecommunications and economic development goals and catapult themselves into the information league of nations. They are liberalizing regulations on foreign investment and foreign ownership and actively promoting the sale of nationalized companies to consortia of domestic and foreign companies. Governments are also auctioning off licenses to foreign carriers to operate cellular and cable television franchises within their borders, as described in chapter 8. Foreign companies—telecommunications carriers and cable television companies in the United States, United Kingdom, France, Germany, and so on—are becoming in this way the most important source of much-needed investment capital and engineering and systems expertise that most third-tier countries need.

Evidently, foreign ownership is a small price for the economic benefits they bring to these countries. The new thrust of the economic development policies of developing countries today is in stark contrast to that of the sixties and seventies when economic nationalism prevailed. The economic development policies that are in vogue today would have been regarded as heresy only a decade ago.

But the superior quality of the education systems and educational institutions of many leading developing nations, such as Hong Kong and Singapore as well as China, for example, along with their industrial policies and the quality of their human resources, among other factors one can argue, may provide them with an important long-lasting advantage over their rivals in other parts of the world. In February 1992, the Educational Testing Service published the results of its assessment of the performance of the education systems of various countries. At the top of the list were several newly developing countries including China and Hong Kong. Far down on the list in thirteenth place was the United States. The quality of the education systems may, therefore, explain to a significant degree the stellular performance of newly developing countries and the declining performance and the deindustrialization of the advanced industrialized economies.

Further evidence of the relative performance of the various countries that make up this new global economic order is provided by The World Competitiveness Report 1990, published by IMD and the World Economic Forum in Geneva, which ranks thirty-three OECD countries according to various indicators.[17] Singapore, for example, ranked number one and Hong Kong either number one, two, or three, in the various categories of infrastructure requirements which includes roads, air transport, port access, telecommunications, and power supply. The United Kingdom ranked between ten and seventeen in these categories while the United States ranked as high as one in telecommunications but as low as six in power supply and port access and number twelve in railroads. In terms of research and development Britain and the United States ranked between twelve and twenty while Singapore, for example, ranked number one in terms of expected future spending. Finally, in terms of total research and development personnel nationwide, Korea, Taiwan, and Singapore ranked one, two, and three, respectively, while the United States and the Britain ranked fifteen and eight respectively. Singapore also ranked number one in terms of its information technology policies and management with Korea a close second and third, respectively.

ADVANCED INDUSTRIALIZED COUNTRIES FIGHT BACK

First-tier countries are fighting these seemingly inexorable global technological and economic development trends and rapidly growing competition from second-tier countries through a variety of industrial and other policies. One of these is by using advanced automation, lean production, and flexible manufacturing techniques to their own strategic advantage to keep production activity along with the associated jobs and economic wealth within their own countries, and some are achieving success. Japan, for example, is well known for the enormous capital investments it has made to foster the development and deployment of robots throughout its economy in part to improve its productivity, its flexible manufacturing capabilities, and its competitiveness, but also to compensate for its aging population and to prepare for a future when it expects a shortage of younger skilled workers. As a result of this policy, Japan boasts that it has more robots than any other country in the world.[18]

American industry is also deploying robots to improve its competitiveness as part of its own industrial policy. Automation in the electronics industry, especially in the manufacture of semiconductors, computers, and telecommunications equipment, as well as radio and television sets, have enabled some American companies to repatriate manufacturing jobs from second-tier countries in Asia. And it has been automation and, as importantly, innovations in management, organization, and management-worker relationships, which it has borrowed to a significant degree from the Japanese, that has enabled American automobile manufacturers to eliminate, for all intents and purposes, the quality, efficiency, and productivity gaps they suffered with Japanese manufacturers in the eighties.

The complete adoption of advanced automation technologies and the building of fully automated plants in some cases provide American companies with one of the few means to become the most efficient producers in the world and create jobs and economic wealth in their home country. American textile companies, for example, have been using advanced automation technologies to gain a strategic competitive advantage in world markets and some are even repatriating their foreign operations. Even low-wage countries cannot compete with some of these fully automated flexible manufacturing plants in Japan and the United States. The experience of Motorola attests to this. In the early eighties, Motorola was devastated by Asian competitors, which flooded the world market with inexpensive radio communications equipment. But it successfully fought back by introducing fully automated flexible manufacturing systems in its plants in the United States. By 1985, it had succeeded once again in dominating the world market, and it has continued to do so since.

Fortune magazine has reported that big U.S. manufacturing companies, like AT&T, Texas Instruments, Xerox, GE Fanouc, and Tandy, have also shifted their production lines back to the United States from Hong Kong, South Korea, and even Japan to take advantage of lower labor costs, higher productivity, faster product development, quicker response, and more rapid delivery times in the United States.[19] Advanced automation and flexible manufacturing techniques permit companies to introduce continuous improvements in product designs and to customize these to local markets. JIT systems allow producers to maintain much lower inventories and provide faster response times. Many of the new technologies—automation, flexible manufacturing, paperless designs, teleconferencing, and EDI, for example—result in tremendous productivity gains especially when used together. They are providing competitive advantages to local manufacturing companies over foreign ones because they favor proximity to the marketplace at a time in which timeliness of response and delivery is critical to meeting customer demands. They also provide the only means of realizing the economic advantages of rapid, high-volume, customized production at costs that are comparable with mass production.

First-tier countries are also being forced to take strategic advantage of their leadership in intelligent technology, their strengths in software, systems design, and computer and network management skills and their advanced computer and communications infrastructures and all of the many application areas that they will spawn in the future. Software, for example, has already become a source of strategic competitive advantage for American manufacturing companies. In a 1994 article in *Fortune* entitled "The Digital Factory," Gene Bylinsky wrote, "Software is becoming more important than hardware—more important than machine tools—in American factories. And smart humans are back, replacing dumb robots.''[20] Whether it is in the form of computer simulation or computer-aided design software, flexible manufacturing systems or virtual, multimedia or workgroup technologies, or the communications networks that make all of these work together, software is powering the come-back of American industry. For it is these that enable IBM to produce as many as twenty-seven completely different products simultaneously, or General Electric, General Motors, or Caterpillar to produce machinery and equipment that is far superior to that of the Japanese.

Japan's Intelligent Manufacturing System project and its Manufacturing 21 project along with America's Twenty-First Century Manufacturing Enterprise strategy are also designed to enhance the competitiveness of their respective economies. The information superhighways that are under development in many countries will increasingly become a source of strategic competitive advantage in the future. The Clinton administration allocated as much as $1 billion in infrastructure megaprojects in 1992. Many of these are targeting software applications and content. It is hoped they will provide the catalytic effect on industry and the economy that the telephone and highway systems have had throughout the twentieth century.

But second-tier (and even third-tier) countries are also adopting similar industrial strategies to gain a strategic competitive edge on first-tier countries. Some, for example, are resorting to more-advanced automation techniques that make extensive use of robotic technologies in an attempt to leap into the first tier. As described above, they are also making better use of their national and global computer and telecommunications infrastructures to compete and make a place for themselves in the new world economic order. And, if member countries of the former Soviet Union succeed in making the transition to a market-based economy and building modern manufacturing and distribution and telecommunications infrastructures at the rate they would like, it is conceivable that they too could leapfrog into the first tier in as short a time as ten years.

The prospects of such a jump, however, appear to be much greater in China or India, or a free trading area in the Pacific in the next decade. Potentially, China is the single biggest market in the world. It is bigger than the markets of the United States, Japan, and Europe combined. If China can harness its human resources and its knowledge and science technology capabilities as well as Japan has done, and there is some evidence that it can, and if it can control its population and make a peaceful transition to democracy, it could well become Asia's and perhaps the world's leading economic superpower within the next quarter century. If this is possible then it is also possible that Asian capitalism, Asian culture and Asian values will dominate the world in a generation.

NOTES

1. A considerable literature has been generated in the past decade on the subject of globalization, global competitiveness and their importance to the national economy, corporate strategy and public policy. Among these are Michael E. Porter, *The Competitive*

Advantage of Nations (New York: Free Press, 1990): Kenichi Ohmae, *Borderless World: Power and Strategy in the International Economy* (New York: HarperCollins, 1990); and Robert Reich, *The Work of Nations* (New York: Alfred A. Knopf, 1991).

2. Lester Thurow, *Head to Head: The Coming Economic Battle Among Japan, Europe, and America* (New York: Morrow, 1992); and Jeffrey E. Garten, *A Cold Peace: America, Japan, Germany, and the Struggle for Supremacy* (New York: Time Books, 1992).

3. For an overview of the industrial policies of leading governments as they pertain to the computer industry, see Kenneth Flamm, *Targeting the Computer: Government Support and International Competition* (Washington D.C.: The Brookings Institution, 1987).

4. Marie Anchordoguy, "How Japan Built a Computer Industry," *Harvard Business Review*, July-August 1990, p. 65.

5. Sheridan Tatsuno, *The Technopolis Strategy: Japan, High Technology and the Control of the 21st Century* (Englewood Cliffs, N.J.: Prentice-Hall, 1986).

6. David Kellar, "TRON: Out of the Limelight," *Computerworld*, 30 November 1992, p. 28.

7. Christopher Farrell, Michael J. Mandel et al., "Industrial Policy," *Business Week*, 6 April 1992, pp. 70–75.

8. Lewis Branscomb, "Does America Need a Technology Policy?," *Harvard Business Review*, March-April 1992, pp. 24–31; also "Technology Policy: Is America on the Right Track?," *Harvard Business Review*, May-June 1992, pp. 140–160.

9. "This Is What the U.S. Must Do to Stay Competitive," *Business Week*, 16 December 1991, p. 92.

10. "Learning from Japan," *Business Week*, 27 January 1991, pp. 52–60.

11. Charles H. Ferguson, "Computers and the Coming U.S. Keiretsu," *Harvard Business Review*, July-August 1990, pp. 55–70.

12. Peter Robinson, *IT Imperatives: Computers and Communications for the 21st Century* (Amsterdam, Holland: Tide 2000 Secretariat, 1992).

13. Rajendra S. Sisodia, "Singapore Invests in the Nation-Corporation," *Harvard Business Review*, May-June 1992, pp. 40–50.

14. "In Southern India, a Glimpse of Asia's High-Tech Future," *New York Times*, 6 October 1991, p. F9. Citicorp, Hewlett-Packard, Lotus Development, Novell, IBM, Unisys, and Sun Microsystems all have partnerships with Indian companies in software and services. See "India's Software Edge," *BYTE*, September 1993, pp. 55–60.

15. "China: The Emerging Economic Powerhouse of the 21st Century," *Business Week*, 17 May 1993, pp. 54–68.

16. "Caribbean Seeks Role as World's Paperless Tiger," *Financial Times*, Spring 1992, p. 7.

17. IMD International, *The World Competitiveness Report 1990* (Lausanne, Switzerland: EMF Foundation, 1991).

18. Depending on the definition of the word "robot," Japan has between 60 and 75 percent of all the robots in the world.

19. Edmund Faltermayer, "U.S. Companies Come Back Home," *Fortune*, 30 December 1991, pp. 106–111.

20. Gene Bylinsky, "The Digital Factory," *Fortune*, 14 November 1994, p. 95.

Chapter 10

Into the Millennium

The electronic technology revolution has already come a long way but it has a long way to go before it is complete. Some of the most dramatic changes, I would argue, have yet to come. This is because the most important will be organizational, economic, sociocultural, and even political and these will take time. Managing these changes could be one of the greatest challenges facing businesses and governments.

It may happen that the information superhighways will never achieve the potential that visionaries have ascribed to them because the task of building them will be too great or too complex from an organizational, legal, or political point of view. They may need to be highly regulated. Perhaps they will concentrate economic power in the hands of a few powerful groups, stateless corporations, or *keiretsu* that operate in multiple sectors in every country of the world. It is also possible that they will enslave us in one way or another or result in massive unemployment. On the other hand, intelligent technology and information superhighways could lead to a great social and economic emancipation of people and enhance democracy. They could be a boon to small, personal, home-based microenterprises. They could also usher in a new age of innovation and entrepreneurship and create opportunities for everyone.

If the history described in this book has a message about the future, it is that many of the developments that visionaries have written about will probably not occur. On the other hand, certain developments will take place that even the experts did not and could not predict. Many of the really important scientific and technological breakthroughs throughout history for the most part were not predictable. Even those who invented them failed to realize their potential in many cases. With these caveats in mind, I believe it is possible to make certain technological, economic, and social forecasts based on trends and experience over the past decades and throughout this century.

Another realization is that science and technology will probably not be a limiting factor in defining what kind of organizations and what kind of economic society we will decide to create in the future. Developments in software, artificial intelligence, biotechnology, and genetic engineering will continue to open up vast opportunities to create new sources of wealth and spur economic growth and social progress. Whether we decide as a society to take advantage of these opportunities and make the necessary changes and sacrifices—and there will likely be sacrifices—are questions that cannot be answered at this time. Certain groups will likely be major beneficiaries of technological and economic progress while others could be big losers. How we deal with the problem of inequality of economic opportunity could well be one of the greatest challenges that governments and the world will face.

TECHNOLOGY TRENDS

Long-term technological and economic trends in the cost and performance of hardware will continue and, if anything, accelerate over the course of the next quarter century.[1] Computers and telecommunications switching and transmission systems will continue to shift from electronic to optoelectronic and photonic technologies[2] with staggering increases in processing power, memory capacities, and transmission and switching speeds and performance. Super-supercomputers, capable of operating in the teraflop range (trillions of floating point operations per second) will probably be on the leading edge of scientific and business applications by the year 2000, and the computers that will be common in the year 2015 could be as much as one thousand times faster. And developments in neural networks and biological computers that mimic the human brain could open up entirely new application areas where traditional sequential and parallel machines have failed.[3] Developments such as these will likely bring incredible intellectually stimulating, creative decision-making power to the computers of hundreds of millions of individuals throughout the world, and this, in turn, will stimulate fascinating productivity-enhancing developments in business through decision-support, workgroup, and virtual reality applications, for example.

Leading-edge innovations will have shifted to sophisticated software applications in the next quarter century and long-awaited breakthroughs will have been made in key application areas, such as expert systems, artificial intelligence, and multilingual speech and voice recognition and synthesis, thus making it possible to hold normal conversations with machines in dozens of languages.

Computers, telephones, and television sets as we know them today will no longer exist. They will be replaced by a variety of advanced multimedia devices with a combination of telephone, television, teleconferencing, blackboard, and telepresence features with powerful, easy-to-use, man-machine interfaces. Wallet-size and wristwatch-size personal digital assistants will also likely have full multimedia and mobile radio and satellite communications capabilities.

Optical fibers along with satellites and cellular and personal mobile radio communications systems will interconnect people in homes and offices and those on the move, wherever they choose to be in the global village, enabling them to go about their day-to-day work activities, to keep informed, and communicate and coordinate their activities by the day, the hour, and the minute. The hundreds of millions of powerful, multimedia personal computers will make many new kinds of economic, cultural, and political activities possible that were never before feasible. People will be able to keep informed, attend meetings, make decisions, and interact with others through the use of groupware software, teleconferencing, multimedia messages and documents, and interactive multimedia databases.

Advanced artificial intelligence features will make it possible for every individual to have his or her own personal software agent. These will increasingly take on the intellectual character of the individual they serve. They will automatically monitor the databanks and communications channels of the world and access and retrieve documents, reports, articles or any kind of content that could interest their owner. These agents will eventually be able to analyze and extract relevant information, create other agents that will report back to themselves and even learn, communicate, and exchange information with their own kind and assemble this for human use. The intelligent infrastructure will evolve in varying degrees into a universal information medium, a universal library medium, a universal retail medium, a universal banking medium, a universal marketing medium, and possibly a universal medium for electronic democracy.

THE FUTURE OF PUBLISHING, BANKING
AND FINANCIAL SERVICES, EDUCATION, AND
HEALTH CARE

Newspaper publishing could become transformed by multimedia technology over the coming decades into a personalized audio, video, and bibliographic medium distributed via electronic storage media or accessed and delivered online and stored and managed locally. Giant newspaper and magazine publishers throughout the world will have been forced by competitive pressures to forge even bigger global alliances to create and manage enormous databanks of information and customize and communicate this information for their clients in homes and offices in every part of the world. Local, national, and international libraries will likely become integrated into a single virtual library accessible throughout the world.

Banks, brokerages houses, investment dealers, and stock exchanges will probably operate in highly decentralized and dispersed office environments but connected with one another by powerful multimedia workstations and efficient, high-capacity telecommunications networks. Stock exchanges and futures, options, and commodities exchanges as we know them today will not have any trading floors, and banks and insurance companies will probably no longer be confined to big buildings in big cities and staffed by hundreds, or even thousands, of central office people. Computers will have completely taken over all of the exchanges of the world. They will be used to gather all of the information from relevant markets around the world, process it, and make decisions on alternative investment strategies based on neural network models and execute trades and make the necessary payments and settlements—all automatically and transparently so efficiently and accurately that no one will bother to check on the details.

The stock exchanges of the future will likely be conspicuous by the absence of people—of brokers, traders, and specialists—as physically active mediators and middlemen in their internal operations. This is because people will not be able to cope with the huge volumes of information needed to play all of the exchanges in the world or cope with the incredibly high speeds at which trading and transactions will occur. These functions too will be delegated to computer software agents which will be programmed to act in the interest of individual traders and their clients. Competition could be among these software-based trading agents, each programmed with the trading philosophies and investment strategies of their investment mentors. Through their personal trading agents, people will be able to play the stock markets of the world, to manage and invest money and wealth, and to trade and transact business on a global scale from a personal computer located anywhere in the world.

The transportation networks will eventually be overlaid with an intelligent infrastructure giving them the capabilities to monitor and control aircraft, trucks, trains, and cars, and keep track of people and freight, and electronic maps will aid navigation of all moving vehicles. Fully automated aircraft navigation and take-off and landing systems and computer-controlled and computer-guided automobiles and highways will likely be common.

Postal services and the education and health care industries will have become mediated in large part by intelligent technology by the year 2015. Doctors, psychiatrists, psychologists, and medical clinics will likely have access to sophisticated, computerized diagnostic equipment. A universal, automated patient records system providing the complete case history of all patients could come into existence by then as well. Expert systems will be capable of complete diagnostic procedures through access to a universal database of baseline data and case studies. Computer-based medical technology such as this could even become available to individuals in the home. Complete computer-based training and education courseware will become increasingly common in the secondary and postsecondary education as well as in the home. Technology could make it possible for a student to take complete courses or complete a year of work or even a university degree from Yale, Harvard, Cambridge, or another international university while remaining at home.

THE OFFICE-, FACTORY-, AND HOME-OF-THE-FUTURE

The office, the factory, and the home will become transformed into fully electronic and intelligent entities with personal computers and communications devices, displays, and so on, becoming embedded into the desks, the walls, and furniture of every kind.[4] The only way people and organizations will be able to cope with the avalanche of multimedia personal and business information and educational, entertainment, and other kinds of intellectual content will be through full computer mediation, and it is this need combined with improved economics and performance of the information and communications infrastructure that will propel the acceptance of this new world. This, in turn, will most likely render obsolete the mountains of paper files and filing systems that are so common in the office of today.

Factories will have become completely electronic and decentralized and distributed throughout the world as well, perhaps by year 2015, with groups of engineers in various countries using computer-based design, simulation, and testing tools to create their products, equipment, and machinery entirely in software, while fully automated plants in other locations perform the manufacturing and assembly operations. All of this computer processing and communications technology and the intellectual power that it makes possible will have diffused throughout every organization and every part of the national and global economies, and it will likely have a massive impact on productivity and efficiency and on the quality of our natural environment.

The home will, in varying degrees, come to resemble an office, a classroom, a theater, a library, a laboratory, an entertainment center, and a computer and communications control center. Robots could be common in the home for, by then, they will have advanced communications, motor controls, and manipulative capabilities enabling them to do everything from performing routine physical household chores to managing massive libraries of entertainment, educational, and information content. As much as 40 to 60 percent of the workforce could be forced by the pressures of global competition to work from home in some capacity a generation from now.

A VIRTUAL FUTURE

Some of the most promising developments will come about as a result of the integration of multimedia, workgroup, and virtual reality technologies which are applied and used in a broadband, intelligent network environment. This will make it possible for many hundreds or even thousands of experts, professionals, and ordinary people throughout the world to collaborate and concentrate their intellectual talents as never before. This will open up incredible opportunities for brainstorming, learning, and strategic thinking. Powerful problem-solving techniques such as this could lead to major breakthroughs in science and technology, engineering, medicine, and health care as well as entertainment and education.

The office-of-the-future will, therefore, come to resemble and indeed become a virtual office; the factory-of-the-future, a virtual factory; the laboratory-of-the future, a virtual laboratory; and the classroom-of-the-future, a virtual classroom. The stock exchange-of-the-future will be a virtual stock exchange. The workplace will become a virtual workplace. The marketplace will become a virtual marketplace, and the economic system will become a virtual economy. The rise of the virtual economy will increasingly make it possible to work and be educated and entertained entirely in an intellectual space.

TELEWORKING, TELECONFERENCING, TELEMARKETING, TELETRADING, AND TELESHOPPING IN A TELE-ECONOMY

The information and communications infrastructures will thus enable us to meet and exchange information and make decisions through teleconferencing media, and market and sell goods and services through telemarketing media. Using the global tele-trading systems, we will be able to play the stock markets and the commodities, options, and futures markets of the world. We could receive much of our education and training through tele-education and tele-training programs, and we could have the opportunity to telework, telecommute, teleshop and teleplay our way through life. We may eventually be able to vote electronically for we may be living in a teledemocracy by then.

THE PROMISE OF THE NEW ORGANIZATION

We will continue to witness spectacular changes in the way we work and organize ourselves in the decades ahead, and we will likely witness the evolution of organizational forms, organizational cultures, and behavior that we can only imagine and many others that we cannot even conceive of today. The structure, operation, and performance of organizations will become increasingly defined by the architectures of their computer and communications infrastructures.

The virtual corporation could be the predominant form of organization a generation from now. It will have no well-defined boundaries, and it will be conspicuous by the absence of hierarchy. It will be a completely horizontally structured and geographically distributed organization. The majority of people will likely be working in small cluster groups that are distributed throughout the world in network-intensive, computer-mediated, interactive environments.

BIG CHALLENGES FOR EVERYONE

The high-tech economy of the future will challenge all of the abilities and capabilities of individuals, businesses, and institutions. Some of biggest challenges will be for governments. The rise of a universal, multimedia infrastructure together with advances in virtual reality, on the one hand, could create tremendous opportunities and initiate a renaissance in learning, education, and creativity. On the other hand, it could become a medium for promoting prostitution, racial hatred, violence, and xenophobia. Activities such as these are already taking place over the Internet. If this proliferates, it could destroy the value of the medium as an enlightening, educational, and democratic force. Such a prospect raises the possibility that the information highways will be highly regulated, policed, and even censored in the future.

The creation of the five-thousand channel, interactive, and on-demand infrastructure could provide the masses with unlimited choice of programming content. It could make everyone a potential broadcaster, for example. On the other hand, it could fragment and possibly destroy the television broadcasting industry as we know it today. It could also destroy the advertising industry. The emerging information and communications multimedium could be completely advertising-free. The likelihood, however, is that it will be dominated by advertising. The information superhighway could, in fact, become a veritable gold mine for the direct-mail marketing industry.

In the years to come, the speed and volumes of computer-directed trading activities and currencies across international borders will continue to increase, and they could render obsolete any prospect for governments and regulators to control and stabilize global economic activity. The prospects of another stock market meltdown such as that which occurred in October 1987, is real and omnipresent. The real danger is that it could cause a complete collapse of the international financial system.

Another set of problems arises as a result of the powerful integrating force of technology. For intelligent technology is one of the most powerful integrating forces the world has ever seen. It is already leading to the convergence and integration of telecommunications and computers and publishing and entertainment industries, and, in the future, it will likely lead to the integration of all of these with banking and financial services, retailing, travel services, securities brokerage and trading and insurance, and investment, and real estate services.

Many of these sectors are already dominated by powerful monopolies. What if these come to dominate and monopolize other sectors of the economy? If the telephone or cable television companies, for example, succeed in using their information highways to expand their monopoly power into home banking, home shopping, home-office, home brokerage, and home investment activities, they could create even more powerful monopolies than they do today. The result could be more, not less, regulation. So what role should governments and regulators play in this coming convergence of the entire economy?

The intelligent infrastructures and the information superhighways in the years to come could also have catastrophic effects on transportation, real estate, and urban development as well. Telecommunications and the intelligent infrastructure are transforming the nature and location of work and many big cities, especially in the United States, are already suffering as the result of the movement of businesses out of the core area into residential communities. There is also a movement of people to cities in the South and West. If the new world of work-at-home and work-on-the-move does develop, which is highly likely, masses of people could decide to leave the big cities and move to small towns and villages and even rural and remote areas. Some may decide to move to other countries and work from there. New towns and villages might spring up in far-away places and even far-away countries, with many of the business, intellectual, and social conveniences that urban dwellers have today but without the stresses, environmental pollution, and other inconveniences associated with urban living. Some of the biggest urban centers in the West would be devastated by the movement of work and jobs to developing countries, for example. Such possibilities as these would likely result in a serious glut of office space in the major cities. Real estate prices would plummet. Roads and highway systems would become underused or obsolete. And governments would lose a major source of tax revenue.

The intelligent multimedia infrastructure of the future could also transform decision making, in general, and democracy as we know it. It could enhance our democratic processes by providing everyone with more information, more choices, and more opportunities to participate in democratic processes. Conversely, it could turn out that the speed, efficiency, and processing and the communications power of our new information and communications machines and infrastructures will become so great that we will have no choice but to delegate decision-making authority to them. Already the world's leading securities, commodities, and currency, options and futures exchanges are being overwhelmed by program trading, and, in the future, computers could entirely take over the trading function worldwide. Traders will not be able to act quickly enough to take advantage of the opportunities to profit. So what is there to stop organizations, government agencies such as the Internal Revenue Service, the market economy, and society itself from being run automatically by computers in the same way? Which organization or organizations will program and audit them?

Ironically, it may turn out that it will be in our collective, democratic interest to delegate an increasing proportion of decision-making power and control in society to intelligent machines in the future. In all likelihood, the new intelligent infrastructures we are building today will free us in some ways but enslave us in others. No technology is perfect. Each solves problems but also creates problems. Some would argue that technology creates more problems and bigger ones than it solves.

THE COST OF OBSOLESCENCE

Technological and economic change and globalization will continue to speed up and accelerate the pace of social and economic change. One of the results will be an acceleration in the rate of obsolescence of our knowledge base, stock of human skills, and experience as well as organizations and social and economic institutions in terms of their ability to cope. In order to work and manage in this new environment, we will need to place even greater reliance not only on technology but organizations and institutions to help us absorb all of this new knowledge more rapidly. The implication is that we will rely much more on our intelligent technologies and intelligent infrastructures than in the past, in education, health care as well as in the office and the home. The speed-up and the obsolescence of everything will drive innovations in our education and health care systems and institutions as we attempt to gain a more decisive source of strategic competitive advantage.

The computerization and telemediation of society is good by many standard measures of economic performance and social progress but it could come at a potentially enormous price. For it means that people may never need to meet face to face except on rare occasions and special circumstances. People will, by necessity, be forced to interact through computer terminals and intelligent networks in their mobile offices and homes in the future wherever these may be located, in order to overcome critically important time, geographic, and distance and cost constraints to economic activity. In many cases, people will seldom, if ever, need to meet one another in person or even to see one another. They will not have time to do so, and they will not need to do so because they will be interacting in an anonymous fashion with hundreds of their own kinds and with machines throughout the world. Some of the offices of the world's leading securities brokerage companies and securities and futures exchanges already resemble these fully electronic, network-based, offices and enterprises of tomorrow.

Sitting at their workstations wherever they are located, people will view the world through the windows of their personal computers connected to a variety of networks, and, indeed, in some ways, people will simply become extensions of computer terminals on a global network. Executives, professionals, managers, and staff will depend on their computers for almost everything they do. The computer- and communications-based infrastructures that are being built today will increasingly become the medium that binds people together as a corporation, a marketplace, an economic system, a nation, and a world community.

In the next decade or more, we could witness the evolution of a new socioeconomic class structure at both the national and global levels as the trickle-down of income and wealth within national economies becomes replaced by a horizontal transfer of wealth among nations. This process is already well underway. In the future, there will likely be the superrich in every country—those who gained their wealth by their own efforts, through innovation, prudent work habits and investments, or through inheritance, or whatever special circumstances and fortunes they find themselves in. There will also be large numbers of relatively well-off professional lawyers, engineers, doctors, scientists, teachers, and educators as well as executives in every country. But, in all likelihood, there will also be a very large underclass of people living at or near the level of poverty and below. Many of these people will have low levels of education and be incapable of coping with the kind of work world described in this book. Many will have never worked a day in their lives. Even some with advanced degrees may find themselves in this class. They may be there simply because they will have been turned off at the prospects of working in the machine-mediated organization or economy of the future. They will be there because they will simply have chosen an alternative life style.

THE FUTURE OF WORK, WEALTH, AND ECONOMIC PROSPERITY

Of the multitude of impacts of technology on people, none is perhaps more worrisome as its potentially adverse effects on work, jobs, employment, and careers, and, therefore, income and wealth. For, in all likelihood, it will only be a matter of a decade or more when computers, robots and intelligent machines of one kind or another will completely take over factories everywhere and perform most of the physical and even much of the nonphysical work of control, monitoring, and coordination that humans have traditionally done. Robots, let us not forget, do not need coffee breaks or unions to represent them, and they work round-the-clock with little supervision. And, as more and more functionality and intelligence are built into smaller and smaller microchips and software, fewer and fewer people will be required to manufacture and test components and assemble them into equipment, machines, and systems. As all industries and all sectors of the economy adopt and use these machines and as virtual work-group technologies become widespread, the whole economy will be affected in the same way.

The implication is that the computerization of society will likely result in dramatic increases in productivity in every sector in the future, and this could eliminate any prospect or potential for job creation in traditional industries. Employment in manufacturing and upstream activities like mining, for example, looks bleak indeed but this is not surprising. Employment in these sectors has been on the decline for decades and is expected to continue declining. The services sector could be especially hit hard by automation in the next decade. Developments in biotechnology and genetic engineering will probably increase productivity and diminish employment in the resource and agricultural sectors. Unlike the technological revolutions that took place earlier in this century, the defense and aerospace industries are likely to shed large numbers even as they attempt to convert to civilian markets. No wonder people are worried about the future of jobs.

Every technological revolution and every economic age have had their share of Luddites and the current age is no exception. But Western societies have coped with the negative impacts of mechanization, automation, and technological change throughout the centuries. During the eighteenth and nineteenth centuries, a massive movement of workers from agriculture into manufacturing took place. Throughout the twentieth century, the millions of workers that were made surplus by mechanization and automation in the resource, agriculture, and manufacturing sectors have been absorbed into the expanding private and public bureaucracies and the services sector. This army of surplus workers found jobs as accountants, lawyers, teachers, professors, doctors, and health care personnel, as well as secretaries, stenographers, bank tellers, sales people, and so on. However, many of these jobs are coming under attack simultaneously by the globalization of economic activity and by computerization which is speeding ahead to pay its last respects to the industrial economy.

Global competition is forcing corporations in every sector of the economy to re-engineer and downsize their workforce using technology as a great enabler. Many corporations, governments, and even entire nations are outsourcing a growing proportion of their manufacturing and services activities to other countries while automating those tasks that remain as quickly as possible so they can remain competitive. The public bureaucracies are coming under the same pressures as private bureaucracies. Declining tax revenues are forcing governments to downsize, deregulate, privatize, and cut spending on defense, social welfare, education, and health care programs.

As globalization gains momentum, more and more low-skilled and low-paying jobs will continue to be transplanted overseas to low-wage countries, thereby displacing domestic workers and contributing to unemployment. Even high-skilled and high-wage jobs will also be threatened in the future. The future looks bleak, indeed, for millions of workers in traditional industries worldwide.[5] If so many traditional jobs are being threatened by the march of technology, what kind of future and what kind of work can people look forward to? Where will the new jobs come from? If they are not in manufacturing or resource industries or in traditional service industries, then what kind of new service jobs will be created? Will these be low skill or high skill? Low paying or high paying? Will the evolving knowledge-intensive sectors absorb all of the people being laid off and coming onto the job market? These are the questions that many people are asking themselves today.

One thing is clear. The record of economic progress over the past two centuries and since the Second World War attests to the fact that major technological and economic transformations are continually taking place without massive loss of jobs and that economic progress creates as many jobs as it destroys, although the nature and quality of these jobs does change dramatically. Technological progress is usually accompanied by a shortage of highly skilled labor. Clearly, one of the unique attributes of our economic system is its ability to regenerate, reinvigorate and re-engineer itself. The same forces of technological change, competition, innovation, and entrepreneurship that displaced jobs and created unemployment in the past also solved them. The question is, Are these forces still as powerful as they were in the past? They probably are.

Clearly, not all traditional jobs will disappear, but they will change in varying degrees. Society will always need working people. Computers and robots cannot do everything—certainly not as efficiently or with the dexterity and imagination of people, at least in the foreseeable future.

Another thing is clear. For the advanced economies of Western Europe, North America, and Asia to grow and prosper in the future, they will increasingly depend on the knowledge-based activities that are created through investments in science and technology, research and development, and engineering. They will depend on the capabilities of entrepreneurs, managers, and innovators to design, develop, and market the many new products and services that consumers in their own countries will need as well as for export to the world's high-growth regions.

Demographic factors will, of course, also play an important role in determining where jobs will be created. With an aging population, considerable job creation and employment growth will probably occur in the health care, tourism, and entertainment industries. The aging population combined with declining birth rates in advanced countries could very well result in a shortage of skilled workers in the early part of the twenty-first century. And let us not forget the environment. In the future, governments and businesses will likely spend huge sums to preserve and protect the environment, and this could become the great generator of jobs in the future. And, with the spread of democracy throughout the world and the transition to Western-style market economies in Asia, South America, and Eastern Europe, world economic growth will increasingly focus on these regions and less perhaps on the United States, Canada, and Japan and the postindustrial countries in Western Europe. These countries are already experiencing an explosion in demand for goods and services and this is creating opportunities for economic growth and employment in the member countries in the triad league of nations.[6]

Since we will be living in a predominantly computer-mediated work environment and a computer-mediated global economy, many of the new jobs and much of the new wealth will likely come from the application of intelligent, multimedia technologies. We will likely need many more technically trained specialists in areas like multimedia software development, systems design, analysis, and administration in network operations, management, and administration as well as in training and education. Jobs will likely be created as well in the future through investments to build, operate, and maintain the information superhighways that are under development around the world.

Some of the most promising areas of economic growth and job creation are likely to be in the information, communications, and entertainment industries, in television, motion picture, and home entertainment production, as consumers continue demanding more and better quality programming content. Innovations in the application of interactive television, computer animation, multimedia, virtual reality, and telepresence look very promising. Job creation and economic opportunity are especially likely in the arts and entertainment industries, especially live entertainment, as more and more people look to more human and creative endeavors to express themselves and escape the stresses of the fast-paced cybernetic age. According to an article in the March 1994 issue of *Business Week*, spending on entertainment and recreation as a percentage of all nonmedical consumer spending rose from 7.7 percent in 1979 to 9.43 percent in 1993.[7] These activities now employ more people than the automobile and related industries.

According to Robert Reich, author of the book *The Work of Nations*, the industrialized world will need large numbers of "symbolic analysts," that is those educated in the use of data, words, and oral and visual representations. These include entertainers, movie producers, corporate executives, engineering consultants, lawyers, and so on. Routine workers face bleak prospects in the future in Reich's view.

The institutional nature of work and employment will also continue to undergo dramatic changes in the future, according to Charles Handy, author of the book *The Age of Unreason*, as the new world of work becomes more decentralized, mobile, flexible, and less structured. Job security will become a thing of the past for large numbers of the population and lifetime careers could cease to exist for many people. Instead of permanent positions, workers will probably be working on one-year, three-year, or five-year contracts, and large numbers of people will be working in part-time positions and holding down two or more jobs in different occupations or in different organizations. Most people will, in effect, be pursuing multiple careers. A growing number of organizations, including governments, will outsource their activities to individuals and groups of individuals working as freelancers and consultants. In all likelihood, large numbers of the workforce will be working in independent teams with contracts throughout the world.

Industrialized countries, however, may never be able to get back to the "full employment" levels of the sixties, in spite of the efforts of their governments to pursue their redistributive and employment equity goals and objectives through a massive overhaul of the institutions of work. One of the most talked-about overhaul schemes is a reduction in the work week, perhaps to a four-day or even a three-day, twenty-four- to thirty- or thirty-five-hour week but, unless this is offset by productivity growth or lower incomes, it will not succeed. Another possibility is to reduce the mandatory age of retirement to fifty. The potentials and possibilities for work sharing could be considerable for many people but these are purely income redistribution schemes. They fail to take into consideration the important fact that everyone involved will have to take a reduction in their income. Unless productivity is improved, the standard of living of entire nations will fall.

In all likelihood, everyone will ultimately be investing more and more of their income and time and effort in keeping themselves informed and educated and keeping up with changing technology and work. Ultimately, much of the effort of every individual will be concerned with generating, adapting to, and managing technological, economic, organizational, and political change. For ultimately, change itself could be the great generator of jobs and the great generator of wealth in the future. This is, after all, the great lesson of history.

NOTES

1. If chip densities continue to increase as they have in the past, according to Moore's Law, the capacities of state-of-art memory chips could possibly reach as much as 10 billion bits a quarter century from now. Even higher densities and much faster chips are possible through developments in quantum-effect transistors which switch on and off with the movement of a single electron. Texas Instruments expects the technology to hit the market by 1998. See *Business Week*, 8 March 1993, p. 87; and "Single Electronics," *Scientific American*, June 1992, pp. 80–85.

2. In 1992, scientists at Rochester's Laboratory for Laser Energetics developed a gallium arsenide photodetector capable of operating at an incredible speed of 510 gigahertz. In 1993, researchers at the Universities of Rochester and Minnesota claimed they had developed a much less expensive photodetector based on silicon that is capable of operating at a speed of 75 gigahertz compared to the speed of one to two gigahertz of the best commercial detectors available.

3. In 1993, *Signal*, the journal of the U.S. Armed Forces Communications and Electronics Association, predicted that in twenty years, the bioelectric approach could lead to extremely fast machines that match the human operator's intellect.

4. The visual theater which researchers at Xerox PARC have developed could become the model office-of-the-future. Microprocessors and communications devices are contained in all office furniture and equipment and even embedded in the walls of the office to create a truly electronic information processing and communications environment.

5. According to the Geneva-based International Labor Organization, both rich and poor nations have already become engulfed in a job crisis that could explode and undermine the social fabric of their society. In a 1993 report, entitled *Defining Values, Promoting Change*, it estimated that 30 percent of the world's labor force is either unemployed or working below the subsistence level. The ILO's Chief of Staff, Ali Taqui, warned that the crisis could reverse the steps toward democracy in Latin America and the former Soviet Union.

6. *The Economist* argued in a special report on the global economy in October 1994 that the third world is now an engine for growth in the rich world. See "A Survey of the Global Economy," 1 October 1994.

7. "The Entertainment Economy," *Business Week*, 14 March 1994, pp. 58–66.

Selected Bibliography

Agarwala, P. N. *The New International Economic Order: An Overview*. New York: Pergamon Press, 1983.

Barnouw, Eric. *Tube of Plenty: The Evolution of American Television*. New York: Oxford University Press, 1970.

Bell, Daniel. *The Coming Post-Industrial Society*. New York: Basic Books, 1973.

Beniger, James R. *The Control Revolution: Technological and Economic Origins of the Information Society*. Cambridge: Harvard University Press, 1986.

Botkin, James, Dan Dimancescu, Ray Stata, and John McClellan. *Global Stakes: The Future of High Technology in America*. New York: Ballinger, 1982.

Boyett, Joseph H., and Henry P. Conn. *Workplace 2000: The Revolution Reshaping American Business*. New York: Dutton, 1991.

Bradley, Stephen P., et al. *Globalization, Technology and Competition: The Fusion of Computers and Telecommunications in the 1990s*. Cambridge: Harvard Business School Press, 1993.

Brand, Stuart. *The Media Lab: Inventing the Future*. New York: Viking Penguin, 1987.

Brock, Gerald W. *The Telecommunications Industry: The Dynamics of Market Structure*. Cambridge: Harvard University Press, 1981.

———. *The U.S. Computer Industry: A Study of Market Power*. Cambridge: Ballinger, 1975.

Brooks, John. *The Telephone: The First Hundred Years*. New York: Harper & Row, 1976.

Carey, James. *Communications as Culture: Essays on Media and Society*. Boston: Unwin Hyman, 1989.

Carneval, Anthony. *America and the New Economy*. New York: Jossey-Bass, 1991.

Chandler, Alfred. *Strategy and Structure: Dynamics of Industrial Capitalism*. Cambridge: Harvard University Press, 1990.

———. *The Visible Hand: The Managerial Revolution in American Business*. Cambridge: Harvard University Press, 1977.

Cohen, Stephen W., and John Zysman. *Manufacturing Matters: The Myth of the Post-Industrial Economy*. New York: Basic Books, 1987.

Coll, Steven. *The Deal of the Century: The Breakup of AT&T*. New York: Simon and Schuster, 1988.

Crandell, Robert W., and Kenneth Flamm, ed. *Changing the Rules: Technological Change, International Competition, and Regulation in Communications*. Washington D.C.: Brookings Institution, 1989.

Crowley, David, and Paul Heyer, ed. *Communications in History: Technology, Culture and Society*. New York: Longman, 1991.

Davidow, William H., and Michael S. Malone, ed. *The Virtual Corporation: Structuring and Revitalizing the Corporation for the 21st Century*. New York: HarperCollins, 1992.

de Sola Pool, Ithiel. *The Social Impact of the Telephone*. Cambridge: MIT Press, 1977.

———. *Technologies of Freedom*. Cambridge: Belknap Press, 1983.

———. *Technologies Without Boundaries: On Telecommunications in a Global Age*. Cambridge: Harvard University Press, 1990.

Dizard, Wilson P. *The Coming Information Age: An Overview of Technology*. New York: Longman, 1982.

Drucker, Peter F. *Post-Capitalist Society*. New York: HarperCollins, 1993.

Egan, Bruce L. *Information Superhighways: The Economics of Advanced Public Communications Networks*. Boston: Artech House, 1991.

Estabrooks, Maurice. *Programmed Capitalism: A Computer-Mediated Global Society*. New York: M. E. Sharpe Inc., 1988.

Feigenbaum, Edward A., and Pamela McCorduck. *The Fifth Generation: Artificial Intelligence and Japan's Computer Challenge to the World*. Reading, Mass.: Addison-Wesley Publishing Co., 1983.

Flamm, Kenneth. *Targeting the Computer: Government Support and Industrial Competition*. Washington, D.C.: The Brookings Institution, 1987.

Forester, Tom. *High-Tech Society: The Story of the Information Technology Revolution*. Cambridge: MIT Press, 1987.

Forester, Tom, ed. *The Microelectronics Revolution: The Complete Guide to the New Technology and Its Impact on Society*. Oxford: Basil Blackwell, 1980.

Galbraith, John Kenneth. *The New Industrial State*. 4th ed. Boston: Houghton Mifflin, 1985.

Garten, Jeffrey E. *A Cold Peace: America, Japan, Germany and the Struggle for Supremacy*. New York: Time Books, 1992.

Gilder, George. *Microcosm: The Quantum Revolution in Economics and Technology*. New York: Simon and Schuster, 1989.

Gutman, Herbert. *Work, Culture and Society in Industrializing America*. New York: Vintage, 1977.

Halal, William E. *The New Capitalism*. New York: Wiley, 1986.

Halal, William, Ali Geranmayeh, and John Pourdehnad, ed. *Internal Markets: Bringing the Power of Free Enterprise Inside Your Organization*. New York: Wiley, 1993.

Hammer, Michael, and James Champy. *Reengineering the Corporation: A Manifesto for the Business Revolution*. New York: HarperCollins, 1993.

Handy, Charles. *The Age of Paradox*. Cambridge: Harvard University School Press, 1994.

———. *The Age of Unreason*. Cambridge: Harvard Business School Press, 1991.

Harvard Business Review Book. *Revolution in Real Time: Managing Information Technology in the 1990s*. Cambridge: Harvard Business School Press, 1990.

Heilbroner, Robert, and Aaron Singer. *The Economic Transformation of America: 1600 to the Present*. New York: Harcourt Brace Jovanovich, 1984.

Hudson, Heather. *Communications Satellites: Their Development and Impact*. New York: Free Press, 1990.

Innis, Harold. *Empire and Communications*. Oxford: Oxford University Press, 1950.

Irwin, Manley Rutherford. *Telecommunications America: Markets Without Boundaries*. Westport, Conn.: Quorum, 1984.

Klein, Burton H. *Dynamic Economics*. Cambridge: Harvard University Press, 1977.

Kuhn, Thomas S. *The Structure of Scientific Revolutions*. Chicago: University of Chicago Press, 1970.

Kurtzman, Joel. *The Death of Money: How the Electronic Economy Has Destabilized the World's Markets and Created Financial Chaos*. New York: Simon and Schuster, 1993.

Lewin, Lenard, ed. *Telecommunications in the United States: Trends and Policies*. Dedham, Mass.: Artech House, 1981.

Luard, Evan. *The Globalization of Politics: The Changed Focus of Political Action in the Modern World*. New York: New York University Press, 1990.

Machlup, Fritz. *The Production and Distribution of Knowledge in the United States*. Princeton: Princeton University Press, 1962.

Mansell, Robin. *The New Telecommunications: A Political Economy of Network Evolution*. London: Sage Publications, 1993.

McLuhan, Marshall. *The Gutenburg Galaxy*. New York: Signet, 1969.

Mills, D. Quinn. *Rebirth of the Corporation*. New York: John Wiley, 1991.

Moreau, R. *The Computer Comes of Age: The People, the Hardware and the Software*. Cambridge: MIT Press, 1986.

Morton, Michael S. et al., ed. *The Corporation of the Nineties: Information Technology and Organizational Transformation*. Oxford: Oxford University Press, 1991.

Noll, Michael, A. *Introduction to the Telephone & Telephone Systems*, 2d ed. Boston: Artech House, 1991.

Nora, Simon, and Alain Minc. *The Computerization of Society: A Report to the President of France*. Cambridge: MIT Press, 1980.

Ohmae, Kenichi. *Borderless World: Power and Strategy in the International Economy*. New York: HarperCollins, 1990.

———. *Triad Power: The Coming Shape of Global Competition*. New York: Free Press, 1985.

Organization for Economic Cooperation and Development. *Information Activities, Electronics and Telecommunications Technologies*. Paris, 1981.

———. *New Technologies in the Nineties*. Paris, 1988.

———. *Technology and the Economy: The Key Relationships*. Paris, 1992.

Pine, B. J. *Mass Customization*. Cambridge: Harvard University School Press, 1993.

Piore, Michael J., and Charles F. Sabel. *The Second Industrial Divide: Possibilities for Prosperity.* New York: Basic Books, 1984.

Pope, Daniel. *The Making of Modern Advertising.* New York: Basic Books, 1983.

Porat, Marc U., and Michael R. Rubin. *The Information Economy,* Washington, D.C.: Department of Commerce, Government Printing Office, 1977.

Porter, Michael E. *The Competitive Advantage of Nations.* New York: Free Press, 1990.

Quinn, James Brian. *Intelligent Enterprise.* New York: Free Press, 1992.

Rees, David W. E. *Satellite Communications: The First Quarter Century of Service.* New York: John Wiley, 1990.

Reich, Robert. *The Next American Frontier.* New York: Times Books, 1983.

———. *The Work of Nations.* New York: Alfred A. Knopf, 1991.

Rogers, Everett M., and Judith K. Larsen. *Silicon Valley Fever: Growth of High-Technology Culture.* New York: Basic Books, 1984.

Rosenberg, Nathan, and L. E. Birdzell Jr. *How the West Grew Rich: The Economic Transformation of the Industrial World.* New York: Basic Books, 1986.

Rubin, Michael Rogers. *Information Economics and Policy in the United States.* Littleton, Colo.: Libraries Unlimited, 1983.

Schumpeter, Joseph A. *Capitalism, Socialism and Democracy.* London: Allen and Unwin, 1943.

Slater, Robert. *Portraits in Silicon.* Cambridge: MIT Press, 1987.

Sobel, Robert and David B. Sicilia. *The Entrepreneurs: An American Adventure.* Boston: Houghton Mifflin Company, 1986.

Stalk, George, and Thomas Hout. *Competing in Time: How Time-Based Competition Is Reshaping Global Markets.* New York: Free Press, 1990.

Sterling, Christopher, ed. *International Telecommunications and Information Policy.* Washington, D.C.: Communications Press Inc., 1984.

Tatsuno, Sheridan. *The Technopolis Strategy: Japan, High Technology and the Control of the 21st Century.* Englewood Cliffs, N.J.: Prentice-Hall, 1986.

Tedlow, Richard S. *New and Improved: The Story of Mass Marketing in America.* New York: Basic Books, 1990.

Thurow, Lester. *Head to Head: The Coming Economic Battle Among Japan, Europe, and America.* New York: Morrow, 1992.

Weizenbaum, Joseph. *Computer Power and Human Reason.* New York: W. H. Freeman, 1976.

Womack, James P., Daniel T. Jones, and Daniel Roos. *The Machine that Changed the World.* New York: Maxwell Macmillan International, 1990.

Zuboff, Shoshana. *In the Age of the Smart Machine: The Transformation of Work and Power.* New York: Basic Books, 1988.

Zysman, John and Laura Tyson, ed. *American Industry in International Competition: Government Policies and Corporate Strategies.* Ithaca, N.Y.: Cornell University Press, 1983.

Index

About the Author

MAURICE ESTABROOKS is an author and senior economist in the Department of Industry in Canada. With more than 20 years experience in information and communications management, he has studied the art and science of strategic thinking and management, and the interplay between technology, corporate strategy, and the market economy in particular. Trained in the physical, social, and managerial sciences, he is the author of a previous book, *Programmed Capitalism: A Computer-Mediated Global Society* which describes the role computers played in the stock market crash of 1987.